CW00405149

TRANSCENDING
TERROR

A history of our spiritual quest and
the challenge of the new millennium

BOOKS

Winchester, UK
Washington, USA

This book is dedicated to the memory of a great father-
James Henry "Harry" Hackett
(1920-1996)

Copyright © 2004 O Books
46A West Street, Alresford, Hants SO24 9AU, U.K.
Tel: +44 (0) 1962 736880 Fax: +44 (0) 1962 736881
E-mail: office@johnhunt-publishing.com
www.0-books.net

U.S. office:
240 West 35th Street, Suite 500
New York, NY 10001
E-mail: obooks@aol.com

Text: © 2004 Ian Hackett

Design: Text set in Rotis Serif by Nautilus Design
Cover design: Sameer Patro

ISBN 1 903816 87 4

A CIP catalogue record for this book is available from the British Library.

Printed by Tien Wah Press (Pte) Limited

CONTENTS

PREFACE AND ACKNOWLEDGEMENTS

———————•●•———————

T his book arose in part from my curiosity about the world's main religions and the apparent absence of an anthology that emphasised their common values. I felt that the availability of such an anthology could be valuable in the light of prophesies about a "Clash of Civilizations" and began to put one together on my retirement from the headship of the International School of London at the end of August 2001. Days later, the world changed dramatically following the "9/11" atrocities. The threat of a clash of civilizations became much more immediate. My original idea of gathering materials for a religious anthology during the course of a leisurely retirement suddenly seemed inadequate in these new circumstances. The book that follows still contains a brief anthology taken from the great religions (in Chapter 10), but the anthology is now accompanied by critical histories of the religions to give an idea of how we got into our current situation, and its closing chapter includes an additional anthology of important ideas that may help us to get out of it. I am therefore indebted not only to the nine men whose historic visions inspired Chapters 1 to 10, but also to the many other men and women whose ideas I have also quoted. These include Aung San Suu Kyi, Robert Barry, Rabbi Tony Bayfield, Yehuda Berg, William Bloom, David Brazier, Jackson Browne, Zarrin T. Caldwell, Nomi Chazan, Andrew C. Clarke, Don Cupitt, Paul Davies, Richard Dawkins, Dorothy Day, Miguel de Unamuno, Kirk Douglas, Michael Douglas, Bob Dylan, Diana Eck, Albert Einstein, Louis Farrakhan, Mohandas Gandhi, Al Gore, Asa Gray, Prince Hassan Bin Talal, Ali Issa

Othman, Christopher Ives, Sharon Janis, David Jenkins, John P. Keenan, Jim Kenney, Irfan Ahmad Khan, Nishida Kitaro, Paul F. Knitter, Arthur Koestler, Hans Kung, Nelson Mandela, Freddie Mercury, N. Muthu Mohan, George Monbiot, Michael Moore, Abdul Rashid Omar, Greg Palast, Jaroslav Pelikan, John Pilger, Alan Race, Seshagir Rao, Ziauddin Sardar, Dorothy L. Sayers, Shlomi Segall, Kirpal Singh, Sulak Sivaraksa, Nathan Soderblom, Thich Nhat Hanh, Evelyn Underhill, Dominique de Villepin, Professor Paul Weller, Adeline Yen Mah, Lin Yutang and Tenzin Gyatso, the 14th Dalai Lama.

I would also like to thank Yasmin Alibhai-Brown, Tony Benn, Richard Coles, Frank Go, John Hackett, Jackie Heather, John Hunt, Sergio Pawel, Jafar Siddiqui and Charlotte Waterlow MBE for reading early drafts of the text and offering valuable encouragement and comments, Julia Hynard for proof-reading the current text, Peter Davies for the text design, Sameer Patro for the cover, Donna Wood, Maria Watson and John Hunt at O-Books, and my wife Mita, for providing support throughout my research and the writing of each draft.

The contents of the present text and any errors that may have crept in are solely my responsibility.

Ian Hackett

INTRODUCTION

———•●•———

This is a book about a human family sharing a wonderful planet in a time when globalization is bringing us together again after several millennia as members of separate groups and civilizations.

Just over half a century ago, we acknowledged our common identity as "We, the peoples" in the United Nations Charter.

Four years ago, at the end of the United Nations' first half-century – one of relative peace and remarkable technological progress – we celebrated a New Millennium with tremendous hopes for the future (albeit hopes tinged with anxieties about a few nagging, mostly greed-related, problems, notably obscene inequalities and world poverty, overpopulation, pollution, global warming, AIDS, resource depletion, moral degeneration, drug abuse, rising crime and the still-real shadow of weapons of mass destruction).

Three years ago – on September 11 – events in New York and Washington dealt a major blow to our hopes and triggered the United States' "War on Terror".

We now live in a world where the evolving re-establishment of human unity, essential for dealing with our global problems and even for the survival of our young civilization, is seriously threatened by renewed division. We live in a world divided between nations or international groups run by leaders high on bravado and self-righteousness, intent on pursuing policies of greed and violence. It is a world that, although still nourished by remarkable technological achievement, is poisoned not only by our greed, but also by the absence of wisdom, vision, humility and capacity for self-criticism, both in our leaders and in ourselves.

A significant dimension of this division is the religious one, but a significant dimension of the solution must be spiritual. These are the dimensions considered here. The book recalls our early separation into tribal groups and traces our religious and spiritual evolution over the last three to four millennia. It highlights the visions of the nine founders of today's great religions. It reviews the ways in which the religions they founded have become so divisive and dangerous. It also argues that a common core in the original visions can still provide us with gateways to real civilization in our newly re-globalized community.

Our religious legacies currently thwart our inchoate unity and hamper our continuing spiritual development. Indeed, they have the potential to destroy us before we earn the right to call ourselves truly civilized. This is why their divisiveness must be challenged. This is why those who have perverted our natural quest must be exposed. This is why those who would use our spiritual search for truth, love and unity to justify the greed, arrogance and hate through which we are now threatened must be defeated.

But in order to put this challenge for the new millennium in context, we need to go back to the times when we, as a species, were first able to think about more than mere day-to-day survival. Ever since those times, we have looked at our surroundings with awe and wonder. We have been in awe of the beauty of the Earth, the immensity of the heavens, the complexity of life and the mystery of the mind. We have wondered about what may be behind it all, whether or not there is any point, any purpose, any guiding light, or any unifying principle. Over the last few millennia, we have been asking questions such as what (if anything) is God? Why are we here? How should we live? What will become of us?

Many have claimed that they have the answers. Many are still searching. Very few of us are indifferent. The spiritual quest is an essential part of what makes us human – an essential part of what differentiates us from the animals who share our planet. It has been initiated independently on every continent and continues into the new millennium.

Over our last three to four millennia, many personalities have emerged and been hailed, either during or after their lifetimes, as visionaries – prophets, buddhas, gurus, or even sons, messengers or manifestations of God. Some of their words have been recorded. The words credited to nine in particular have given rise to the religions considered here. They have all generated ways of thinking and living that transcend the simple material world of our five senses. But the religions they started have also taken on lives of their own and been used to dominate, even terrorize, their own or other people's societies.

Most of the world's people now belong to societies that follow one or more religions that have their roots in the words credited to the central characters of this book, each of whom has a dedicated chapter. The chapters vary in length according to the age and global influence of the different religions. The book seeks to bring together the highlights of their founders' visions, showing their core congruence with regard to essentials, such as the importance of living a good and honest life based on love and unselfishness. It also seeks to explore the problem of why our religions, despite their common goals, continue to divide rather than to unite us.

Over the last three to four centuries, our scientific and technological advances have brought us together as a single interdependent community in One World for the first time since the earliest pioneering human groups split away from our common ancestors in Africa. For the first time since the dawn of civilization, we really have to learn to live together again. We already recognize this to some extent. The creation of the United Nations in the aftermath of World War II is a small testament to that recognition.

Unfortunately, due to the differing traditions arising from our responses to religious questions, and due to the arrogance of religious fundamentalists and of some of our leaders, religion has often become more of a battleground than a spiritual quest, more of a threat than a means of healing divisions. God's name has been used to justify acts such as developing and using weapons of mass destruction – chemical, biological or nuclear – or bulldozing homes and murdering families, flying passenger planes into office blocks, blowing up leisure facilities, and even, by some governments, to justify the use of full-spectrum overwhelming force to impose their national goals on weaker nations. Such evils make it absolutely essential that we open our minds to self-criticism so that our quest for truth also becomes a quest for unity. We can no longer afford to arrogantly proclaim one approach while remaining ignorant of others. We can no longer afford not to recognize the values of other approaches or the flaws in our own. There is a real and growing risk that, without unity, our quest for truth may be prematurely terminated.

A majority of Earth's people and their leaders either promote, accept, or exploit the idea of God. Inevitably, their interpretations vary. They range between visions of a benevolent bearded old man, who was somehow able to create the Earth and the heavens in six days, to something nebulous and beyond comprehension: something that both encompasses the universe and controls it, either through taking decisions on a moment to moment basis and, therefore, being something worth praying to, or through the strict application of first principles, the understanding of which constitutes the ultimate goal of scientific inquiry.

The truth may fall somewhere within this range and, if, indeed, it is the truth, it is, by definition, one truth, and must govern all valid religious claims and scientific conclusions.

Any and all contradictions between the great religions, plus all those ideas that have been scientifically disproved, can be attributed to human error or worse. The ideas in question range from entertaining nonsense to dangerous dogma. Growing minorities, particularly in the West, have questioned some of the more bizarre accretions of their various religions, and even gone on to reject spirituality and morality in general. Others, particularly in materially impoverished societies, cling desperately to their own religious "truths." Both groups are dangerous.

The aims of this book are:

▷ to look at our quest for truth in the light of the historical records of utterances credited to nine visionaries in particular, insofar as the fruits of their visions allow

▷ to review some of the ensuing human ideas and activities that have led to so much historical and continuing division and unnecessary suffering

▷ to contemplate our continuing quest

Each of the chapters on the visionaries – Zarathustra, Moses, Atharva, Lao-tzu, Siddhartha Gautama (the Buddha), Jesus, Muhammad, Nanak Dev and Mirza Husain Ali Nuri (Baha'ullah) – opens with a brief introduction placing the visionary in his historical context, and continues with sections entitled:

▷ *The Vision – Selected Highlights*

▷ *The Legacy*

The visions presented are taken from English translations of holy books of the religions based on their teachings – the Gathas, the Torah, the Mundaka Upanishad, the Tao Te Ching, the Dhammapada, the Bible, the Koran, the Guru Granth Sahib and the Gleanings from the Writings of Baha'ullah. The visions are all sub-divided into the same sections:

▷ The Nature of God

▷ God's Purpose and Human Responsibility

▷ Worship

▷ Prayers (including poems, proverbs or psalms)

▷ Prophesies

These sections are used again in the 10th chapter, where *Collected Visions – Extended Highlights* from each of the great religions are brought together.

This arrangement was chosen to facilitate comparison. It allows us to see how far the similarities provide evidence that the words may constitute a genuine attempt to communicate divinely inspired truth. It also allows the contradictions to alert us to the possibilities of the "human error or worse" that we need to watch for.

The concluding section of each of the first nine chapters, *The Legacy*, provides a brief history of the religions spawned by the visions of their founders and of the impact each religion has had and continues to have on our common heritage and on our environment.

The final chapter adds comments about the significance of some key recent developments in our scientific and environmental understanding and in our continuing political folly. It also includes a selection of quotations from modern thinkers in the fields of science, religion and politics, and attempts to suggest what all of this means for the prospects of humankind: whether we will be able to continue to home in on the truth, or whether we're destined to deal in greed, arrogance, dogma and division until they destroy us. Readers' comments on any aspect of the book are welcome.

1
ZARATHUSTRA &
GOD'S LIGHT

———————●●●———————

E ver since we have been able to record our thoughts, we have sought or
suggested explanations for our existence and questioned whether or not
we share our environment with more powerful and unseen beings. Since
long before we learned to read and write, since long before we learned the
skills of agriculture and began to live in settled communities, we have
imagined gods and demons all around us. These have been described by J G
Frazer as innumerable spirits "in every tree and flower, every brook and river,
every breeze that blew and every cloud that flecked with silvery white the blue
expanse of heaven."[1] Among hunting tribes, the greater spirits were often
identified as male and associated with the sun, the sky and the stars. As tribes
settled and became more pastoral, their gods tended to become female and
associated with the bountiful Mother Earth until the male principle eventually
enjoyed a revival, often in tandem with the advent of literacy, during the
earliest periods of war and imperialism.[2] Spirits associated with the wind, the
rain, animals, birds and the dead were also revered, as were some living rulers.

Some of our earliest written records – hieroglyphics from the Nile basin of
5,000 years ago – show that the gods of the sun and the river were central to
ancient Egyptian worship.[3] More recent records from Egypt also provide the
earliest written evidence of monotheism – the idea of a single "creator;" one
wholly exclusive God, ruling all else.[4] This evidence comes from the reign of
King Amenophis IV (Akhenaten), in the form of references to Aten, The Great
One.

Monotheism in Egypt did not survive the death of Akhenaten (c.1360 BC), but
humanity's experience of God has since recurred often, sometimes
independently, sometimes among those who have had contact with earlier

monotheistic cultures.[5] Indeed, several ancient Sumerian and Egyptian folk tales and hymns reappear in the Torah and the Bible. One example of the latter is Psalm 104 (See Chapter 10), a re-working of Akhenaten's "Hymn to Aten."

Around the time that monotheism was making its first appearance in Egypt, nomadic Aryans spreading through central Asia and Chinese settling in East Asia were also providing contexts that would lead to the monotheistic experience. For the Aryans, the first evidence still available to us came at around 1300 BC through the prophet, Zarathustra Spitama.[6] For the Chinese, early evidence of the quest would eventually be recorded by in the Tao Te Ching (The Way and its Virtue) credited to Lao-tzu (the Old Master) around 530 BC.

The westward migration of the Aryans from central Asia to Mesopotamia, the land of the fertile valleys of the Tigris and Euphrates (now Iraq), paved the way for the revelations that would also spawn Judaism, Christianity and Islam plus the Sikh and Bahai faiths; and the Aryan migration to the Indus valley in the south provided the context, via the Vedas and Upanishads (particularly Atharva's Mundaka Upanishad), for the enlightenment of Siddhartha Gautama, the Buddha, in India. Each of these religions is considered in the following chapters.[7]

First though, a brief look at Zarathustra Spitama, the fruits of whose visions were expressed in the form of a number of prayers or Gathas. Originally transmitted orally, these were written down some time after his death and 17 of them were eventually collected as part of the Zoroastrian Avesta several centuries later.

Zarathustra was born into a nomadic Aryan tribe in central Asia, wandering lands that are now part of Russian steppes. The Aryans of the time were nature worshippers who venerated a series of deities associated with the sun, moon, fire, earth and water, alongside higher gods of war (Intar), justice (Asha) and the sky (Uruwana). A further Aryan god, Mithra, associated with light, loyalty and obedience, and also seen as the provider of cattle, came to be revered above all of the others.[8] There is also evidence that their religions included fire worship and blood sacrifice at crude altars.[9]

Apart from the evidence of Zarathustra's name, which translates as camel keeper, little is known of his early life, but it is believed that the Gathas followed a series of visions he experienced between the ages of 30 and 40, and the original language of the Gathas dates them somewhere between 1400 and 1200 BC.

The extracts of the translations that follow show Zarathustra's recognition of a single creator, God, also referred to as Ahura Mazda, the Lord of Light. They are presented in the five clearly defined sections chosen for use with all nine of the present book's collected religious texts:

▷ The Nature of God

▷ God's Purpose and Human Responsibility

▷ Worship

▷ Prayers

▷ Prophecy

Selected highlights appear below.

Extended highlights, presented alongside highlights from the other eight faiths covered, can be found in Chapter 10.

THE VISION – SELECTED HIGHLIGHTS

On The Nature of God

Who in the beginning, at creation, was the Father of order?

Who established the course of the sun and stars?

Through whom does the moon wax then wane?

Who has upheld the Earth from below and the heavens from falling?

Who sustains the waters and plants?

Who harnesses swift steeds to winds and clouds?

Who, O God, is the Creator of good purpose?

What Craftsman created darkness and light?

What Craftsman created sleep and activity?

Through Whom exist dawn, noon and eve which remind us of our duty?

Who fashioned power and devotion?

Who made the child respect the parent?

By these questions, O Lord,

I help to identify You as Creator of all things through the Holy Spirit.[10]

God created corporeal life
And acts and words, through which one who has free will expresses choices.[14]
God is all-seeing and not to be deceived.[16]

On God's Purpose and Human Responsibility

Meditation teaches the best things to be uttered.[17]
Learn the commands which God has given.[21]
Seek to satisfy those who are poorly protected.[22]

On Worship

Truly, praising, I shall worship you, O God of truth, good purpose and power
We worship with reverence for God, who offers us support.[25]

Prayers

I shall serve You with good purpose.
Grant me the gifts of both worlds – of matter and mind – through Your truth.
I shall praise you in song as never before.[29] God help me.[32]

Prophecy

God has promised by truth and good purpose that there shall be wholeness and immortality within God's realm, strength and perpetuity within God's house.[43]
If you abandon this teaching, then there shall be woe for you at the end.
Such is the power by which God gives what is better to the honest poor.[46]

See Chapter 10 for further highlights from the vision of Zarathustra.

THE LEGACY

From the internal evidence of the Gathas[47] we know that Zarathustra's son and a local leader named Kavi Vishtaspa were among the first people to accept Zarathustra's teaching. Other Aryan communities on the steppes and in Eastern Iran subsequently adopted this monotheistic religion, but Zarathustra was killed, probably while in his 70s, during an attack on his community by a still-nomadic Aryan tribal group, long before his teaching had spread beyond his own community. The teaching, now known as Zoroastrianism, continued to be preached by those of his followers who were moved to become missionaries. As it diffused through the polytheistic Aryan tribes and communities, however, it was elaborated in a number of ways:

▷ The Magi, a hereditary priestly caste, who claimed to control spirits and interpret the movement of stars, initially opposed Zoroastrian monotheism, but later became priests of the new religion.

▷ Worship at fire temples, controlled by the Magi, became a central feature.

▷ Abstract qualities of right thought and understanding, power, truth, holy spirit, order, devotion, perfection, wholeness, health and long life, or immortality, became associated with minor deities.

▷ The primitive perception of darkness as the opposite of light, rather than the absence of light, was combined with Zarathustra's reference to God as the Lord of Light (Ahura Mazda), giving rise to the idea that there was also a lord of darkness (Ahriman or The Devil).

▷ The concepts of Paradise, Hell, Afterlife, Resurrection, and The End of the World were also read into Zarathustra's words, and interpreted with very simple, literal and immediate imagery.

▷ The word, *saoshyant*, used to describe an enlightened person, living a life of good purpose, became associated with the idea of a Savior who would appear at the end of the world.

It was this modified Zoroastrianism that became the state religion of the Persian Empire established under Cyrus the Great around 550 BC. It had drifted a long way from Zarathustra's original vision, but was, nevertheless, an important unifying religion for the Persian emperors and their subjects, and Cyrus the Great's empire, centered in what is now Iran and Iraq, was much more humane than that of the Babylonians he displaced.

Fire temples were built throughout the Persian Empire, often adorned with carvings combining a bull's body, a man's head and a bird's wings. The fires that were kept burning in the temples were seen as holy and surrounded by elaborate rituals.

The religion prospered for many generations under Cyrus and his successors, despite tensions between dualists, who saw God (Ahura Mazda) and the Devil (Ahriman) as equals in battle, and monotheists, known as Zurvanites, who sought to retain the concept of One God above all.

Cyrus conquered Babylon in 538 BC, making the Persian Empire the most powerful in the region, a situation that lasted for more than 200 years. At its height, the empire stretched from what is now Libya in the west to the borders of India in the east.

One of Cyrus' acts on entering Babylon was to release all the members of the hierarchies of Babylon's subject tribes and petty kingdoms that had been held captive in the city for years beforehand. These captives included Jews, who were allowed to return to Jerusalem and encouraged to rebuild their temple there. The release of the captives of Babylon was an act that was typical of the just and open Zoroastrian rule of the Persians, further evidence of which has been found in inscriptions left by Cyrus' successor, Darius (522-486 BC), which include the following:

"A Great God is Ahura Mazda, who created this excellent work we see around us, who created happiness for man, who bestowed wisdom and energy on Darius the king. By the favor of Ahura Mazda, I am a friend to the right; I am not a friend to the wrong. It is not my desire that the weak man should have wrong done to him by the mighty; nor is it my desire that the mighty man should have wrong done to him by the weak. What is right; that is my desire. I am not a friend to a man who is a Lie-follower. I am not hot-tempered. What things develop in my anger, I hold firmly under control by my willpower. I rule firmly over my impulses."[48]

The Persian Empire was eventually conquered by Alexander the Great in 334 BC – over a century after Darius' death. Alexander's rule lasted only eight years, but, during this time, many priests were slaughtered, temples destroyed and much Zoroastrian literature lost. However, the Gathas and the "Good Religion" survived Alexander and his warring successors to become the guiding religion in Iran for a further millennium, first under the Greek Seleucid Dynasty (312-141 BC), then the Arsacid Parthians (141 BC-AD 224) and the

Sassanian Persians (AD 224-651). During this time, the religion, almost inevitably, became associated with the empires that adopted and manipulated it. The corruption of imperial leaders and their priests and the confusion caused by the monotheist/dualist debate continued until, eventually, from AD 636, the religion fell, along with the Sassanian Empire, under the onslaught of Arab imperialism and Islam[49] (see Chapter 7).

Although Zoroastrianism did not spread significantly beyond the bounds of these pre-Islamic empires, its teachings had a profound effect on Judaism and hence on Christianity.[50] It also survived the Arab conquest of Iran as a minority religion, despite more slaughter and other incentives to mass conversion to Islam.

The first Muslim caliphs imposed a poll tax on non-Muslims and, by AD 700, Arabic had replaced Pahlavi as Iran's official language, but Zoroastrians remained a considerable minority and were able to translate many Zoroastrian works into Arabic. Persecution of non-Muslims intensified, however, and, in AD 917, a small group of Zoroastrian pioneers sailed east from the Persian Gulf for Gujarat. They became known there as the Parsis. In 936 the local Hindu Rajah recognized an autonomous Zoroastrian colony in the village of Sanjat. By the end of the 12th century, Parsis had settled in many towns along the coast of Gujarat, but, in 1297, Gujarat was conquered by Muslims (under the Sultan of Delhi) and the Parsis again suffered from the introduction of a poll tax on non-Muslims.

Back in Iran, the remaining Zoroastrians were a dwindling minority. Their numbers were reduced particularly sharply during the reign of Shah Abbas II (1642-67) who ordered their forcible conversion to Islam and murdered refusers, most notably at the Massacres of Isfahan (1665).

In India, on the other hand, Parsi numbers and influence continued to grow. At the end of the 14th century, when North India was invaded and Delhi sacked by the warlord, Timur, Gujarat became an independent sultanate. It was subsequently incorporated into the Mogul Empire that dominated India up to the 17th century, but, in 1661, the city of Bombay was acquired and developed by the British, who granted the Parsis religious freedom. This prompted many of them to move from Gujarat to Bombay, where they worked within the British imperial system and eventually built a thriving community. They now number some 100,000 around Bombay plus twice as many in the worldwide Parsi diaspora.

In the 1820s Parsis set up Bombay's first printing press. In 1851, they founded

The Zoroastrian Reform Society, which clarified the primacy of the Gathas and confirmed Zoroastrianism as a monotheistic religion. In 1854, they founded The Society for the Amelioration of the Conditions of the Zoroastrians in Persia, which was instrumental in achieving the abolition of the Persian poll tax on non-Muslims in 1882, and the choice of Tehran for the First World Zoroastrian Congress in 1960. Today, Parsis in India own many large hotels, stores and factories and are well known for their generosity to good causes.

Their creed is: "Good Thought; Good Words; Good Deeds." Faith and devotion are not enough. A Parsi must live up to the creed of good thoughts, words and deeds. The religion specifies four duties:

▷ Worship God selflessly

▷ Be loyal and obedient to the teachings of Zarathustra

▷ Fight against Evil

▷ Have confidence in the laws of nature and God's Will

For all Zoroastrians, the fight against evil must be non-violent. Evil must be conquered by love. Parsis work and pray for world peace, for tolerance and respect for all peoples, whatever their color, race or religion. A Parsi is expected to be fully involved in the world, working for the good of others and believing that we can all develop spiritually in this life and that it is God's purpose that this world should eventually become a place of goodness and love. Parsis have no country and do not claim one, so they can look at international problems more impartially than most and are dedicated to world peace.[51]

With such a sound creed and outlook, it is surprising that the numbers of Zoroastrians and Parsis in the world should now be so few (less than a million). Perhaps this is a consequence of the forcible destruction of Zoroastrianism in its homeland by Islam and the subsequent decisions of Parsis to remain a community intent on survival rather than evangelism.

The subsumption of faith within community means that Zoroastrianism, despite its antiquity and virtues, is clearly never destined to become a religion that will bring the world peace that its founder hoped for. Indeed, some of the Parsis' decisions, such as opposing marriage outside the faith, refusing to accept the children of Parsi women married to non-Parsi husbands as members of the faith, and refusing to admit outsiders into their temples, are likely to ensure that they remain a dwindling minority. However, the contribution of

Zarathustra's vision to the continuing search for truth and unity should not be underestimated. It was Zarathustra who, through the Gathas, provided civilization with the first lasting visions of spiritual light and the unity of God. Although we seem to have lost the plot in the three millennia that have followed, the Gathas still provide a foundation for an approach to spiritual truth insofar as our understanding will allow, and insofar as it is needed to make the world a place of goodness and love.

Or, in the words of one of 20th century's best-known Zoroastrians, Farook Bulsara, aka Freddie Mercury of Queen:

One man/One goal/One mission
One heart/One soul/One solution
One flag – of light/One God/One vision
One flesh/One bone/One true religion
One race/One hope/One real decision
Give me one vision
No wrong/No right
Let me tell you there's no black & white
No blood/No stain
All we need is one world/One vision
A vision of one sweet union
Give me your hand
Give me your heart
There's only one direction
One world/One nation/No hate
Just give me one vision.[52]

Long before the time of Zarathustra, the one race – one family – of humans that emerged in Africa had spread throughout the world and become thousands of communities, developing in varying degrees of isolation and interacting with fear and suspicion. Now, however, as we enter a new millennium, modern trade and communication have brought us all back together. We must now live together as one community – one family again – albeit with much acquired diversity. If we fail to do this, we risk destroying ourselves. It is time to rebuild a vision compatible with unity, and the foundation Zarathustra gave us over three thousand years ago provides a reference point from which that vision can still be built, a theme we will return to after considering the worlds, visions and legacies of our next eight prophets.

2

MOSES &
GOD'S LAW

———•●•———

When Cyrus the Great, the Zoroastrian Emperor of Persia, invaded Babylon in 538 BC, he liberated the Jewish leaders held captive by the Babylonians and encouraged their return to Jerusalem and the rebuilding of the Jewish temple there. This act facilitated a development in Jewish religious and literary creativity that would eventually lead to the production of the Jewish Torah and the Christian Bible's Old Testament. The Books of Moses became a fundamental part of both and, hence, of Jewish and Christian doctrine. They also provided an important part of the context for the holy book of Islam, the Koran. Retrospectively, we can see that Cyrus the Great's liberation of the Jews from Babylon was clearly a key event in the development of the world's religions.

Prior to their liberation, the Babylonian Jews were already putting together some of the stories that would become the Torah. These consisted of collections of the oral traditions of the Hebrews, the 12 tribes of Israel, and included many re-workings of old Mesopotamian and Egyptian stories.[1] They were brought together and presented as a comprehensive history – from the creation of the world to the deliverance of the Hebrews from an earlier period of captivity in a foreign land, Egypt, and on to the rise and fall of the Kingdom of Israel. The history covers the story of Adam, the first man; of Abraham, Isaac and Jacob/Israel, the forefathers of the 12 tribes of Israel; of Israel's sons and their move to Egypt; of the Israelites' descent into slavery in Egypt; and of the birth, life and death of Moses, the prophet, who, with the help of God, was able to lead the Israelites out of bondage in Egypt.

During their Babylonian captivity, the story of an earlier deliverance was bound to have been a part of the folklore that would resonate. Faith in God and adherence to religious practices would also have been important for identity preservation, giving hope for the future. It is not surprising, therefore, that the idea of a direct relationship between God and the Jews was the major theme running through all these books and their stories of the people's history.

The Books of Moses cannot, of course, be read as a reliable world history and much of the writing suggests that Yahweh, the god of the Torah, was just another tribal god.[2] But the story of the Creation is definitely the story of a universal God and many of Moses' Laws have a universal application. God's Law, as presented in the stories of Moses, also appears to fill a gap in the pre-existing monotheism: the rules of behavior spelled out by Moses may well be aspects of the Good Purpose so important to Zarathustra in the Gathas. Although Zarathustra made many references to Good Purpose in the Gathas, those that have survived give very little information about what he actually meant by this term. The books of Moses therefore provide our earliest evidence of a detailed moral code associated with monotheism.

The selected highlights of the Vision that follow as the Jewish contribution to the quest for God's truth are taken principally from the Books of Moses. The extended highlights presented in the Collected Visions (Chapter 10) also include selections from the much later collections of Proverbs and Psalms. All the selections are part of both the Jewish canon and the Christian Old Testament.

THE VISION – SELECTED HIGHLIGHTS

On The Nature of God

God is the Lord. There is no other. God is the Rock. All God's works are perfect. All God's ways are just. God is without iniquity.[3]

In the beginning, God created the heavens and the Earth.[4]

On God's Purpose and Human Responsibility

Have no other gods before God. Do not make, bow down to, or serve any graven image or likeness of anything that is in the heavens above or in the earth beneath.

Do not take the name of God in vain.[5] Honor your father and your mother, so that your days may be long in the land that the Lord your God gives you.

Do not kill. Do not commit adultery. Do not steal. Do not bear false witness against your neighbor. Do not covet your neighbor's house, wife, servants, ox, ass, or anything else that is your neighbor's.[6]

Do not make yourselves gods of silver or gold.[7]

Do not lie. Do not deceive one another. Do not oppress your neighbor or rob him.

Do not oppress the poor and needy hired servant. Do no injustice in judgment.

Do not be partial to the poor or defer to the great. Judge your neighbor fairly.

Love your neighbours as yourself. And when strangers sojourn in your land, do not do them wrong. Love them as yourself. Have the same law for the sojourner and the native. Do not pollute the land. Love and serve the Lord your God with all your heart and with all your soul and with all your might. These words shall be upon your heart. Teach them diligently to your children and talk of them when you sit in your house, when you walk by the way, when you lie down and when you rise. Respect the Lord and walk in God's ways.[8] Better a patient man than a warrior: one who controls his temper rather than one who takes a city. Discipline your children and they will bring you peace. They will bring delight to your soul.[9]

On Worship

Sing to the Lord, for God is highly exalted.[10]

Prayers

I will sing to the Lord for God is highly exalted. The Lord is my strength and my song. This is my God, I will praise and exalt Him. Who is like You, O Lord, among the gods? Majestic in Holiness, doing wonders.[10] Let the Lord go with us. Forgive our iniquity and sin and take us for Your inheritance.[11]

May the Lord bless you and keep you.

May the Lord's face shine upon you, be gracious to you and give you peace.[12]

Prophecy

God will reign for ever and ever.[10]

We need have no fear of false Prophecy.[13]

See Chapter 10 for further highlights from the vision of Moses (+ Proverbs & Psalms).

THE LEGACY

The words generated by Moses' vision and collected in the Jewish Torah show clearly that he, like Zarathustra, was an early prophet of monotheism. The influence of the ethics contained in these words, particularly in the Ten Commandments, has since been evident not only in Judaism and Christianity, where they form part of the canon, but also in Islam, Sikhism and the Bahai Faith and, to some extent, in the Universal Declaration of Human Rights. Indeed, it could be argued that Moses remains the most widely influential of all nine prophets considered in this book, especially as the Talmud, a later part of the Jewish canon, also contains such examples of universal spiritual advice as:

▷ You must forgive those that transgress against you before you can look to forgiveness from God.

and:

▷ The charities of life are worth more than all ceremonies.

Another universal – but more mystical – tradition known as Kabbalah also developed within Judaism and is enjoying a revival today. Kabbalah is a largely oral tradition of the master/pupil type common in eastern religions like Buddhism (see Chapter 5). It claims the patriarch Abraham as its founder and, among its formative adherents, Rabbi ben Akiva who was skinned alive by the Romans in first century Judea (see below).

The earliest extant written work referred to by Kabbalists is the third-century *Sefir Yezira* (The Book of Creation), but Kabbalists also refer to lost works going back as far as the second century *Zohar*, written by Shimon bar Yochai and re-discovered by Moses de Leon in 13th-century Spain, and even to *The Book of Formation* attributed to Abraham. Kabbalism's current revival is not limited to the Jewish community and some of its insights can be found quoted in Chapter 11.

But the next part of this chapter looks at the Torah – the heart of the Jewish canon – and its relationship to Jewish history and the modern state of Israel.

The Torah provides no evidence of Hebrew missionaries spreading the good news in the way the early Zoroastrians did. The orthodox rabbinical Judaism that emerged was an essentially tribal, then ethnic phenomenon. The Books of Moses (Genesis, Exodus, Leviticus, Numbers and Deuteronomy) were actually compiled over several centuries following Moses' death. They contain many additions to his monotheistic teaching. The writings, which still form part of the Torah and the Christian Bible, also illustrate confusion, idolatry, barbarity, misogyny, racism and genocide among a group of 12 small nomadic tribes, the Hebrews or Israelites. These negative aspects in the chronicles were no doubt typical of the tribal religions of this time and region and many of them faded in significance as Judaism (and Christianity) developed.

Had this remained the case, there would be little value in mentioning them as part of Moses' legacy for today. But, for many Jewish (and Christian) fundamentalists, some, if not all, of these aspects have re-emerged as a significant part of the religious mind-set following the creation of the modern state of Israel, particularly within Israel's National Religious Party and the Likud-led coalition government last re-elected in 2003. Each aspect is, therefore, illustrated briefly in introducing our short review of Jewish history.

1. The confusion between God and man goes back to Genesis 6:

> ▷ When men began to multiply on the earth, the Sons of God saw that the daughters of men were fair, and took to wife such as they chose ... The daughters of men bore children to them. These were the mighty men of old.

This early confusion led to the emergence of an anthropomorphic vision of God absent in eastern religions, and to the idea, peculiar to Judaism, that the children of Israel, specifically those who continue to follow the Jewish religion, are God's chosen people with a God-given right to occupy and rule all the Biblical lands. The specific extent of this God-given right is referred to repeatedly in the Books of Moses, Joshua and Judges and is returned to below in the contexts of both Biblical history and current fundamentalist goals.

2. The early Israelites' flirtations with polytheism and with idolatry in the form of a golden calf are condemned in Exodus, but the visual image of angels is accepted and detailed instructions for the making of an ark for the stone tablets of the Ten Commandments suggest the need for some form of material connection with the spirit of God, if not a visual graven image:

▷ Behold, I send an angel before you to guard you and bring you to the place I have prepared.

▷ Make an ark of acacia wood. Overlay it with pure gold, within and without. Make a mercy seat of pure gold with two cherubim of gold on the two ends ... A lamp may be set up to burn continuously in the tabernacle of the ark.

The idea of the need for a burning lamp echoes a ritual that crept into Zoroastrianism, that other early monotheistic faith. This may have been due to common roots or just coincidence, but, unfortunately, most of the religious developments and rituals that have emerged in these and other religions since have tended to emphasize exclusivity over common ground.

3. Examples of the advocacy of violence referred to above are rife in Genesis. They range from the advocacy of blood sacrifice to bloody rituals with babies and extremes in punishment:

▷ Taking the blood of oxen, Moses threw it upon the people.

▷ He that is eight days old shall be circumcised.

▷ Whoever curses his father or mother shall be put to death.

Genesis also shows an acceptance of slavery:

▷ When a man strikes his slave and the slave dies, he shall be punished.

and a less than humane attitude toward animals:

▷ When an ox gores a man or woman to death, the ox shall be stoned, but the owner of the ox shall be cleared.

In Exodus, there are tales of even greater inhumanity and bloodthirstiness, notably with regard to intolerance and punishment:

On finding the people worshiping the golden calf, Moses is quoted as asking:

▷ Who is on the Lord's side? Come to me.

and adding to those who came:

▷ Thus says the Lord, God of Israel, "Let every man put on his sword and go from gate to gate throughout the camp and slay his brother, his companion and his neighbor." The sons of Levi did according to the word of Moses, and about 3,000 of the people fell that day.

The general application of such barbarity is reinforced in Leviticus:

▷ Whoever blasphemes the name of the Lord shall be put to death; the congregation shall stone him.

4. Evidence of misogyny appears in both Exodus:

▷ You shall not permit a sorceress to live.

and Leviticus:

▷ If a woman conceives and bears a male child, she shall be unclean seven days; if she bears a female child, she shall be unclean two weeks.

5. The racist and genocidal sentiments start in Genesis, where God is quoted directly as saying to Abraham:

▷ Go from your country and your kindred to a land I will show you. I will make you a great nation. To your descendants I will give the land from the river of Egypt to the Euphrates – the land of the Kenites, Kenizzites, Kadmonites, Hittites, Perizzites, Rephaites, Amorites, Canaanites, Girgashites and Jebusites.

God also spoke to Abraham's descendants:

▷ I will send my terror before you and throw into confusion all against whom you shall come.

This theme continues in Exodus:

▷ I will drive the Canaanites out until you possess the land from the Red Sea to the Sea of the Philistines. All this land I will give you for all time.

It recurs in Numbers:

▷ The Lord said to Moses: "Send men to spy out the land of Canaan, which I give to Israel."

and:

▷ They took possession of the land of the Amorites.

The first explicit celebration of genocide follows:

▷ They warred against Midian as the Lord had commanded and slew every male. They took captive the women and their little ones. They took as booty all their cattle, flocks and goods. They burned their cities and all their encampments.

Numbers goes on to state that Moses was angry because the Midianite women and children had been spared. He commanded that the Israelites:

▷ Kill every male child and kill every woman who has known man by laying with him, but keep all the virgins alive for yourselves.

Racist promises and genocidal intentions continue in Deuteronomy:

▷ When the Lord your God brings you in to the land you are to possess and gives many nations over to you, nations greater and mightier than yourselves, you must utterly destroy them; make no covenant with them; and show no mercy to them.

▷ Make no marriages with them.

▷ You shall be blessed above all peoples.

▷ You shall destroy all peoples that the Lord will give over to you. Your eye shall not pity them.

Several of these aspects of the Israelite legacy have contributed to more than three millennia of almost continuous conflict between Israelites, then Jews and Israelis, on the one hand, and their neighbors on the other. Between 900 BC and 1945, the Jews were usually the underdogs and victims in this conflict, but, with the establishment and expansion of Israel, the new Jewish state in Palestine, they have become the oppressors again.

The creation of the state of Israel was initially a consequence of Western guilt and sympathy following the Jewish holocaust under Nazi Germany, but its recently renewed expansionism under Ariel Sharon has generated a situation that constitutes a blot on our civilization and could even threaten its survival. The 2003 US road map to peace may yet offer a way out, but Sharon does not yet seem ready to take it seriously or approach it pragmatically. Stating an intention to maintain the current violent occupation of Palestine until the anti-Israeli retaliation of all terrorist groups and refugees stops is effectively saying no to peace. It would be an impossible task for the Palestinian

Authority, even if it had a normal government's powers, to maintain such a high level of security. Would any reasonable government dedicated to social reform in a country ever state that the reform will start only when that country's crime rate has fallen to zero? Does the Israeli government really want peace, or does it have a different agenda? Its fundamentalists certainly do. They have their God's agenda, as incorporated in the books of Moses (see above) and in the books of Joshua and Judges (see below).

The history of the three millennia from Moses' death to the current Middle-East Crisis – from the leadership of Joshua to that of Sharon – is briefly reviewed here, so that the reader can relate the current Israeli occupation of Palestine to its religious background.

The books of Joshua and Judges that follow the Books of Moses document a growing frenzy of serial genocide as the Israelites take over their Promised Land "from the wilderness and this Lebanon as far as the River Euphrates, to the Great Sea toward the going down of the sun."[14]

The first victims claimed are the inhabitants of the ancient walled city of Jericho:

> ▷ The people raised a great shout and the walls fell down flat, and they went up into the city and took it. They utterly destroyed all in the city, both men and women, young and old, oxen, sheep and asses, with the edge of the sword, and they burned the city and all within it, except the silver and gold and the vessels of bronze and iron, which they put into the treasury of the House of the Lord.[15]

The archaeological record suggests that the walls Jericho have been breached on several occasions, but always by the setting of brushwood fires around them, rather than by a great shout. Archaeology also suggests that Jericho had actually been a deserted ruin for hundreds of years at the time the Israelites were colonizing Canaan (c1100 BC).[16] Nevertheless, this story in Joshua remains a horrific description of the early Israelites' idea of God.

After Jericho, the Joshua story moves to the city of Ai:

> ▷ I have given into your hand the king, his people, his city and his land. You shall do to Ai as you did to Jericho; only its spoil and its cattle you shall take as booty for yourselves.

and:

> ▷ Israel smote them (the defenders of Ai) until none survived or escaped,

but the King of Ai they took alive and brought to Joshua. All Israel entered Ai and smote it with the edge of the sword. Those who fell that day were twelve thousand – all the people of Ai – Joshua did not draw back his javelin until he had utterly destroyed all the inhabitants. Israel took the cattle and the spoil as booty, according to the word of the Lord. Joshua burned Ai and made it forever a heap of ruins, as it is to this day. He hanged the King of Ai on a tree until evening, when his body was taken down and cast at the entrance of the city, and he raised over it a great heap of stones, which stands there to this day.[17]

Next on Joshua's list was Gibeon, but the Gibeonites surrendered, so

▷ Joshua made them hewers of wood and drawers of water for the House of the Lord.[18]

He then headed for Jerusalem. The King of Jerusalem got together an alliance against the Israelites, but we are told:

▷ The Lord threw them into a panic before Israel, who slew them with great slaughter and chased them by the way of the ascent of Beth-Horan. As they fled, the Lord threw great stones from heaven upon them, and they died.[19]

Then Joshua spoke to the Lord in the sight of Israel:

▷ "Sun, stand still at Gibeon, and moon in the valley of Aijalon." The sun and moon stood still until the nation took vengeance on their enemies.[20]

When Joshua and the men of Israel had slain all except the remnant that had entered the fortified cities, they went to Makkedah.

▷ Joshua took Makkedah and smote it and its king with the edge of the sword until none remained. When the King of Hazor heard of this, he sent to the kings of the northern hill country. They came out with all their troops – a great host. The Lord gave them into the hand of Israel, who smote them until there were none remaining. Then he took their cities and smote them with the edge of the sword, utterly destroying them. The people of Israel took the spoil of the cities and the cattle for their booty.[21]

▷ Joshua then wiped out the Anakim, a people great and tall, from the hill country.[22]

The book of Joshua ends with his death and is followed by the book of Judges, named for the Israelites' leaders during the years before the Kingdom of Israel was established. It tells how the Israelites were punished by having to serve other leaders when they failed to follow their god, Yahweh, and mixed with other tribes, and how they were led to further heroic exploits when they returned to him. The first Judge was Othniel:

▷ The Spirit of the Lord came upon him, and he judged Israel; he went out to war and the Lord gave Cushan-Rishathaim [the King of Mesopotamia] into his hand, so the land had rest for forty years, then Othniel died, and the people of Israel did what was evil in the sight of the Lord and became subjects of King Eglon of Moab.

Then came Ehud.

▷ "Follow after me," Ehud said, "for the Lord has given your enemies, the Moabites into your hand." So they went down after him, seized the fords of the Jordan against the Moabites, and allowed none to pass over. They killed about ten thousand of the enemy, all strong, able-bodied men. Not a man escaped. So Moab was subdued that day under the hand of Israel and the land had rest for eighty years.[23]

The pattern of sin, repentance and triumph was repeated under the Judges, Deborah and Gideon, and still "the people of Israel did what was evil in the sight of the Lord and served the gods of Syria, the Ammonites and the Philistines"[24] until:

▷ The Spirit of the Lord came upon Jephthah. Jephthah crossed over to the Ammonites to fight against them, and the Lord gave them into his hand. He smote twenty cities with a very great slaughter.[25]

▷ Then Jephthah gathered all the men of Gilead and fought with the Ephraimites. They took the fords of the Jordan and held them against the Ephraimites. When any Ephraimite said, "Let me go over," they said to him, "Are you an Ephraimite?" When he said, "No," they said, "Say shibboleth," and he said, "sibboleth" for he could not pronounce shibboleth, so they slew him. They slew forty-two thousand Ephraimites at that time.[26]

After Jephthah died, "the people of Israel again did what was evil in the sight of the Lord, and the Lord gave them into the hand of the Philistines for 40 years."[27] They were then delivered by another Judge, Samson. Samson married a Philistine, but doubted her fidelity. He set her a trap by giving her the solution to a riddle that he later put to the Philistine men of the town of Ashkelon. When they provided the solution he said, "If you had not plowed with my heifer, you would not have found out my riddle." The Spirit of the Lord came mightily upon him and he went down to Ashkelon and killed 30 men of the town.[28] Samson's wife's father subsequently found her another husband, so Samson caught 300 foxes, tied them tail to tail, with torches tied between them, lit the torches and set the foxes among the Philistines' grain fields and olive orchards. Following these acts of terrorism (or resistance – the terms are just the two sides of the same coin) the Philistines came to Judah and demanded that they turn Samson over to them. The people of Judah agreed to this, but when the Philistines came for Samson:

▷ The Spirit of the Lord came mightily upon him. The ropes on his arms became as flax that has caught fire, and his bonds melted off his hands. He found the jawbone of an ass, and with it he slew a thousand men.[29]

Eventually, Samson was caught again by the Philistines, blinded and imprisoned, then:

▷ The lords of the Philistines gathered to rejoice, and to offer a great sacrifice to Dagon, their god, for they said, "Our god has given Samson our enemy into our hand." When the hearts of the people were merry, they said, "Call Samson to make sport for us." So they called Samson out of the prison, and took him to the Temple of Dagon, where he said to the lad who led him by the hand, "Let me feel the pillars on which the temple rests, so that I may lean against them." The temple was full of men and women; all the lords of the Philistines were there, and on the roof there were about three thousand men and women looking on. Samson called to the Lord, "O Lord God remember me, I pray, and strengthen me only this once, that I may be avenged upon the Philistines." He grasped the two middle pillars upon which the temple rested, and leaned his weight upon them, his right hand on one and his left on the other. "Let me die with the Philistines," he said. Then he bowed with all his might and the temple fell upon the lords and upon all the people that were in it. So those he slew at his death were more than those he had slain during his life.[30]

Samson's final act was committed some 3,000 years before the terrorist attacks of September 11, 2001 on the World Trade Center in New York, but, if we rely on the death toll quoted from the Book of Judges, then, in terms of the percentage of the world's population killed, it still remains the world's worst ever terrorist suicide spectacular. Yet, like the Israelites' exploits that preceded it, this episode is still remembered – by Christians as well as Jews – as an act of divinely inspired heroism!

The canon goes on to tell of Israel's subsequent victories over the Philistines; of the establishment of a Kingdom under Saul, and of King Saul's downfall following his failure to destroy the Amalekites according to Yahweh's instructions:

▷ Totally destroy everything that belongs to them. Do not spare them. Put to death men and women, children and infants, cattle and sheep, donkeys and camels.[31]

It continues with stories of a golden, but still warlike, age under King David. One of David's key exploits was the capture of Jerusalem from the Jebusites. David's son, Solomon, succeeded him and built the Israelites' first temple in Jerusalem, but the Kingdom was split between Judah and the Northern tribes when he died. Throughout the stories of division and decline that followed, Israel's political reverses are related as consequences of the Israelites' failures to follow Yahweh.

The Assyrian Emperor, Shalmaneser V, conquered the Northern Kingdom of Israel in the 720s BC. He removed the northern Israelites to Assyria and then entered Judah and besieged Jerusalem in 701 BC. This is where the stories begin to mesh with the recorded histories of other peoples of the region. As a chronicle of events from this time forward, the Jewish canon can be seen as a combination of reliable history on the one hand and folk tales of prophets and their prophesies on the other.

Most of the stories of the prophets from the times of Israel and Judah's decline were written either during the Babylonian exile, or shortly after the return to Jerusalem. They were largely canonized by 200 BC and have not been substantially re-edited since Rabbi Akiva ben Joseph's Masoretic text of around AD 100 when the Jews' continued existence was threatened by the Roman Empire. Yahweh's earlier lust for serial genocide faded, but was replaced by occasional exploits of mass murder, such as when his prophet, Elijah, ordered the killing of 450 prophets of Baal[32] and again when:

▷ The angel of the Lord went forth and slew 185,000 in the camp of the Assyrians.[33]

As we have seen, exploits such as these did not prevent the Assyrian conquest of Israel and the Assyrian exile of all the leading Israelites, except those from the tribe of Judah. The ancient Israelites were subsequently lost to history. Today's Syrians and Lebanese, plus the Palestinians currently being displaced and decimated by Jews "returning" from as far afield as Europe, America and Ethiopia to the new state of Israel, will no doubt include many of their descendants. The indigenous people may even be the Israelites' true heirs in terms of genes rather than religious dogma.

Ancient Judah escaped the Assyrian conquest and occupation suffered by the rest of the old Kingdom of Israel, but the Babylonian invasion came about a century later when the Babylonians were displacing the Assyrians as the main imperialist power in the region. When Jerusalem fell to the new conquerors in 597 BC, the Jewish leadership was exiled to Babylon. The first Jewish diaspora dates from this time with many of those left behind moving as refugees to Egypt and other relatively safe areas.

One of the most moving Psalms sings of the Babylonian exile:

▷ 137. By the rivers of Babylon we sat and wept
When we remembered Zion.
There on the poplars we hung our harps
For there our captors asked us for songs.
Our tormentors demanded songs of joy.
They said, "Sing us one of the songs of Zion!"
How shall we sing the Lord's song in a strange land?

The exile lasted until the Persians took Babylon in 538 BC. The liberation is recorded in 2 Chronicles 36.22-23:

▷ In the first year of Cyrus, King of Persia, he made a proclamation throughout the land:

Thus says Cyrus, King of Persia: "The Lord, The God of Heaven, has given me all the kingdoms of the Earth, and he has charged me to build him a House at Jerusalem, which is in Judah. Whoever is among you in all his people, may the Lord his God be with him. Let him go."

The canon takes the history of Judah and the Jews into the fifth century BC. The exploits described in these ancient writings, along with the subsequent history of the Jews, constitute a still-continuing roller-coaster ride with the Jews becoming victims more often than victors and with their heroic exploits giving way to a series of reverses, culminating in the Nazi holocaust of the 20th century, which, in its turn, has spawned the re-emergence of the fundamentalists' hopes of a return to past glories as God's chosen people.

The return of the Babylonian Jews to Jerusalem from 538 BC was initially resisted by the locals, but, in 520 BC, Zerubbabel, a descendant of King David, was appointed Persian Governor of Judah and he was able to lead not only a successful return, but also the rebuilding of the temple. In 458 BC, he was followed by Ezra, the scribe and prophet, and, in 445 BC, the walls around the temple were rebuilt under the leadership of Nehemiah.

Persian influence in the development of Judaism is evident during this period. Examples include the appearance, in the Book of Job, of Satan, an errant angel of God, who becomes the Devil, and the development of the idea of the pit or Sheol as the antithesis of Heaven and home of the Devil. These ideas later find a home in the Heaven and Hell of Christianity and Islam.

When Alexander the Great, King of Macedon, conquered the Persian Empire in 334 BC, Judah came under Macedonian control and Greek influence. On his death in 323 BC, the country passed to Ptolemy I as part of a Greek empire centered upon the new city of Alexandria in Egypt. In 220 BC, it passed from the Ptolemaic to the Seleucid Greeks and was ruled from Antioch to the north (now in Turkey).

A Jewish revolt under the Maccabees (166-164 BC) drove the Greeks out, and a treaty with Rome in 161 BC gave some security to limited Jewish independence. In 152 BC, the Seleucids recognized the Jewish High Priest as the ruler of Jerusalem, and in 142 BC Simon Maccabee established full independence for a fundamentalist Jewish state.

He was succeeded by John Hyrcanus (134-104 BC). John attempted to repeat Joshua's conquest of the Promised Land. To this end, he demolished the cities of Samaria, Scythopolis, Adora and Marissa, whose inhabitants were forcibly converted to Judaism or slaughtered.[34]

John's successor, Alexander Jannaeus (103-76 BC) continued the expansion. His ambition led to a civil war between fundamentalists and rebels that cost some 50,000 lives.[35] Following the fundamentalists' victory, Alexander Jannaeus crucified 800 rebels and had the throats of their wives and children cut in front of them as they hung.[36]

On Alexander's death, his widow, Salome, ruled from 76-67 BC, then, under her chief minister Antipater, Judea became a protectorate of the Roman Empire. Initially, Roman Judea thrived, with peace bringing rapidly expanding trade, especially under Antipater's son, King Herod the Great (37 BC-AD 4), who separated the high priesthood from the crown and rebuilt the temple, but ruthlessly put down any opposition. Judea's prosperity under Herod led to a return of many Jews from other parts of the Roman Empire, but the drift from strict Judaism led to divisions between Romanizers and fundamentalists.

A significant Jewish teacher of this period who attempted to heal the divisions was Rabbi Hillel (60 BC-AD 10). He emphasized the spiritual importance of pursuing wisdom and knowledge rather than wealth and power:

> ▷ Do you wish to know the law of God? Love peace and cherish one another. If you do not win the respect of others, you will lose their respect. If you do not increase your knowledge, it will diminish. If you refuse to learn, your mind will grow in ignorance. If you use your abilities solely for your own benefit, you will commit spiritual suicide. Do not be confident of your own wisdom and goodness. Do not condemn another person until you have been in the same place as that person and reacted differently. The more you obey God's laws, the more fully you will love. The more you study, the wiser you will grow. The more advice you receive, the more enlightened you will become. And the more good you do, the more peace you will enjoy. Do not delay until tomorrow because tomorrow never comes.[37]

Hillel's advice of two millennia ago remains as universally valid today as it was then, but, during his lifetime, it was either not communicated well enough, or communicated but not acted upon. Either way, Hillel's wisdom was no match for the encroachment of Roman imperial might and the inevitable violent resistance. On Herod's death, direct rule from Rome was imposed, leading to a Jewish revolt under Judas of Gamela (AD 6) and the succession of Herod Agrippa I as Rome's puppet king.

This was the environment in which another Jewish reformer, Jesus of Nazareth, grew up, preached briefly and was crucified. His followers, notably Saul of Tarsus (St. Paul) went on to develop the new religion of Christianity (see Chapter 6).

Jewish resistance to Roman occupation continued. Revolts against Rome followed in AD 44, 52-60, 66-72 and 132-135. At the time of the first of these revolts, the Jewish population of the Roman Empire was around seven million out of a total population of 70 million (census under Emperor Claudius, AD 48). This included a Jewish population of two-three million in the areas currently occupied by the state of Israel. The cities of Alexandria, Babylon and Rome also had large Jewish populations and there were also an estimated million Jews living beyond the boundaries of the Empire.[38]

Following the revolt of AD 66, up to a million Jews were either killed or sold as slaves. The Romans tore down Herod the Great's temple (AD 70) and laid siege to the last Jewish stronghold, the hill fort of Masada, where around 960 fundamentalists committed mass suicide in AD 72 rather than surrender to Rome. The final revolt of AD 132-135 led to the destruction of Jerusalem and the construction of a Roman city over the ruins, a city from which Jews were excluded. In the religion of the Jewish diaspora, the local synagogues replaced Jerusalem as focal points for worship.

During the long decline of the Roman Empire, many Jewish villages survived in the Middle East and Jewish traders continued to practice their businesses successfully in cities and towns throughout the empire. Some adhered to the old faith, others converted to Christianity. Those accepting Christianity were instrumental in developing a religion that became the official religion of Rome, then the main religion of Europe and, subsequently, the Americas, Southern Africa and Australasia (see Chapter 6).

Those that held on to Judaism developed an identity that kept them separate from their host communities. This separate identity was reinforced by their religion's ban on marriage to non-Jews. Judaism also forbade professional money-lending (usury) within the Jewish community, but not without. As Christianity and later, Islam, also banned usury as a profession, non-Jews often relied on Jews for loans. This eventually gave a negative twist to outsiders' views of Judaism. The association between Judaism and Jesus' crucifixion twisted Christians' views even further.

In AD 313 the Roman Emperor Constantine moved his capital to Byzantium and adopted Christianity as his empire's official religion. Although he was tolerant of other religions, Christian persecutions of Jews (and pagans) in his Byzantine Empire soon followed. In 388 a Christian mob, instigated by their bishop, burned down a synagogue in Callinicum on the Euphrates.[38] From the 420s, there were pogroms against Jews in Palestine and Samaria. Their synagogues and villages were burned. They were barred from government office and armies; the Hebrew language was outlawed. In 527 Samarian Jews were virtually destroyed after rising against the Emperor Justinian.[39]

Jews also suffered occasional persecution outside the Roman Empire. In 455, the Sassanid Emperor of Persia, Tazdiger III, banned the Sabbath.[40] This led to a Jewish rebellion and the establishment of a small independent Jewish entity that survived for seven years before being retaken by the Sassanids. Apart from this episode, the Jews fared relatively well in Persia. So much so that they celebrated when the Persians took Jerusalem from the Byzantines in 624. They soon paid a high price, however, as the Byzantines retook the city five years later and massacred the Jews there. Jews were also massacred further south in Medina, where the Muslims beheaded Jews who would not convert to the new religion of Islam (see Chapter 7). But when Muslim armies defeated the Byzantines in 636, the few remaining Jews of the defeated empire fared better than the Christians and were generally tolerated – as long as they, like other non-Muslims, paid the poll tax.

The Jewish population of Christian Spain, on the other hand, suffered extensive persecution. They responded by aiding the Muslim armies entering Spain in 711 and subsequently prospered in Muslim Spain. Their influence in the new Muslim capital, Cordoba, was extensive and Granada became a virtually Jewish city.

Despite this, conversions to Christianity and Islam continued. By 900 the worldwide Jewish population had fallen to around a million. Then, when fundamentalist Berber Muslims conquered Southern Spain, prominent Jews in Cordoba were assassinated and the Jews of Granada were massacred. There was further persecution following the Almohad conquest of Southern Spain in 1146. Synagogues were burned and the remaining Jews were forced to convert to Islam or to wear a humiliatingly silly outfit called the shikla or, if spared this, to dress completely in yellow.[41]

Persecution of Jews also returned elsewhere in the Islamic world. In addition to the intermittent persecution that pre-dated the Muslim conquest continuing in Alexandria, Jews were forced to convert to Islam or wear yellow badges from 1121 in Baghdad and from 1198 in Yemen.

However, Jews fared far worse in Christian Europe, particularly from the time of the First Crusade (1095). Persecution in France was widespread before this, but forced conversions and massacres throughout Europe now became commonplace. There were major massacres in Rouen and the Rhineland in 1096. Jews were expelled from France in 1182. There were massacres in York in the 1190s and a spate of blasphemy and usury arrests throughout England from 1278, leading to the hangings of around 300 Jews and the expulsion of Jews from England in 1290. Medieval Christians depicted them as agents of the Devil who had tails and sacrificed Christian boys. They were expelled from town after town throughout Europe, being forced to leave their assets behind. They were ritually snowballed every winter in North Italy, unless they paid protection money.

There were major anti-Jewish riots in Seville in 1378 and 1391, and even conversion to Christianity failed to placate some of their neighbors in Spain: there were anti-*converso* riots in the 1440s in Toledo, and in the 40s, 60s and 70s in Ciudad Real. With the Spanish Inquisition from 1481, up to 2,000 Jews were burned at the stake, and up to 50,000 killed in all, including up to 13,000 *conversos*. The Spanish Inquisition went on until 1790, but, in 1492, the year Christians completed the re-conquest of Spain from the Muslims, an Edict of Expulsion forced some 200,000 Jews and *conversos* to leave the country. About half went to Portugal[42] and the rest traveled into other parts of Europe, or to North Africa and the Middle East. By the 1540s, the inquisition was hitting hard in Portugal as well. Many Jews, including *conversos*, were expelled from Lisbon in 1550 and some joined a much wider exodus to the New World.

This New World had been discovered by Christopher Columbus, probably a *converso* himself, in 1492, and, by 1549, the colony of Brazil had a *converso* governor-general in Thomas de Souza. However, in 1645, the Jews were expelled from Brazil. Many moved to the West Indies and set up plantations, but 23 refugees from Recife moved to Dutch New Amsterdam in 1654. The local authorities tried to evict them, but were overruled by the Dutch imperial government. They finally gained full civil rights as New Yorkers 10 years later when the settlement became British New York. This event can be seen as the birth of American Jewry, one Jewish community whose successes have far outweighed their reverses, and continue to this day. Their contributions in banking, retail, science, literature and entertainment have been out of all proportion to their numbers. For example, in 1792, when New York's Jewish population was still only a few hundred, Jews were instrumental in the foundation of the New York stock exchange. By 1820 there were 4,000 Jews in the USA, rising to 250,000 by 1880, 4.5 million by 1920, and around 10 million, in a total population of 260 million, today, including some two million of the eight million Americans in New York City. Jewish entrepreneurial skill is responsible for many of New York's 19th-century landmark developments, including Bloomingdale's and Macy's department stores, and much else of what makes today's USA what it is. Sigmund Lubli, a Philadelphian Jew, was a pioneer of the film industry and Jewish Americans are predominant in that industry today, not only as studio owners and producers, but also as directors and actors. The contributions of American Jews in other aspects of the entertainment industry have also been remarkable. For example, American popular music would be nowhere near as rich as it is without the input of such songwriters as the Gershwins, the Hammersteins, Irving Berlin, Jerome Kern and Bob Dylan, to name but a few.

By and large these contributions have not come from fundamentalist Jews, and many have been either critical of, or bemused by, the fundamentalist outlook. Film megastar, Kirk Douglas, for example, admits that "the more I study Judaism, the less Jewish I become"[43] and Bob Dylan expresses his bemusement in song:

> God said to Abraham, "Kill me your son."
> Abe said, "Man, You must be putting me on."
> God said, "No."
> Abe said, "What?"
> God said, "You can do what you want, Abe, but
> the next time you see me coming, you better run."
> So Abe said, "Where do you want this killing done?"
> God said, "On Highway 61."[44]

The contributions of Jewish individuals and families in the old world have been no less remarkable. They have included the writings Maimonedes (eg *Guide of the Perplexed,* c1190) and Spinoza (*Ethics,* 1677), Daniel Bomberg's printing press in Venice (1520); the works of David Ricardo and Karl Marx in the 19th century and the defining 20th-century works of Einstein (*Special Theory of Relativity,* 1905; *General Theory,* 1915), Freud (*The Interpretation of Dreams,* 1900; *The Ego and the Id,* 1923) and Kafka (*The Trial,* 1924; *The Castle,* 1926; *Amerika* 1927), plus contributions from innumerable other more recent scientists, philosophers and writers.

The Jewish creative spirit in other fields has also been significant. In the 1570s, Daniel Rodriguez built the Adriatic port of Split for Venice. From the 18th century, the Rothschilds and Hambros were pioneers in international banking.

The Reuters were pioneers in news. Europe's leading artists included the Jews, Pissarro, Chagall, Modigliani and Leibermann.

In spite of contributions such as these, the situation for Jewish communities in Europe remained precarious for most of the last half of the last millennium. Anti-Jewish riots in Cracow and Lithuania in 1495 led to the first expulsions of Jews from eastern European communities. In Venice, Jews were confined in the walled *Ghetto Nuovo* in 1515; Levantine Jews were confined to the *Ghetto Vecchio* in 1541, and a *Ghetto Novissimo* was built in 1633. By the 1650s, the walled ghettos of Venice housed some 5,000 Jews. Walled ghettos were also built in other European cities, both to protect and to confine the Jews.

Jews fared particularly badly in the Papal States: a walled ghetto was built in Rome in 1555 and throughout the 16th century Jews were expelled from other Papal Italian towns and duchies or subjected to forced baptisms.

In Berlin the synagogue was sacked in 1572 and the Jews were expelled in 1573. They were also expelled from Frankfurt in 1614, but invited back in 1630. They probably fared worst of all in Russia and Ukraine, however, where thousands were converted, expelled or drowned during the reign of Tsar Ivan the Terrible (1530-84) and where, at the end of the Thirty Years War (1618-48) over 6,000 were massacred by Cossacks at Bar and Narol. As many as 30,000 Jews were killed during that war in which some 300 Jewish communities in Central and Eastern Europe were destroyed.

For much of this time Poland was considered the safest place in Europe, but, by the late 18th century, Russian expansion brought the Polish Jews back under the Tsars and, while most of Europe was becoming less dangerous, Jews in the Russian Empire continued to live precariously, especially after the Odessa pogrom of 1871. In 1881 there were more pogroms throughout Russia and the Ukraine. During the 1890s Jews were expelled from Moscow and other Russian cities. Between 1903 and 1911 there were yet more pogroms and expulsions. The Russian Empire was on the point of collapse, however, and many Jews were involved in the anti-imperialist struggle, including Leon Trotsky, who subsequently became the Red Army commander following the fall of the empire in 1917. In spite of this, pogroms resumed after the revolution in the new Soviet Union and in Poland.

Back in England, Jews had been readmitted since 1656. In 1745 Samson Gideon became the first Jew to enter the House of Lords and, in 1858, Benjamin Disraeli, the son of a Jew, became the British Prime Minister.

Jews were readmitted to most Italian states during the 1700s and, in 1748, they were readmitted to Prague, having been expelled only three years earlier. They were also allowed back into France, but subjected to a poll tax until 1784. In 1789 the French Revolution gave them full civil rights as "French citizens of the Mosaic Faith," while rejecting the separatist idea that there could be a "nation within a nation." In 1796-8 the Italian ghettos were liberated by Napoleon and, in 1812, Jews were recognized as full citizens of Prussia.

The 19th century saw the emancipation of Jews in all of Europe, apart from the Russian Empire, but toward the end of the century, anti-Jewish ideas were becoming a feature of right-wing political parties such as The League of the French Fatherland. In 1879, the Anti-Semitic League was founded in Hamburg and, by 1886, the League's first German deputy was elected amidst rising anti-Jewish mob violence.

In the early 20th century German anti-Semitism remained a minority trait, and German Jews identified strongly with their country as well as their religious community. During World War I (1914-18) 31,500 Jews won Iron Crosses for service to Germany. In the aftermath of Germany's defeat, however, Adolf Hitler's violently anti-Semitic Nazi Party rose to power and, from 1933, the Nazi regime claimed six million Jewish lives, most of whom were rounded up and gassed during World War II (1939-45), an atrocity unparalleled before or since, in a war that claimed an unprecedented total of 25 million lives.

The guilt and sympathy that spread through Europe and America following the Holocaust was a major factor in the decision of the UN, founded in 1945, to accept the creation of the state of Israel in Palestine in 1948, a decision which facilitated the mass migration of Jews from Europe and America to Palestine and the displacement of the Palestinians, who were forced to pay the price for Europe's guilt. This decision turned the Jews from victims of attempted genocide back into perpetrators, as they repeated their quest of 3,000 years earlier to conquer the "Promised Land."

The wars of independence and expansion in 1948, 1956 and 1967, the Yom Kippur War of 1973 and the continuing determination of the current Israeli regime (subsidized by $3 billion a year of US Aid) to deny land and civil rights to Palestinians have so far cost the lives of around 20,000 Jews, 50,000 Palestinians and up to 30,000 Arabs from neighboring countries. Israel's 1982 invasion of Lebanon alone cost 30,000 lives – almost all of them civilian.

These numbers continue to rise relentlessly. Ariel Sharon's extremist Zionist government remains in control in Jerusalem and an uneven war of attrition continues between Israel's American-supplied military machine and a defenseless Palestinian refugee population, reduced to a level of desperation that leads many of them to applaud the atrocities of suicide bombers (see below).

Modern Zionism – the movement to establish a Jewish State – was a product of the late 19th century. Earlier in that century there were few signs of its existence. In 1836 a German rabbi had asked the Frankfurt Rothschilds to finance the purchase of land around Jerusalem in the Ottoman province of Palestine, but his request had been rejected. At that time the Jewish population of Palestine was a mere 600 out of a world Jewish population of over six million. World Jewry held that Jews were "no longer a nation, but a religious community"[45] and that "in the civilized world [the Jew] has found at last not only justice and freedom, but almost a certain recognition."[46]

However, a small minority of Jews adopted the idea of Zionism and, in 1896, the publication of Theodore Herzl's *Der Judenstaat* propelled its author to the forefront of the movement. Herzl was born in Vienna in 1860. He never learned Hebrew and had previously advocated the conversion of all Jews to Christianity as a solution to their problems of acceptance in Europe. Zionism was still rejected by the Rothschilds, who refused even to see Herzl, although they were by then financing Jewish agricultural colonies in Palestine. Baron Maurice de Hirsch, another prominent Jewish millionaire philanthropist, also rejected Zionism. He was happier financing Jewish colonies in Argentina.

In 1897 the First Zionist Congress was held in Basel and Britain was subsequently persuaded to offer some of its imperially held land in Cyprus, Egypt or Uganda as a possible site for a Jewish homeland. At their Seventh Congress in 1905, however, the Zionists decided that only Palestine would be acceptable.

By the start of World War I the Jewish population of Palestine had risen to 85,000. This fell to 60,000 during the war, but many Jews fought with the British and, in 1917, they were rewarded with a letter from Foreign Secretary Balfour to Lord Rothschild declaring that Britain would look favorably on the establishment of a Jewish homeland in Palestine. The peace treaty that followed the defeat of the Ottoman Empire made Palestine a British Mandate and immigration took its Jewish population to 500,000 by 1939. Palestine received 62,000 Jewish immigrants in 1935 alone.

Following anti-immigration riots in 1936, the British decided to restrict Jewish immigration to 12,000 per year. After another Palestinian revolt in 1937, many Jews, including Albert Einstein, who turned down an offer of the presidency of Israel, expressed a preference for the restoration of peace with the Arabs over the creation of a Jewish state. The immigration limit was then amended to 75,000 over the next five years. This was to be followed by a suspension of further Jewish immigration without the consent of the Palestinians.

But British policy was changed dramatically following the outbreak of World War 2, the sinking of refugee ships, the holocaust and increasing Zionist terrorism in Palestine. In 1945 there were 500,000 Jews in Palestine. By 1948 the Zionists had their State of Israel.

The Jewish population had by then risen to over 600,000, but there were still 1.3 million Palestinians on the land. Terrorism and expulsions quickly reduced this number by more than a million, leaving only 160,000 Palestinians, now renamed Israeli Arabs, on their former land. It began the world's worst ever refugee crisis and led to the series of Arab-Israeli wars mentioned above and the ongoing Palestinian *intifada*. The world's total Palestinian population has now reached six million, including just under one million in the state of Israel, two million in Israeli-occupied Palestine and two million in refugee camps around Israel's borders. The world's Jewish population is around 20 million, including six million in Israel and occupied Palestine.

The modern Zionist terror campaign began in the 1930s with the Irgun militia and the Stern Gang blowing up British tax and immigration offices and police stations in Palestine. It continues to this day, and has now become part of a two-sided war of attrition between the Israelis, using their multi-million dollar American-equipped army to retain control over Palestinian lands occupied in 1967, and the dispossessed Palestinians, fighting back with everything at their disposal, from stones to suicide bombers. The use of terror by the Palestinian resistance can be traced back to the 1960s. The Palestinian Liberation Organization, led by Yasser Arafat, supported the terrorists between 1967 and 1993, but has renounced terrorism since then. Nevertheless, fringe Palestinian terrorist groups such as Hamas continue to flourish. Arafat, now President of the Palestinian Authority, continues to condemn the terrorism of both sides, but appears unable – many Israelis say unwilling – to control some Palestinian groups.

But the first major atrocity in the current half-century-plus of terror in

Palestine was committed in July 1946. A group from the Irgun militia blew up the HQ of the British Mandate government in the King David Hotel in Jerusalem, killing 91 civilians, including 28 British, 41 Arabs and 17 Jews. Their leaders were Israel Levi and Menachim Begin. The latter gained further notoriety in 1948, when he led the massacre of around 250 villagers in Deir Yassin. He went on to become Israel's Prime Minister in 1977 and to invade Lebanon in 1982. Begin's defense minister was Ariel Sharon.

Sharon had come to prominence in October 1956 when leading a group of commandos who blew up 45 houses in the village of Qibya, killing 69 Palestinians. He was forced to resign as defense minister in 1982, following his complicity in the massacre of 800 Palestinian refugees by Lebanese Christians in camps near Beirut. By 1999 he was back – as Prime Minister – re-elected in 2003 and again reducing his country to the level of a terrorist state in order to pursue the supposedly divinely sanctioned goal of a pure Jewish homeland with continuing attacks, killing both terrorist suspects and innocent civilians and provoking ever more Palestinian acts of revenge. Between 1967 and 2000 195,000 Jews were settled in the occupied Palestinian territories. From 2000, under Sharon, the settlement rate was dramatically increased – another 100,000 in just three years. Palestinian reaction has included around 100 suicide bombings. There was a lull and even a short-lived reversal following the acceptance of the US road-map in March 2003, but this had passed by the summer with settlers returning to make Palestinian farmers destitute by destroying more and more olive groves, some of them dating back to Roman times. And in October 2003, the government announced plans for 600 new Jewish homes in the occupied territories in direct contravention of the road-map agreement.[47] Decisions like this will continue to provoke desperate reactions, including more suicide bombings, thus giving legitimacy to further attacks in a vicious cycle taking the country ever closer to a genocidal final solution; continually reducing the chances of finding a way to achieve peace and harmony in a multicultural state. In addition to the 100,000 lives lost in the Israeli-Arab wars of 1948-82 (see above), the death count for the terror campaigns since 2001 currently stands at around 2,500 Palestinians, including 340 children, and 400 Israelis, including 60 children, plus around 10 times these numbers injured on both sides. The rate of killing has increased significantly since 2002 when the Israeli government decided that killings of Palestinians by the Israeli army no longer warranted investigation.

The continuing pursuit of Sharon's goal is more likely to bring us to World War III than it is to bring peace to anyone. This would be the worst possible legacy of Judaism. The tradition has given us great teachers – from Moses, Hillel and Jesus to Einstein – but it has also given us perpetrators of genocide, terror and ruthless ethnic cleansing, from Joshua and Samson to Ariel Sharon and his supporters.

The use of religion for racist ends will have to be overcome if civilization is to survive to allow humanity's quest for unity and peace to continue. In this respect, there are hopeful signs, both within Israel and among Jews of the diaspora. These include the restraining influence of Israelis like Nomi Chazan, former deputy speaker of the Knesset, the emergence of the organization, Courage to Refuse, among Israel's reserve soldiers, and the views expressed by Rabbi Tony Bayfield, head of the Jewish Reform Movement in Britain. Nomi Chazan recognizes that Israel cannot crush the will of an entire people "as no-one should know better than the Jews"[48] and Courage to Refuse is an organization of young Israelis who reject the current government's expansionist policies and have vowed not to serve as soldiers in the territories occupied by Israel since 1967. In the words of their spokesperson, Shlomi Segall:

> ▷ Ariel Sharon will tell you that Israelis are fighting a war for survival against a bloodthirsty enemy. Not so. Sharon and his cronies are fighting a colonial war to keep his pet settlement project in place, to perpetuate the Israeli occupation and the subjugation of the Palestinian territories. It is a one-sided war with a not-so-covert purpose of destroying any hope of a Palestinian homeland. Although Sharon and his government are the elected and legitimate representatives of the State of Israel, he and his generals do not represent the basic values that Israelis – Jews and Arabs – stand for; so to criticise the current government of Israel is not to attack the people of Israel, and is definitely not anti-Semitic. By branding any criticism of the suffering he inflicts on the Palestinians as anti-Semitic, Sharon is enlisting something sacred for the vile colonial and expansionist ends he pursues. [No-one should] lend a hand to such a despicable attempt to desecrate the memory of Jewish suffering, and to use it to justify the oppression of another people.[49]

Rabbi Bayfield has addressed members of both Jewish and Christian faiths as follows:

▷ [It is] about time that we stood up against the fundamentalists within our respective traditions and stood together in affirmation of the shared values we claim to believe in ... Remember Yigal Amir who took the law into his own hands and murdered [moderate former Israeli Prime Minister] Yitzhak Rabin in the name of Judaism. Remember Baruch Goldstein who rose in the night after reading the book of Esther and murdered [29] Muslims at prayer ... Today you reap huge anger, radicalization, the desire for revenge – are you surprised? When will your misguided lust for empire and power end? Why do you need to own the whole world, which is actually God's? Fundamentalists, in their fear and insecurity, claim to have a monopoly on truth and more. They seek to seize power and so impose their authority on others. It is a desperate and disastrous phenomenon. It has led to 250,000 fundamentalist Jews clinging on to land which must, in justice, become part of the State of Palestine. It has led to coalition governments in Israel that reflect neither the democratic will nor the ideals of Judaism. It has led to a situation in the United States where Churches have been captured and seduced by men like Pat Robertson and have become a major obstacle to American participation in aid, development and the eradication of poverty in the Third World. You have made globalization a nightmare by making it an instrument, not for spreading education and welfare and eliminating hunger, but for trampling the brotherhood and sisterhood of humanity under foot. You have sought to impose democracy, free trade, and human rights primarily to win economic advantage. [But] you have resisted democracy, free trade and human rights [where] they threaten your hegemony and stand as an implied criticism of your culture ... You show no humility. You reveal only arrogance. You have not been prepared to be even moderately self-critical. You have performed small acts of goodness and kindness, but you have failed when it comes to the big picture and the tough issues. You speak of peace, but you train children to hate and arm them with terrible weapons. You have raped and exploited the Third World and created the conditions in which despair and terror are rife.[50]

When the rich world as a whole and the US and Israeli governments in particular recognize that those blessed with wealth and power should use it to support justice; when they heed Israeli and Jewish voices like those of Nomi

Chazan, Shlomi Segall and Rabbi Tony Bayfield, then we may be able to deal effectively with both the Middle-East problem and the much wider problem of world poverty. Until then, both these problems will overshadow the potential good for the world inherent in Moses' vision. They will remain major obstacles to the rebuilding of our human family, to the achievement of real civilization on Earth, and to the continuation our common spiritual quest. The 2003 road map to an Israel/Palestine peace settlement may yet provide a solution to the narrower of these problems but, without more goodwill from all sides, even this small step will turn out to have been just another false start.

3
ATHARVA & GOD'S ESSENCE

O ver 4,000 years ago, soon after the world's first urban civilizations had taken shape in the valleys of the Nile, Tigris and Euphrates, a separate Bronze Age culture was developing its own civilization in and around the Indus valley further east. The Indus civilization blossomed between 2,500 and 1,700 BC and produced its own writing, arts, sculpture and town planning.

The archaeological evidence from many sites shows that this was a relatively advanced and peaceful culture with extensive irrigation and sewage management schemes in many of its towns, but without the fortified structures and religious monuments of the Middle East. Its writing survives on seals and tablets, but has yet to be deciphered. Its towns disappeared from history during the second millennium BC and were not rediscovered until the end of the second millennium AD. We are not certain about how the civilization disappeared. It may have succumbed to floods, epidemic diseases, nomadic incursions, or some combination of these, but, on the basis of available archaeological evidence, there were no great struggles between civilizations.

Nomadic Aryan tribes moved into the region from Iran around 1500 BC. The settled survivors of the Bronze Age Indus valley culture, despite their one-time development, were no match for the invading Aryans, with their horses, spoked wheels and iron weapons.

In the centuries that followed an Indo-Aryan culture quickly developed. It produced a sophisticated written language, Sanskrit, and an extensive literature that includes some of the oldest religious texts still in existence. These are the Vedas (Sanskrit for Knowledge or Wisdom).

The Vedas are generally polytheistic and their deities are very similar to the pre-Zoroastrian deities of the Aryans. For example, the Vedas include hymns to Indra and Mitra who are almost identical to the Iranian Intar and Mithra, gods of war and honor. The Vedas also expound the concept of the caste system, which still survives, albeit illegally, in India today. The four main castes were the brahmins (or priests), the kshatriyas (kings, warriors and aristocrats), the vaishyas (traders and professionals) and the shudras (peasants and servants). The rigid hierarchy and separation of the castes was almost certainly introduced to prevent the invading Aryans from being assimilated by the conquered indigenous people.

The surviving Vedas have been collected as four groups: the Rig Veda (a compilation of over 1,000 everyday hymns), the Yajur Veda (hymns for sacrificial rites), the Sama Veda (hymns for chanting) and the Atharva Veda (magical rites of the fire priests). In addition to the older hymns, the Vedas include the Brahmanas (writings which detail the Indo-Aryan ritual ceremonies), the Aranyakas ("forest" teaching for religious retreats) and the Upanishads (meaning "sit down close" – philosophical writings).

The Upanishads are generally the most recent of the Vedas and most of them were probably first written down between 1000 and 800 BC. More than 200 Upanishads survive and 10 to 20 of these are still revered in Hinduism as the Principal Upanishads. They include the Mundaka Upanishad (see below).

Some of the Upanishads mark a move from polytheism to the idea of a single supreme unity, a recognition of the existence of God as the Creator and Protector of everything (Brahman), whose Holy Spirit (Atman) reaches out to everyone. Like other ancient religious texts, they existed as oral traditions passed down through generations before being committed to writing. The Mundaka Upanishad claims its source as God's "eldest son, Atharva"[1] saying that he received his knowledge directly from God and that "Atharva, in olden times, told Angiras. He, in his turn, taught it to Satayavaha, son of Bharadvaja and the son of Bharadvaja to Angiras, both the higher and the lower knowledge."[2]

The word mundaka derives from the root, *mund* (to shave), suggesting that the text of this Upanishad is presented as simple truth, shorn of obfuscation. In referring to its source as Atharva, God's eldest son, the writer is clearly indicating a significant teacher, not just a generic Aryan fire priest of old. He is distinguishing the source of the Mundaka Upanishad that follows from the earlier polytheistic Atharva Veda.

THE VISION – SELECTED HIGHLIGHTS

On The Nature of God

1.1 There are two kinds of knowledge, as those who know God declare, the higher as well as the lower. Of these, the lower includes the Rig Veda, the Yajur Veda, the Sama Veda, the Atharva Veda, phonetics, ritual, grammar, etymology, metrics and astronomy, and the higher is that by which the Undecaying is understood – that which is ungraspable; beyond family, beyond caste, beyond sight or hearing, without hands or feet, eternal, all-pervading, omnipresent, exceedingly subtle. It is the Undecaying that the wise perceive as the source of beings. As a spider sends forth and draws in its thread, as plants grow on the earth, so from the Imperishable arises the universe.

2.1 This is the truth. As from a blazing fire, sparks issue forth by the thousand, so beings issue forth from God, and to God they return. God is without and within, beyond breath, beyond mind, pure and higher than the highest immutable. From God are born life, mind, senses, space, air, light, water and earth. From God, all the seas and the mountains; from God flow rivers of every kind; from God come all plants and their juices, through which, together with the elements, the inner soul is upheld.

3.1 Vast, divine, of unthinkable form, subtler than the subtle, God's spirit shines forth, farther than the far, yet here, near at hand, set down in the secret place of the soul, and even here it is seen by the intelligent. God is not grasped by the eye or by other senses. But, when one's intellectual nature is purified by the light of knowledge, then one, by meditation, sees God, who is without parts.

On God's Purpose, Human Responsibility and Prayer

1.2 The immature, living in ignorance, think "we have accomplished our aim." Those who perform rituals do not understand the truth because of attachment and sink down wretched when their worlds are exhausted. These deluded men, regarding sacrifices and works for gain as most important, do not know any other good. Having scrutinized the worlds won by works, let us arrive at non-attachment.

2.2 God in whom the sky, the earth and space are woven with the mind and all living breath, know Him alone as the One. Dismiss other utterances. This is the bridge to immortality.

On Worship and Prophecy

3.2 The wise, who, free from desires, worship God, pass beyond the seed. Those who entertain desires, thinking of them, are born here and there on account of their desires, but, for those who are perfected souls, desires vanish, even here. Just as the flowing rivers disappear into the ocean, casting off name and shape, even so, the knower, freed of name and shape, joins the Divine, higher than the high. One who knows God joins God; crossing over sorrows, crossing over sins, liberated from the knots of the soul, becoming immortal.

See Chapter 10 for further highlights from the vision of Atharva.

THE LEGACY[3]

Among the tribes and states of the Indian sub-continent of up to 3,000 years ago, the monotheism of the Upanishads was a concept discussed only among the literate and intellectual minority. The Brahmins and other teachers who accepted it did so in such a way as to accommodate the earlier Vedas and other local beliefs, and in such a way as to protect their own status. The idea of a universal Soul led to a superstitious view of reincarnation in which individual souls of humans and animals could retain their individuality from one life to another in a cycle of being, returning at different levels, according to the merit they achieved in each life. This fitted in nicely with the existing caste system, if not with the spirit of the Upanishads.

The idea of a single God or permanent entity beyond human understanding, but One with which humans could nevertheless find unity, was seen as being beyond the reach of the masses. Thus the religions that emerged – and which, 2,000 years later, would be given the generic name Hinduism by Muslim invaders – produced the concepts of a divine trinity consisting of Brahman the Creator, Vishnu the Preserver and Shiva the Destroyer, with destruction seen as an inevitable and essential part of the cycle of being.

Each god of this divine trinity became identified with a material icon, and was accepted as a valid object of devotion through which contact with God could be made. Hinduism also postulated four stages within a human lifespan – the first for training and education, the second for working and/or raising a family, the third for the loosening of bonds, and the fourth for the holy life – and the religion accepted a trinity of ways to approach God:

(i) through wisdom or knowledge (eg of the teaching of the Upanishads),

(ii) through good living (eg following the lifestyles advocated in the Upanishads)

and/or

(iii) through devotion to God.

With respect to devotion, and in view of the subtle and impersonal nature of the One Supreme Being referred to in the Upanishads, it was acceptable to approach God through more personal images, or avatars, that the masses could relate to. In addition to Brahman, Vishnu and Shiva, God could be approached through the old gods of the Vedas, although these declined in importance, and through a variety of other avatars, including Shakti, a female partner for Shiva, and new heroes from Sanskrit puranas (legends), especially two major epic poems, the Mahabharata and the Ramayana, both of which are filled with sentiments conducive to the building of a national identity. The central story of the Mahabharata (Great India), is that of a civil war between tribes led by two branches of the same family, and can be seen as relating to an ideal unification of the tribes of North India. The Ramayana is shorter and tells of the adventures of its eponymous hero, King Rama, as he travels south from his capital, Ayodhya in North India, on a quest for justice against the demon king of Ceylon, kidnapper of his wife, Sita. In the story, both Rama and Sita are portrayed as god-like: Rama in his honesty, sincerity and love for his fellow creatures; Sita in her purity and kindness. Both are now important avatars for many Hindus.[3]

Another important Hindu avatar is Krishna. He appears in the most influential episode of the Mahabharata, the Bhagavad Gita (The Song of God), an episode that was probably added many years after the original story. It tells of Krishna, an incarnation of Vishnu, appearing as a charioteer to advise the warrior Arjuna, who is suffering from a moral dilemma as he prepares for battle. Krishna's advice clearly draws on the Upanishads, but it uses the concept of Spirit to belittle mortality and excuse killing on the basis of the idea of reincarnation, and it uses the concept of duty to glorify war:

> The wise grieve not for those who live and they grieve not for those who die,
> for life and death shall pass away.
> As the spirit of our mortal body wanders on in childhood, youth and old age,
> the spirit wanders on to a new body.
> Interwoven into God's creation, the spirit is beyond destruction.
> If any man thinks he slays, and if another thinks he is slain,
> neither knows the ways of truth.
> The eternal in man cannot kill.
> The eternal in man cannot die.
> As a man leaves an old garment and puts on one that is new,
> the spirit leaves an old body and puts on one that is new.
> Think also of your duty and do not waver.
> There is no greater good for a warrior than to fight in a righteous war.
> There is a war that opens the doors of Heaven, Arjuna.
> Happy the warrior whose fate is to fight such a war.
> To forgo the fight for righteousness is to forgo duty and honor.[4]

This kind of religious glorification of war has also crept into other religions. It is a chilling reminder, for example, of the way the God of the Old Testament is often used to sanction atrocities (see Chapter 2). Similarly, the idea that "there is a war that opens the doors of Heaven" returns in Islam in the way some Muslims interpret the idea of Jihad in the Koran. Indeed, today's Islamic suicide bombers are comforted by a belief that their actions serve them as a ticket to Paradise (see Chapter 7).

In contrast to this aspect of later Hinduism, the Upanishads also provided part of the context in which some very different Indian teachings emerged during the sixth century BC. Teachings that, like Zoroastrianism and Moses' Ten

Commandments, do not sanction killing. These included the teachings of Nataputta Vadhamana (c600-527 BC), who would be renamed Mahavira, meaning great hero, and Siddhartha Gautama (c560-483 BC), who would become known as the Buddha, meaning enlightened one. Both these teachers spawned new religions that still survive. The followers of Mahavira are the Jains (meaning victors), and those of Siddhartha, the Buddhists (see Chapter 5). Although their teachings gave rise to separate religions, both Mahavira and the Buddha were also accepted as teachers (or even avatars) within the various Hindu traditions.

The Jains recognize Mahavira as the last in a line of 24 teachers of their faith in the current cycle of the universe. All of them are revered as tirthankaras, meaning bridge-builders. Mahavira was born into a higher caste near Pataliputra (now Patna, Bihar) then the capital of the north Indian state of Magadha. He abandoned his family for the life of a wandering ascetic. He rejected the Vedas and the caste system, and taught that escape from the cycle of birth and rebirth could be achieved by right faith or knowledge and right conduct. The essence of right faith was to recognize all living things as having a valuable and eternal soul, while rejecting material things as transient, soulless and evil. His instructions for right conduct were: don't kill; don't lie; don't steal; abstain from sex, and renounce all pleasure in material objects. He taught that a fully spiritual life required non-attachment to material things and his injunction to avoid killing extended to all animal life (*ahimsa*).

In order to live according to his teaching, Mahavira traveled completely naked except for a facemask to ensure that he didn't accidentally kill insects he may otherwise breathe in. He carried a brush to sweep the road ahead of him, so that he would not kill anything by treading on it. To avoid forming new attachments, he never stayed in the same place for more than one night, except in the monsoon season. He earned reverence and the name, Mahavira, great hero, for his feats in conquering ridicule and persecution through maintaining his austere and non-violent lifestyle in the face of numerous provocations.

He traveled and taught for around 30 years and, by the time of his death in his 70s, had attracted a sizable community of followers. Although the original attractions of Mahavira's teachings would have included their simplicity and egalitarianism, the religion soon spawned its own priests and temples. At its first council of monks in Pataliputra, it split into two sects over the issue of traveling naked: the digambaras (sky clad) would wear no more than a loin cloth, while the shvetamabaras (white-clad) accepted the wearing of simple white clothing. The latter soon became the dominant sect and included Chandragupta (c320-293 BC), the founding emperor of the Mauryan Dynasty, among its adherents: after establishing a north Indian empire around his capital at Pataliputra, Chandragupta abdicated to become a Jain monk. Today there are several million Jains throughout India and in Indian communities around the world, and Mahavira continues to be recognized within the wider Hindu tradition, particularly for his teaching on non-violence, vegetarianism and transmigration of souls.

Like Mahavira, Siddhartha Gautama rejected the Vedas and the caste system and advocated a non-violent, non-acquisitive lifestyle. He too attracted a significant following during his lifetime. It eventually spread even more widely – far beyond India. His vision will be presented and his legacy reviewed in Chapter 5.

With regard to the Hindu legacy, however, it should be mentioned here that, in most of what is now India, Buddhism spread rapidly and, within 250 years of Siddhartha's death, it had become the established religion, thanks to Ashoka (268-233 BC), the third Mauryan emperor, who converted to Buddhism following his retrospective revulsion at the carnage he had caused in expanding his empire far beyond the Ganges basin. In the peaceful golden era that followed, Ashoka left numerous Buddhist (and Jain) texts in rock and pillar edicts all over the Ganges and Indus basins and deep into the south of the Indian peninsula. Following Ashoka's death, the Mauryan dynasty survived until 181 BC, but its influence waned and the influence of Buddhism waned with it. In contrast to the growth of Buddhist religions beyond India, the teachings of Buddha within India became more and more diffused through the mix that is Hinduism.

From the second century BC until around AD 320, India was divided into a patchwork of mini-states and continued to suffer from invasions from the north. The caste system survived and became more extensive and entrenched. Some unity was re-established in 320 under Chandra I, founder of the Gupta dynasty, initially based around the Ganges basin cities of Ayodhya, Vaisali and Varanasi (Benares). Chandra's successor, Samudra, then expanded Gupta influence down the southeast of the peninsula and his successor, Chandra II, expanded the Empire west to the Arabian Sea. By the end of this second golden era, six separate knowledge systems were recognized and accepted across most of India:

(i) samkhya – an essentially atheist view of the spirit/matter duality

(ii) yoga – differing from samkhya in recognizing a Supreme Being, and requiring its disciples to remain chaste, to avoid harming living things, to pursue inner calm and control, and to practice specific physical positions (asanas), breathing exercises and meditation in order to facilitate this pursuit

(iii) mimansa – accepting the stipulations of the Vedas as a means of escaping from the cycle of death and rebirth

(iv) vaisheshika – an atheist view of a universe made up of nine elements

(v) nyaya – a development from vaisheshika advocating the pursuit of scientific investigation and logical analysis

(vi) vedanta – accepting the end of the Vedas, ie the Upanishads

During the sixth century AD, India again lapsed into division and, although its influence later spread east to Indonesia (Hinduism became the established religion in Java and its dependent islands, and survives to this day in Bali), India's old religions at home had to face new challenges from the north and west.

Muslim invasions of India date back to the eighth century (see Chapter 7). The Muslim Sultanates of Delhi were India's most powerful states from the 12th to 15th centuries, and Muslim Mogul Emperors ruled most of India from the 16th to 18th centuries.

One reaction to the introduction of Islam to India was the birth of another new religion, Sikhism (see Chapter 8). Another was the development of Hinduism as an anti-colonial and nationalist religion. This continued during the rise of European power in India from the 18th century, contributing to the fall of the British Raj in 1947. It is still present today in the form of the BJP, the Bharat Janata Party (Indian People's Party) that currently rules the nominally secular democratic and federated nation-state of India (see below).

The exposure of Indians to Christianity (see Chapter 6) and other Western ideas was also followed by the foundation of many specific reform movements and modern adaptations of the Hindu traditions. These included:

▷ The Brahmo Samaj (God Society). Founded by Raja Rammohan Roy

(1774-1833) the society is based on a revival of the study of the Upanishads combined with a Western approach to science and education. It became very influential in the last days of the Raj with the support of Dev Tagore (1817-1905) and his son, the Nobel Prize winner, Rabindranath Tagore (1861-1941).

▷ The Arya Samaj (Aryan Society). Founded by Swami Dayanad Saraswati (1824-83) the Arya Samaj is a "back to the Vedas" movement and is still influential in India.

▷ The Ramakrishna Mission. Founded by Swami Vivekananda (1862-1902), a disciple of Ramakrishna Paramahamsa (1834-86) who had revived the One Supreme God teaching of the Upanishads, this Mission now carries out social, educational and medical work around the world.

Swami Vivekananda travelled to the US for the 1893 World Parliament of Religions in Chicago, staying on until 1900 and setting up Vedanta Society Centers in Boston, Portland, Providence, Pittsburgh and Los Angeles. He was the first of many Indian gurus who came to the West as missionaries. The most influential of the rest was probably the Maharishi Mahesh Yogi, who brought Transcendental Meditation to Europe and America in the 1950s and enjoyed fame in the sixties as the Beatles' guru. His legacy lives on in Maharishi International University in Fairfield, Iowa, many TM Centers worldwide and Natural Law Parties contesting elections in several countries.

Another Hindu reformer whose influence reached beyond India was Mohandas Gandhi (1869-1948), guru of the nominally secular Congress Party. Gandhi acquired the epithet, Mahatma (Great Soul), during India's independence struggle, combining the principle of duty from the Bhagavad Gita with that of non-violence from the Yoga school of Hinduism in his political activism, but also demonstrating the influence of Mahavira and of western thinkers such as Thoreau, Ruskin and Tolstoy in both his words and his deeds.

Gandhi's own additions to the Atharvan and later Hindu ethical legacies for the world were manifold. They included an identification and excellent summary of what he called our seven social sins:

1. Politics without principles

2. Wealth without work

3. Enjoyment without conscience

4. Knowledge without character

5. Business without morality

6. Science without humanity

7. Religion without [self]-sacrifice.[5]

Gandhi lived to see the achievement of India's independence in 1947, but was grieved by the fact that it was marred by religious strife between Hindus and Muslims, by the acrimonious division of the country into India and Pakistan, by mass migrations of Hindus from Pakistan and Muslims to Pakistan, in which some 14 million people were displaced and one million died. His campaigning for religious tolerance led to his own assassination at the hands of a Hindu extremist.

Despite this, India went on to develop as a stable democratic state over the next 30 years, with the Congress party winning election after election. Then, in 1977, the fundamentalist Hindu party, Janata, came to power.

India has swung between Congress and Janata (now the BJP) ever since, but the 1998 return to power of the BJP, whose supporters had already been allowed to demolish a mosque in Ayodhya while the BJP controlled the state government there, was accompanied by attacks on Christian, Muslim and Sikh targets all over India. Within weeks, the new BJP government also detonated India's first nuclear weapons and tested delivery missiles that they had named Agni after the Vedic god of fire and thunder.

A further tragic clash of fundamentalisms occurred in 2002. A group of Muslims attacked a train carrying Hindu pilgrims from Gujarat to the birthplace of their avatar, Ram, in Ayodhya. Several people were killed. Instead of treating the attack as a criminal act to be dealt with under the law, Gujarat's Chief Minister, the BJP's N D Modi, called for vengeance. Mobs of armed Hindus took to the streets on a murderous rampage, killing Muslims and looting and burning their shops and businesses. The rampage left a death toll of least a thousand (government estimate) and perhaps as many as two thousand (Muslims' estimate).

The legacy of the Upanishads in general and Atharva's Mundaka Upanishad in particular could still contribute to the human quest for unity and a universal approach to God, as exemplified by the Brahmo Samaj, the Ramakrishna Mission and the Mahatma, Mohandas Gandhi, but Hindu fundamentalism is currently leaving India prey to the ungodly influence of extreme nationalism and intolerance.

Such fundamentalism, given the ongoing dispute with Pakistan over Kashmir, constitutes just one more threat to civilization. If this threat is to be overcome and a secular and peace-loving Indian democracy is to prevail, the wealthy elite of India and those in power outside India – particularly in the US and the UN – will need to do all they can to help deal with the conditions that are feeding this reactionary fundamentalism.

4
LAO-TZU &
GOD'S WAY

To the east of the Pamir Mountains and north of the Himalayas some 4,000 years ago, when the people settling in the valleys of the Nile, Tigris, Euphrates and Indus were developing their now long-gone civilizations, and when nomads still wandered freely over the lands that would become the rest of today's nations, the people of the Yellow River Valley in Honan were settling in the communities that would become China, the world's oldest and largest nation. These people were united under the Hsia Dynasty by 2200 BC.

Like their contemporaries to the west, the people of the Hsia Dynasty developed polytheistic religious ideas. They carried out ritual sacrifices to their gods. They also practiced ancestor worship and divination. These practices continued during the Shang Dynasty (c1766-c1122 BC). Indeed, ancestor worship and divination can still be found in Chinese culture today, but Chinese monotheism also has deep roots. It can be traced back to the Shang period, along with writing and the production of elaborate bronze art, some of which still survives.

Under the Shang priest-kings, God was referred to as Shang-ti, the Sovereign on High. The priest-king was Tien-tzu, the Son of Heaven. He was invested with Tien-ming, the mandate of Heaven.[1]

A long period of prosperity under the Shang Dynasty began to falter in the 11th century BC. Tribes began to switch their allegiance to other leaders, notably those of the Chou clans moving in from the north.

When the Chous had established a new dynasty, they attributed the fall of the Shang priest-kings to their indifference to crime and the complaints of the people, to their lack of virtue and to "the rank odor of drunken orgies felt on high."[2] From the start of the Chou Dynasty, the leaders continued to recognize one God (Shang-ti), but their vision became less that of a personal, anthropomorphic God, and more that of one nebulous all-encompassing Power[3] along the lines described by Zarathustra and the Upanishads. Although there is no evidence that Zarathustra's teaching reached China until much later, God was recognized in the same way as the rewarder of morality and the punisher of immorality. Morality was seen as more important than making sacrifices.

The Chou Dynasty lasted until 249 BC. It was accompanied by the development of feudalism and by the widespread building of schools, but its early serenity was lost during the reign of King Yu (781-771 BC). Yu taxed the people heavily, squandered China's wealth and lost much territory to tribes of invading nomads.[4] In the troubled times that followed, the feudal system collapsed and much of China was split into warring states.

Many philosophers offered explanations for the loss of the golden age and the ways to revive it. One concept to emerge was that of the yin and the yang, complementary qualities described in the I-Ching (Book of Changes). The yin (shady side of a hill) was the spiritual quality of darkness, coolness, and dampness. The yin was seen as female and was associated with the earth, the moon and shadows. The yang (sunny side of a hill) was the material quality of lightness, brightness, warmth and dryness. The yang was seen as male and was associated with the sun. When these forces worked in harmony, life would be as it should be. During the dark days of the declining Chou Dynasty, the harmony of yin and yang had been lost, but faith survived. In the words of Chiu Kao from the Shu Ching (Book of Documents), "God is not cruel. People bring evil upon themselves."[5]

It was during this troubled period that Li Ehr (or Li Po-yang) was born – around 600 BC – in Ku Xian, some 400 miles south of Beijing. He worked as the keeper of the royal archives in the court of the Chous until around 530 BC, when he is said to have left the court and traveled west to China's borders.[6] Although few details of his time as a teacher have survived, he was destined to become known as Lao-tzu (The Old Master) and one story suggests that, when he reached the Hankukan Pass on China's western border, he was recognized by a guard and persuaded to write his teachings down.[7] They became the Tao Te Ching, the Book of The Way of Virtue and its Power[8] or of The Divine Intelligence of the Universe.[9] The selections that follow are taken from several of the many English translations of the various Chinese versions that are still available.[10]

THE VISION – SELECTED HIGHLIGHTS

On The Nature of God

1.1 The God that can be described is not the enduring and unchanging One – the Originator of Heaven and Earth, the Mother of all things – the Mystery.

1.2 Where the Mystery is the deepest is the gate of all that is subtle and wonderful.

25 Before the world existed and the sky was filled with stars, there was Something complete and beyond definition; silent, beyond all substance and sensing, standing alone and undergoing no change, reaching everywhere and in no danger. It has always been here and always will be. Everything comes from It. It is the Mother of Everything. Its Way is great. It is greater than the heavens, greater than earth, greater than kings. Humanity is schooled by the earth. The earth's nature is derived from Heaven. Heaven's nature follows the Way.

On God's Purpose and Human Responsibility

1.1 The way that can be trodden is not the enduring and unchanging Way.

1.3 Without desire we must be found, if the Way's deep mystery we would sound.

But if desire within us be, its outer fringe is all we'll see.

12 Too much color blinds the eyes. Too much music deafens the ears. Too much taste deadens the mouth. Too much riding drives you crazy. The wise seek to satisfy the craving of the belly, but not the desires of the eyes.

13.3 If you can put yourself aside, you can do things for the whole world, and if you love the world like this, then you are ready to serve it.

15.3 Who can make muddy water clear? Let it be still and it will become clear. It may be hard to wait for mud to settle, but if you can, then you can act. If you follow the Way without pretension, you will never burn yourself out.

46 Greed is the seed of the apocalypse.

On Worship

51.2 Every living thing should bow to the Way and its virtue.

Prophecy

43 Those who live violently die violently.

46 When the Way prevails in the world, the war-horses may be sent to draw carts.

When the Way is disregarded in the world, war-horses will breed in the borderlands.

61 A great state is like a low-lying estuary. It is a place where all the lesser states mingle and merge. If a great state takes a low place, it wins over the trust of smaller states.

79.3 In the Way of Heaven there is no partiality; it is always on the side of the good.

32 A ruler who follows the Way is like a river reaching the sea, gathering the waters of the streams as he goes.

30.4 and 55.4 All that is not in accordance with the Way soon comes to an end.

33.2 Those who follow the Way will last forever.

See Chapter 10 for further highlights from the vision of Lao-tzu.

THE LEGACY

After writing down the Tao Te Ching, Lao-tzu is reported to have left it with the border guard, Yin Hsi, and gone upon his own way.[7] The teachings were not widely disseminated until it was taken up by Chuang-tzu (369-286 BC) whose interpretation and development of the Tao were presented as a counterweight to Confucianism, a philosophy of government that was then gaining support across China. Confucius (Kong Fu-tzu or Zhuang Zi, 551-479 BC) was a younger contemporary of Lao-tzu and is reported to have met the Old Master while the latter was still working in the library of the Chou court. After the meeting, Confucius is reported to have described Lao-tzu as a flying dragon who rode the wind and clouds up in the sky.[11]

Confucius' main work, The Analects, is a practical guide designed for maintaining a feudal order through respect for traditional values and the use of a meritocratic civil service. He also edited much of China's earlier writing, including the I Ching, set up an extensive legal framework and elaborated rigid social traditions for the guidance of political and social life. In the Analects, he wrote: "I have transmitted and do not create anew. I am faithful to the men of old and love them."[12] When China was united again under the Chin Dynasty (221-207 BC), a new imperial legalism was adopted as the state philosophy and many old books were burned, but the Tao and some of Confucius' writings survived.

During the subsequent Han Dynasty (202 BC-AD 220), Confucianism became the main philosophy of Chinese government and continued to be taught in schools until 1905, while the teachings of the Tao were developed along two distinct paths. On the one hand, the Tao was interpreted and reinterpreted as a spiritual philosophy among intellectuals, and on the other, it was taken up by the masses, although only to be incorporated into earlier local religions, both monotheistic and polytheistic. Both these developments still lay claim to the name of Taoism, even though, to quote the Tao Te Ching: "The Way that can be named is not the true Way."

Compared to the teaching of the Tao Te Ching, the writings of Confucius were practical rather than spiritual and communalist rather than individualist. Despite this, Confucianism also spawned religious cults over the two millennia that followed Confucius' death. In 1503, however, the Chinese government ordered the removal of images of Confucius from temples and had them replaced with wooden tablets inscribed with his teachings. From 1503 to 1906, he continued to be officially revered, but not as a deity. He became "Master Kung, the perfect teacher of antiquity."[13]

For most of the time from the Han dynasty until the early 20th century, Confucianism and Taoism co-existed comfortably in China and among Chinese communities elsewhere without making much impact among non-Chinese. Many Chinese also remained receptive to new ideas, whether developed internally, or introduced from outside. Buddhism (see Chapter 5) reached China during the Han Dynasty and was widely accepted as a complement to the indigenous spirituality.

Following the fall of the Han Dynasty and the division of the kingdom, Confucianism fell temporarily from favor, while Taoism and Buddhism thrived. Both of these philosophies influenced Chinese culture dramatically, ushering in a golden age of temple building and painting. The landscape paintings of Li Ssu-hsun, Wu Tao-tzu and Wang Wei in particular used the relative scales of their tiny people and pagodas against backdrops of misty mountains and tranquil waters to give an impressive feel for their respect for nature and awareness of humanity's humble place within it.

The Chinese invented printing in the sixth century. This allowed wider distribution of Taoist and Buddhist texts. In the seventh century, the country was reunited under the Tang Dynasty (618-906), the first Manual of Feng Shui was printed, Chan (Zen) Buddhism was developed, and Zoroastrianism, Manicheism, Nestorianism and Islam all reached China through contacts with Persian and Arab traders. All these introductions had their influence on Chinese religions, but the indigenous Taoism and Confucianism remained at the core.

During the final years of the Tang Dynasty, the Confucian classics were printed and widely circulated and, after another period of division, Chinese unity was re-established under the Confucianist Sung Dynasty (960-1279). This was not the best of times for Buddhism and Taoism. The former was rejected as foreign and the latter rejected as too overlain with primitive superstition.

The Sungs were eventually overthrown by the invasions of Mongol Khans in the 13th century and were followed by the Mongol Yuan Dynasty (1260-1368).[14] Taoism enjoyed a revival under the Yuan Khans and Tai Chi exercises became a part of the tradition of Yuan Dynasty China.[15] This was also the period during which western Christian explorers and missionaries first reached the country.

The Pope sent a number of envoys to the Khans, but, as contacts increased, the Khans became less and less impressed by the West. When Mangu Khan received the Franciscan missionary, William Rubruck, as an envoy of King Louis of France, he told him:

▷ We Mongols believe that there is only one God, but, just as God has given fingers to the hand, He has given different ways to men.

And:

▷ He has given you Christian scriptures, but you do not observe them.[16]

Although the Khans adopted Chinese ways, they were always seen as foreign imperialist rulers and, by the 1350s in a time of famines, the peasants began to revolt against them. The White Lotus Society, a revolutionary sect that sprang from the masses and claimed Buddhist and Taoist inspiration[17] was a key part of the reaction against Mongol rule. It paved the way for the replacement of the Khans by the indigenous Ming Dynasty (1368-1644). The Mings were subsequently replaced by the Ching (Manchu) Dynasty (1644-1912).

Western Christian missionaries continued to be received in China during the Ming and Ching Dynasties, but, as more and more quarreling sects arrived, their message was compromised and their influence diminished. One key argument among the Christian sects was whether the Chinese words, Shang-ti and Tien, could be accepted as having the same meanings as the God and Heaven of Christianity.[18]

Other Western impacts did little to help mutual spiritual understanding. The Spaniards brought tobacco. The Portuguese brought opium. Chinese attempts to ban the opium trade prompted a British invasion in 1839.

China continued to suffer at the hands of the West throughout the 19th century and many blamed the conservatism of their Confucian philosophy for their relative weakness. Adeline Yen Mah has summarized the roots of this criticism admirably:

▷ For over 2,000 years, the sole purpose of education in China was to study the works of Confucius so as to pass the imperial civil examinations and become a magistrate. The importance of mathematics in the study of science was never recognized in Imperial China. Mathematics was considered a waste of time since it did not help one pass the examinations. Without an adequate numerical alphabet, mathematical thought could not develop and science could not advance.[19]

Some reformers advocated fighting fire with fire by adopting Western education and values; others, including Kang Yu Wei (1858-1927), presented visions that owed more to the Tao. While a candidate in the Confucian examinations of 1894, Kang organized a reformist petition and sent it to the

Emperor Kuang-hsu. He was subsequently appointed to the emperor's court in 1898 and began to implement his reforms (The Hundred Days Reform), until a conservative backlash led to a violent coup against Kuang-hsu, and his replacement by his mother, the Empress Tzu-hsi.

Manchu conservatism managed to defeat this attempted reform. Kang Yu Wei was forced to leave China. But the Dynasty's days were numbered. It was overthrown in 1912 and replaced by a republic that embraced western capitalism and social democracy. From soon after its inception, however, the republic suffered from continual strife. This included civil wars in the 20s and 30s, a Japanese invasion in 1937 and a communist revolution following the defeat of Japan in 1945. These violent upheavals cost tens of millions of lives.

The communists finally secured power in Mainland China in 1947 and replaced its inchoate capitalism and democracy, and its residual indigenous philosophies, with another import from the West, atheist Marxism-Leninism, albeit given a Chinese gloss as Maoism. This was taken to extremes in Mao's Cultural Revolution of 1966-76, when the famine following the farm collectivization of the Great Leap Forward cost another 20 million lives.

China's government has modernized the country and introduced a number of market-orientated reforms since this catastrophe, but it still remains in the hands of the Communist Party and persecution continues. Among its current victims are the adherents of one particular branch of Taoism, the Falun Gong. This organization was created in 1992 by Li Hongzhi (b1951), and banned by the government in 1999. Li now lives in exile in the USA, but the Falun Gong claims a membership of over 70 million in China, exceeding that of the Communist Party. Falun Gong embraces the values of "truth, compassion and tolerance." It promotes the enhancement of personal well being through a program of physical exercises. Since 1999, thousands of Falun Gong practitioners and leaflet distributors have been beaten, arrested, tortured and sentenced to jail terms of up to 18 years. There are currently over a thousand detained in China's mental hospitals and up to 25,000 in labor camps, yet the Falun Gong is still enjoying phenomenal growth. This is just one sign that the values of the Tao Te Ching are definitely enjoying a revival in China and, more and more, they are being noted and applied by people around the world.

As the world's most populous country with one of its fastest-growing economies, China is certainly a place to watch in the new millennium. It is set to become one of the major players on the world stage. One view of history emerging from the country even postulates that, just as the 19th and 20th centuries were the British and American centuries respectively, the 21st is destined to be the Chinese century: "The pendulum of history will swing from the *yin* ashes brought by the Cultural Revolution to the *yang* phoenix arising from its wreckage."[20]

This could be interpreted as dangerous, in the "Clash of Civilizations" sense, but it is not the inevitable interpretation. The Chinese Century may be the one in which the Tao enters the global political arena. The Chinese Century may be the one in which the prophesies of the above-mentioned Kang Yu Wei bear fruit. Kang predicted that progress to complete peace and equality throughout the world was inevitable in the long run:

▷ Like the rushing of water through a gully; nothing can check it.[21]

This prophecy, recalling Chapters 32 and 61 of the Tao Te Ching, was expressed in Kang's *Ta Tung Shu* of 1884-5. He is quoted further below:

▷ Nowadays disarmament conferences are being held ever more frequently, and whenever states make treaties, they are based on the principle of disarmament, nevertheless, so long as the boundaries of states are not abolished, and until the strong and the weak, the large and the small, work together, then to plan for disarmament will be like ordering tigers and wolves to go vegetarian – it must fail.

▷ Peace cannot be achieved without disarmament. Disarmament cannot be achieved without the abolition of state sovereignty. It is certain that One World will be achieved, although it may take an age and be a complicated task. Confucius' era of complete peace with equality, the Buddha's Lotus World and Lao-tzu's Mount Tan Ping are realities, not empty imaginings. Within the next hundred years, all monarchical and autocratic forms of government will be swept away, republican constitutions will be enacted everywhere. Democracy and equality will burn brightly. We will form alliances, disarm, establish a universal legislature, then we will gradually achieve One World.[21]

In the 1890s Kang predicted that this achievement would take two to three hundred years. By his death in 1927, he had revised his estimate to one hundred years. World events since then have included some of the most destructive ever, and ill omens still abound (see the closing paragraphs of Chapters 2, 3, 6 & 7) but the legacy of the Tao remains one of hope and, with sincere attempts at mutual understanding and co-operation, we may still be on course for the fulfillment of Kang's prediction.

5

SIDDHARTHA GAUTAMA & THE FOUR NOBLE TRUTHS

———————————●●●———————————

Siddhartha Gautama (the Buddha) was born in the southern foothills of the Himalayas around 563 BC.[1] He was raised in a society influenced by the Vedas and Upanishads (see Chapter 3). His socio-political environment was one of agricultural villages and small towns organized as a network of competing tribal republics and kingdoms around the Ganges basin of northeast India. The main regional power was Magadha. The Maghadan capital, Pataliputra – now Patna, Bihar – was the region's main city.

Siddhartha was a prince of the Shakya clan. His father, King Suddhodana, ruled an area around the hill town of Kapilavastu, in what is now Nepal. As a boy, he knew only the grounds of the family's opulent palaces and was shielded from the poverty and squalor of the surrounding towns and villages, not only by the palace walls, but also by his family's determination to protect him from all unpleasant sights; they kept him fully occupied and amused within palace grounds. The stories of the Buddha's childhood suggest that his secluded upbringing was his father's response to the prophesies of wise men that Siddhartha would become either a great emperor or a wandering spiritual leader. The enforced seclusion was intended to promote the former outcome. This was not to be.

One key story tells of a prophet by the name of Kondanna who predicted that Siddhartha would one day see four special signs that would lead him to reject his palace and family for the simple meditative life of a wandering ascetic. This was the outcome the family sought to thwart. Siddhartha's mother died within days of his birth, but his father provided the boy with the best available academic and physical education and all the comforts he believed a young prince could wish for.

Although far-reaching, Siddhartha's education was conducted wholly within palace walls and specifically excluded any reference to poverty, which was widespread, or to sickness, old age or death. The palace grounds contained beautiful gardens with fountains, ponds full of fish, bird life and water lilies. Siddhartha was waited on by young attendants and entertained by musicians and dancing girls. Although always of a non-violent disposition, he regularly won contests in martial arts, including archery and horse riding. Soon after puberty, he was married to his cousin, Yasodhara, who bore him a son, Rahula.

However, despite this responsibility, Siddhartha became overwhelmed by boredom and restlessness. He decided that it was time he learnt more of life beyond the protected confines of the palace grounds. The story goes on to tell that Siddhartha summoned his groom to take him on journeys of discovery by chariot beyond the palace walls. During these excursions, he saw, for the first time in his life, a man who was old, wrinkled, hunched up and toothless, another who was covered in sores, rolling on the ground, too weak to stand and crying in pain, a third, whose body was being carried in a funeral procession, and a fourth, who was slightly built and simply dressed, but seemed to be at peace with the world. Siddhartha reflected on these four signs, realized that there was something seriously deficient about his own way of life, and decided that he would have to change it. Shortly after his first excursions into the wider world, his father arranged a feast to celebrate the birth of Rahula. It was during this feast that Siddhartha resolved to act on his decision and to renounce his comfortable, but superficial world, and to begin his quest to live a more meaningful life. As all in the palace slept following the feast, he woke his groom and they quietly slipped away on horseback to the River Neranjara. At the riverbank, Siddhartha dismounted. He removed his princely clothes and jewelery, shaved his head and instructed his groom to return all his things to the palace with a message that he would return when his quest was complete.

Siddhartha then crossed the river and traveled on to the cities of Benares (Varanasi) and Pataliputra seeking out well-known gurus. He studied with one after another until there was nothing more that any of them could teach him, but he did not find enlightenment through them, so he joined a group of five wandering ascetics. Together, they practiced self-control and self-mortification: going without food, sleeping on hard ground, and leading a very uncomfortable life in general, in the hope that this would enable them to achieve enlightenment through spiritual purity.

Siddhartha persevered with this lifestyle until he became so weak that he would collapse from hunger and exhaustion. Some six years after he had first crossed the river, a shepherd found him in just such a state and took care of him. On regaining his strength, Siddhartha told his five companions that he no longer accepted that enlightenment could be achieved through ascetic extremism, and that, having already rejected the wealth and luxury of his princely upbringing, he was now going to continue his search by following a middle way between these two extremes. His companions were disappointed in this decision and left him.

Following his separation from the five ascetics, Siddhartha regularly sat to meditate under a banyan tree in the village of Gaya to the south of Pataliputra. A young mother called Sujatha befriended him and brought him rice and milk. Then one day in May, on the night of a full moon, he bathed in the river, ate a meal of rice and milk, and sat to meditate with a firm resolve to remain until he had achieved enlightenment. He reflected on his childhood, his marriage and family, the four signs he had seen on his journeys around Kapilavastu, his years with the gurus and the ascetics, and the kindness of the shepherd and young mother who had supported him during the most recent phases of his search. He battled with and overcame thoughts of temptation and, with fresh determination, continued to meditate until his mind became pure and clear, and ready to be bathed in the truth. He emerged from this meditation the next morning in a state of perfect peace and happiness. He now understood the meaning of life. He had been reborn fully enlightened – a buddha. He had risen above the mundane concerns about the cycle of birth and rebirth that dogged so many of his (and our) contemporaries. He had found Nirvana – a state of supreme peace and infinite joy – and he was ready to dedicate the rest of his life to spreading the good news.

After sitting for six more days under the banyan tree and then spending a further six weeks in Gaya, Siddhartha traveled a hundred miles north to Isipatana (Sarnath), near Benares to begin his mission. The deer park in Isipatana had been a regular haunt of Siddhartha and his companions during his ascetic years. He believed that he may find these former companions there and that they would be the people most likely to appreciate the vision he had to share.

Although Siddhartha's former companions were indeed there in the deer park, their first reaction was to try to ignore him. However, they could not avoid seeing that he now had a new and special aura. They became drawn to him and willing to listen to what he had to say.

In Siddhartha's first sermon, he outlined the Four Noble Truths, which were to become the core of Buddhism. These have been passed on many times, both orally and in written form, in many versions and many languages. The oldest surviving written version is part of the Pali canon, which dates back well over 2,000 years. The Four Noble Truths presented here are a composite drawn from several versions.[1] The rest of the Buddha's vision that follows comes from the Dhammapada (The Way of Perfection).[2] The usual selection on The Nature of God is not included. The Buddha had no words to add to those already available on this matter. For a follower of the Buddhist way, an understanding of the nature of God can only come with enlightenment, the path to which starts with the Four Noble Truths.

THE VISION – SELECTED HIGHLIGHTS

The Four Noble Truths

It is noble to realize that suffering is an integral part of life, involved in birth, in ageing and sickness, in death and loss, in parting from loved ones, and in longing for that which we do not have. It is therefore noble to be aware of the world's afflictions and to be compassionate.

It is noble to acknowledge that the key causes of suffering and sorrows are our passions: desire, lust, craving, selfishness, greed, and attachment to material things.

It is possible to rise above suffering and achieve enlightenment by overcoming such passions. This is the way that will allow us to deal with the world's afflictions and to strive towards attaining better state of mind (Nirvana) and hence a better world.

Nirvana can be attained by keeping to The Middle Way – avoiding the extremes of pursuing wealth or living as an ascetic – and by following the Noble Eightfold Path: (i) right views and understanding (ii) right thoughts and intentions (iii) right speech (iv) right action (v) right livelihood (vi) right effort

(vii) right awareness, mindfulness, and (viii) right concentration, contemplation and meditation.

On God's Purpose and Human Responsibility

(from the Dhammapada)[2]

146 How can there be laughter, how can there be pleasure, when the whole world is burning? When you are in deep darkness, will you not ask for a lamp? 151 The glorious chariots of kings wear out; and the body wears out and grows old, but the virtue of the good never grows old and can therefore teach the truth. 273 The best of all truths are the Four Noble Truths. The best of states is freedom from passion. The best of ways is the Noble Eightfold Path. Whoever goes this Way travels to the end of sorrow. 177 The noble find joy in generosity. 211-2 Do not become addicted to pleasure, for its loss will bring pain. There are no fetters for those who rise above pleasure and pain. They are free from fear and sorrow. 256-7 Do not attempt to settle matters in violent haste. Calmly consider what is right and what is wrong. Face differing opinions with truth, non-violence and peace. 289 Those who are virtuous and wise understand the truth, then strive with all their might to follow the path to Nirvana.

On Worship

141 Neither fasting nor squatting in a meditative pose can purify those who harbor doubts and desires.

Prayers

197-201 O let us live in joy; in love among those who hate; in health among those who are ill, in peace among those who fight. O let us live in joy, although having nothing. In joy, let us live like spirits of light.

Prophecy

126 Those who do evil may go to Hell and the righteous to Heaven, but those who are pure find Nirvana.

See Chapter 10 for further highlights of the Vision of the Buddha.

THE LEGACY

When the five ascetics accepted the Buddha's first sermon in the deer park at Isipatana (Sarnath), they became his first disciples. The number of his followers quickly grew to around 60. Together they formed the first Buddhist community or sangha. The Buddha then instructed his disciples to do as he planned to do himself: to spread the new teaching from village to village.

Having achieved enlightenment and been born again at Gaya at the age of 35, the Buddha spent the remaining 45 years of his life traveling and teaching, thus showing that his enlightenment was not an end in itself, but a new beginning. The fact that he continued to work for a better world until his death at 80 suggests that he found in this way of life a continuing reinforcement and renewal of his enlightenment, and that the Nirvana that he taught about is not some other-worldly illusion, but a state of mind that can be attained during this life on earth – a feeling of communion with the supreme universal wholeness, or God, that Zarathustra, Moses, Atharva and Lao-tzu had experienced before him.

The Buddha's teaching spread quickly throughout the kingdom of Magadha and its neighbors and the Buddha himself traveled to the Rajagaha Palace in Pataliputra (Rajgir, Patna), the Magadhan capital, where he was well received by King Bimbisara. The king respected the Buddha's rejection of the caste system and ritual sacrifice, and accepted the teaching of the Four Noble Truths and the Noble Eightfold Path as the way to achieve enlightenment. He did not go as far as making Buddhism the state religion, but did facilitate the spread of the new religion by providing parks and buildings for the monks, and the Rajagaha Palace was the venue for the world's first Buddhist Great Council attended by hundreds of Siddhartha's disciples within a year of his death around 483 BC.

The king of the neighboring state of Koshala, which now controlled the lands of the Buddha's Shakya clan, also patronized the new religion. When the Buddha returned to his hometown of Kapilavastu, the people flocked to see him. He visited his father, King Suddhodana, and stayed in the palace for a few days, before continuing with his mission.

During the Buddha's stay, his wife and many of the royal family immediately accepted his teaching, but Suddhodana could not do so, and initially resisted the suggestion that the Buddha's seven-year-old son, Rahula, should be taught to follow the path. The idea that another Gautama generation should reject the Shakya inheritance was not one Suddhodana relished. He was, however, finally persuaded that the Way of the Buddha had more to offer Rahula than the wealth and privilege of his royal inheritance, so Rahula too was raised as a Buddhist and became a monk.

By the time the Buddha died in Kushinara in the Malla republic, the new religion was well established throughout north India. The local kingdoms and republics had enjoyed a period of relative peace and prosperity, but Suddhodana and Bimbisara were already dead and the royal families of Magadha and Koshala soon became involved in territorial wars. A second Great Council was held around 380 BC, hosted by the neighboring Licchavi Republic in its capital of Vesali, but it would be more than another century before Buddhism would again enjoy significant royal patronage.

In 327 BC Alexander the Great led his armies into the northwest corner of the Indian sub-continent and the local reaction to this alien threat soon led to the birth of a new indigenous imperial dynasty, the Mauryas. The first Mauryan emperor, Chandragupta (321-297 BC), established his rule throughout north India before retiring to become a Jain (see Chapter 3).

Chandragupta was succeeded by Bindusara (297-68) and Ashoka (268-233). Ashoka's rule can be divided into two distinct phases. In the first, his armies protected the empire's boundaries and then extended them across most of the Indian sub-continent. In the second, having vanquished his enemies, he was converted to Buddhism, rejected violence and set about spreading the religion throughout his domains. Evidence of the extent of these domains can still be seen in rock and pillar edicts from Kandahar (now in Afghanistan) in the northwest to Yerragudu (near Madras) in the southeast. Ashoka hosted the Third Great Council of the Buddhist faith at Pataliputra and sent missionaries throughout his empire and beyond: across his northern and western borders – as far as Syria, Egypt and Macedonia – and also to South India, Sri Lanka and Burma. The mission to Sri Lanka, which included visits by his own son and daughter, Mahinda and Sanghamitta, was particularly fruitful. By the time of this mission, the banyan tree at Gaya, where the Buddha first attained enlightenment, had become a place of pilgrimage and, when missionaries planted a cutting from this tree in Sri Lanka's capital, Anuradhapura, this city also became a place of pilgrimage. It remains so to this day. It is also the home of the Mahavihara (Great Institute) and is still a major center of learning, although the Sri Lankan capital has since moved to the southeast coastal city of Colombo.

Buddhism continued as the major religion in India and its neighboring regions following Ashoka's death, but was associated with Mauryan imperial rule, and, by the time the dynasty collapsed around 180 BC, it had returned to the status of a minority religion, although Buddhist ideas continued to influence some strands of Hinduism (see Chapter 3).

Buddhism lived on in the Himalayan kingdoms of Bhutan (now 80% Buddhist) and Nepal (now 25%), but continued to fade in its homeland. The proportion of Indians regarding themselves as Buddhists fell to less than 10% over the next two millennia and declined further under Muslim and British rule. By the time of India's independence from Britain in 1947, only around 1% of Indians classified themselves as Buddhists. The new government was sympathetic to Buddhism, however. It put a Bengali Buddhist monk in charge of the temple at the site of Buddha's enlightenment in Bodh-Gaya, and has supported the construction of several Buddhist Peace Pagodas (see below).

There has also been some evidence of a grassroots Buddhist revival since independence, particularly among intellectuals and "untouchables," but the proportion of Buddhists in India has still not risen much above 1%.

The fate of Buddhism in Sri Lanka was totally different. It had been brought by missionaries rather than by an imperial conqueror and peacefully became the central part of the culture. By 100 BC, the Pali Canon was written here in the form in which it still survives. The Canon includes the Dhammapada – from which the words used in the Vision section (above and Chapter 10) – were taken. Buddhism did, however, become a much more devotional religion, with the Buddha being regarded as a god rather than a teacher or prophet.

Key prayers, which still form part of Sri Lankan buddhist worship, start with the following chant:

> ▷ Honor to the blessed One, the exalted One, the fully enlightened One. I go to the Buddha as my Refuge. I go to the Dhamma as my Refuge. I go to the Sangha as my Refuge."[3]

Vows to abstain from killing, stealing, sexual misconduct, lying and the use of intoxicants are then followed by offerings of flowers, lights and incense to the

Buddha, who is normally represented by a golden statue.

Buddhism soon became established as the state religion in Sri Lanka, even to the extent that possession of a holy relic, "the Buddha's tooth," was accepted as conferring the right to the throne; and it was from Sri Lanka that Buddhism spread throughout Southeast Asia: to Sumatra, Malaya, Siam (Thailand), Cambodia and Laos. Buddhist missionaries from Sri Lanka also traveled to Burma, following the footsteps of the earlier Ashokan missionaries. The Buddhism taken to, and still widely practiced in, these countries, is now generally referred to as Theravada Buddhism[4] to distinguish it from later variations, collectively known as Mahayana Buddhism[5], practiced widely in the rest of Asia (see below).

Theravada Buddhism remained the state religion in Sri Lanka until the island became part of the British Empire in 1802, even though parts of the country had been ruled successively by Tamils, Portuguese, and then the Dutch and British East India Companies during the intervening two millennia.

The Tamil incursions from South India started in 846 and continued until the early 11th century, when most of the island came under the Tamil Chola Dynasty following the conquests of Rajaraja (1001-4) and his son Rajendra (1014-17). In the later 11th century, the indigenous King Vijayabahu (1065-1120) led a Sinhalese revival, and his successors gradually reversed Tamil control during the 12th century. Then the Portuguese landed in 1505, the Dutch East India Company took over their holdings in 1658 and the British East India Company gained control of the island in 1796.

By independence in 1948, Sri Lanka's population was around 70% Buddhist (mostly the Sinhalese), with significant Hindu (Tamil), Muslim and Christian minorities. The government continues to resist the secessionist aims of the Tamils, who live in the north and the east of the island, and the violence between Sinhalese and Tamils between 1983 and 2002 cost around 64,000 lives. Despite the nominal Buddhism of the vast majority of the Sinhalese, Sri Lankan government policy toward its Tamil population prior to the 2002 ceasefire owed little to the Buddha's teaching. It must also be said, however, that any sympathy for the Tamil cause among the majority Sinhalese must have been damaged by the terrorist atrocities of the Liberation Tigers of Tamil Elam committed between 1983 and 2001. These included over 100 suicide bombings and the assassination of President Premadasa (1993).

In Burma (Myanmar), 90% of the population still espouses the Theravada faith, although suffering under a repressive military dictatorship. Burma first became a united country under King Anawrata (1044-77). He patronized Buddhism and his Shwe Dagon Pagoda, in Rangoon, is one of the greatest shrines to the Buddha. Burma was then conquered by the Mongols under Kublai Khan in 1287 and not reunified until 1758, when Alaungapaya established the Konbaung dynasty. The country subsequently fell to British India in 1885, following the "Teak Wars". It achieved limited self-government in 1937, was occupied by Japan from 1942-5 and gained full independence in 1948, but remained divided between socialists, communists and secessionist Shan, Kachin and Karen hill tribes. In 1954-56, however, Burma hosted the Sixth Great Buddhist Council, which re-edited the sacred scripts and produced a new canon.

Following Burma's democratic elections of 1990, the winning National League for Democracy was prevented from taking office by a military junta, and the NLD leader, Aung San Suu Kyi, was arrested. Although she was awarded the Nobel Peace Prize in 1991, she remained in prison until 1995 and then lived under restrictions amounting to virtual house arrest until 2002 before being re-arrested in 2003. The blatantly unbuddhist military dictatorship still controls the country, but Aung San Suu Kyi enjoys tremendous popular support and continues to do all she can to propagate her dream of making both Burma and the world "a better happier home for all of us by constructing the heavenly abodes of love and compassion in our hearts. Beginning with this internal development, we can go on to the development of the external world with courage and wisdom."[6]

Also spreading from Sri Lanka, Theravada Buddhism became established in Sumatra and Malaya by the eighth century. It was patronized by the Sailendra Dynasty, which ruled much of the island and peninsula until the 13th century. From the 14th century the religion had to compete with the arrival of Muslim and Christian invaders from further west. The Sultanate of Malacca was established in 1403 and dominated the region until the arrival of the Portuguese in 1511. Control then passed to the Dutch, then to the British and then to the Japanese, until 1945, when Sumatra was claimed as part of the new state of Indonesia, and Malaya was returned to British rule. Malaya subsequently became part of the independent Federation of Malaysia in 1963. Theravada Buddhists currently make up around 1% of the population of Sumatra and 20% of the population of Malaya. Indonesia and Malaysia also have small Mahayana Buddhist populations, following later introductions of the faith from China, and Indonesia's heritage includes one of the world's largest Buddhist monuments, built in the mid-nineteenth century, at Borobudur in Java.

The spread of Theravada Buddhism to Siam, Cambodia and Laos bore more lasting fruit.

The Thais first came to Siam in the 13th century under pressure from Mongol expansion further north. They established a kingdom around Sukhotai and eventually adopted the pre-existing Buddhist faith. An early king arranged for a Theravadin teacher to be sent from Sri Lanka and he was subsequently appointed as head of the Siamese Buddhist order, which the king joined. The Thais survived the expansionist pressures of Muslim and Christian powers to become the only Southeast Asian country never to suffer from a period of Western colonization. Today Siam is officially called Thailand. It is a constitutional monarchy with its capital in the port city of Bangkok. Its racially mixed population is 80% Thai, 12% Chinese, 4% Malay and 3% Khmer. Although 94% of this population is nominally Buddhist, many have succumbed to Western influence. In the words of one leading Thai Buddhist, "Today Bangkok is a third-rate Western city. The department stores have become our shrines," and "this new religion of consumerism exploits the minds and bodies of the young and is entirely dysfunctional. Modern Siam is an eroding society. It has 250,000 monks and twice as many prostitutes."[7]

The Buddhist history of Cambodia goes back to before the time of the Khmer Empire that ruled the region from the sixth century to the 15th. The remains of many Buddhist temples in the old Khmer capital of Angkor bear testament to its influence during that period. Under pressure from Thai invaders, the Cambodian capital was moved south to Phnom Penh in the 15th century. The country subsequently suffered from invasion and colonization by the French (1863-1940), Japanese (1940-45) and French again (1945-53). Then North Vietnam's communist Viet Cong occupied border areas during their war against American-backed South Vietnam (1954-75). The country also suffered from bombing by the Americans and from a takeover by the communist Khmer Rouge (1970-79) who wiped out millions before being overthrown by Cambodian and Vietnamese troops. Modern Cambodia is a constitutional monarchy with a population that is 94% ethnic Khmer and 88% Buddhist.

In Laos, Theravada Buddhism became the official religion when it was adopted by King Fa Ngoun in 1353, but tribal traditional beliefs remain common. Since 1893, the country has come under French, Japanese and communist control, and has become a major center for opium production. About half its population still espouses Buddhism.

While the Buddhist influence in these Southeast Asian countries is based largely on the Sri Lankan Theravada Buddhism of the Pali Canon, the Buddhist religions of the rest of Asia were more of a graft on pre-existing beliefs, and many Buddhist teachers, both in Asia and in the west, have simply taken Buddhist philosophy as a starting point on which to build their own personal philosophies or belief systems. The myriad philosophies or religions that have arisen from these processes are generically known as Mahayana Buddhism.[5]

Buddhism in China goes back over two thousand years, arriving both directly from North India and, via the silk route, from Afghanistan. Its interaction with Taoism in China has already been outlined (see Chapter 4). It remains particularly vibrant in Taiwan, from where the Buddha Educational Foundation has distributed millions of copies of hundreds of Buddhist texts worldwide, and in Tibet and Inner Mongolia (see below).

Much of today's Afghanistan was part of Ashoka's Indian Empire during the third century BC. Buddhism survived there alongside Zoroastrianism, which had spread from the west, and a variety of tribal religions until the Muslim conquests of the eighth century (see Chapter 7). It was the state religion under King Kanishka (cAD 78-101), whose career and conversion followed a pattern similar to Ashoka's. He had many monasteries built and is also credited with convening the Fourth Great Buddhist Council. Most of the Buddhist monasteries in Afghanistan were destroyed soon after the Muslim conquests, but the cave monasteries of Bamiyan in the north survived until the 21st century, along with a 177-foot statue of the Buddha. These were destroyed in the summer of 2001 by the short-lived Muslim fundamentalist Taliban regime.

Early Buddhism in Tibet was strengthened in AD 750 with the mission of an Indian Theravada Buddhist Monk, Padmasabhava, and the building of a monastery in Samye, completed in 787. Four separate sects of specifically Tibetan Buddhism emerged by the 11th century. Dominant among these was, and is, the Gelugpa order with two sub-sects whose leaders are revered as the Dalai Lama and Panchen Lama. On the death of a Lama, a search is mounted among Tibet's baby boys to find his replacement, seen as a reincarnation of the dead Lama. The Dalai Lama leads the "yellow monks" and is revered as the "living Buddha." The Panchen Lama leads the "red monks."

The Dalai Lama was also the effective ruler of Tibet until it was conquered by the Mongols in 1206 and, although Tibet has been claimed by China since the fall of the Mongol Empire, successive Dalai Lamas remained in the capital, Lhasa, as spiritual leaders until 1959, when China's suppression of Tibetan Buddhism led the 14th Dalai Lama, Tenzin Gyatso, to flee to North India to establish a government-in-exile in Dharamsala in the state of Himachal Pradesh. The Dalai Lama continues to be revered by Tibetan Buddhists around the world. He also enjoys the respect of a far wider public as a result of his actions of peaceful protest, and his speeches and writings on Buddhism, ethics and peaceful resistance to Chinese oppression in Tibet. He was awarded the Nobel Peace Prize in 1989.

On hearing of the award, while attending an ecumenical conference in California, he pointed out that:

▷ As a Buddhist monk, my concern extends to all members of the human family and, indeed, to all sentient beings who suffer. I believe all suffering is caused by ignorance. People inflict pain on others in the selfish pursuit of their own happiness or satisfaction.[8]

He went on to refer to the "Common Human Religion" and stressed the need to complement the human rights ideal by developing a widespread practice of universal responsibility based on "love, the will to others' happiness; and compassion, the will to others' freedom from suffering."[8]

Following the Dalai Lama's exile from Tibet, the 10th Panchen Lama became Tibetan Buddhism's leader within the country. On his death in 1989, his "reincarnation" was born in the hills and located by the Buddhist elders, but he was kidnapped by the Chinese authorities when he was six years old and, if still alive, remains a political prisoner in Beijing.

In 1906, the Tibetan provinces of Ladakh and Sikkim were taken by the British. Ladakh is now part of Indian Kashmir. Sikkim achieved independence in 1947, but became an Indian protectorate in 1950 and an Indian state in 1975. Both areas remain largely Buddhist.

During the Mongol rule of Tibet, the Khans adopted Tibetan Buddhism themselves. It subsequently became the state religion of Mongolia and spread as far west as Russia's Volga basin, where the Russian Republic of Kalmykia still has a large proportion of Buddhists. Kalmykian Buddhists were instrumental in organizing the first All-Russian Buddhist Congress in Moscow in 1927. Some of them have also moved further west – to the USA – where they have built a temple in Freewood Acres, New Jersey.

The Buddhist Kingdom of Mongolia was conquered by China in 1911 and, with the support of the Soviet Union, became the Mongolian People's Republic in 1924. Following the failure of an anti-communist rebellion in 1932, many Mongol Buddhists fled to the Chinese province of Inner Mongolia.

Buddhism reached Korea, Japan, Vietnam and Indonesia via China, very gradually during the first millennium. Significant proportions of the populations of each of these countries still espouse some form of Mahayana Buddhism: 20% in Korea (North, 2%; South, 28%), 74% in Japan, 55% in Vietnam and 1% in Indonesia.

A variety of Chinese schools of Buddhism, including the meditation-based Chan (Zen) Buddhism, have developed in China and Korea. The Korean form of Chan Buddhism, known as Son Buddhism, is the main form practiced there today, but there are many sects. These include the indigenous Chogye Zen sect and a number of imported Japanese schools. Many Korean Zen Masters have also taken their schools to the West, particularly to the USA.[9]

Buddhism reached Japan before it became a unified state in the seventh century. It was adopted by several local leaders and spawned the idea of Amida Buddha, a mythical or cosmic Buddha representing the wisdom and compassion contained in the Buddha's enlightenment. After unification, the Emperor Shomu (724-49) had Buddhist temples and monasteries built in every province. Various esoteric rituals were introduced, however, and the extent of the drift from the Buddha's teachings is clear from the evidence of monastic wealth and power, guarded and enhanced by "warrior monks" or *sohei*. By the 12th century, the ascetic warrior approach to "enlightenment" had been complemented by "easy path" devotional schools claiming that followers could enter "the Pure Land" of Buddhist enlightenment by the repeated chanting of simple formulae. One of the Pure Land schools was that of Nichirin Shonen (1222-82). The Nichirin School promoted a simple formulaic approach aggressively with a very unbuddhist intolerance of other schools and became a mass sect that went on to support Japanese militarism in the early 20th century.

Despite, or perhaps because of, all its variations, Japanese Buddhism never completely displaced Japan's indigenous religion, Shinto. Originally primitive nature worship, Shinto was revived in the 18th century by the Japanese leadership as a nationalist response to the growing threat from Western colonialist powers. Hereditary military leaders, the Shoguns, had become the effective rulers of Japan, with the emperors continuing as mere figureheads, but, following Japan's humiliation in being forced by the USA to abandon its policy of isolationism in 1854, the Shogunate fell. Power was returned to the Imperial line with the Meiji Restoration of 1868. Shinto became the official state religion and the emperors were regarded as divine descendants of the Sun God. Japan modernized and became an aggressive colonial power itself until 1945, when this policy led to the atom-bombing of Hiroshima and Nagasaki, and Japan's surrender to the USA, bringing World War II to an end. The Emperor then renounced his claim to divinity and became a constitutional monarch.

Since 1945, most of the varieties of Japanese Buddhism, including the Zen and Pure Land schools, have enjoyed a revival. Many new schools have also emerged, but, with a few exceptions, Japanese Buddhists have begun to come together, regarding each other as complementary flowerbeds in the same garden. Japanese Buddhism in general is returning to more recognizably Buddhist ethics. One of the Nichirin schools, the Japan-Bharat Sarvodaya Mitrata Sangha, led by Nichidatsu Fujii (1885-1990) has dedicated itself to the construction of Peace Pagodas in Japan, India and all over the world, including two in England – at Battersea Park in London and at Willen Lake in Milton Keynes. Another school taking its message ("Be lamps unto yourselves. Work out your own salvation with diligence") around the world is the Sangha of the Soka-Gakkai (Value Creation Society) International led by Daisaku Ikeda.

Vietnam became Buddhist as part of China over a thousand years ago and, following independence in the 10th century, Vietnamese emperors used Buddhist monks as advisors and declared Buddhism to be the official state religion. Vietnamese Buddhism subsequently developed as a synthesis of the Chan and Pure Land forms. It survived French and Japanese occupation (1859-1954), but suffered persecution during the 1954-75 Vietnam War, under the regimes of both the communist North and the American-backed South. In the South, Buddhists advocated peaceful resistance to the war and, in 1963, Dictator Ngo Dinh Diem responded by banning all celebrations of Buddha Day. The killing of eight Buddhists protesting against the ban in Hue, on May 8, 1963, led to demands for apologies and reparations to their families and triggered widespread hunger strikes. These were met by a violent clampdown on all peace protestors. On June 11 a Buddhist monk, Thich Quang Duc, took disciples and journalists to the center of Saigon and, with the help of a fellow monk, covered himself in petrol and burned himself to death as an anti-Diem protest. Other self-immolations followed. Rather than accept the inevitable, however, Diem reacted by introducing martial law, banning all public gatherings, suspending all civil liberties and, with American aid and assurances, escalating the war. By November that year, Diem had been assassinated by his own generals in a US-backed coup and, in 1968, American bombing of Hue destroyed virtually all of Vietnam's most important Buddhist temples. Nevertheless, by 1975, the Vietnamese people had humbled the world's greatest superpower and finally become an independent nation again.

Thich Nhat Hanh is another Vietnamese monk who became a leading anti-war activist and opponent of repression in the South. He was forced into exile during the 60s, but has since achieved worldwide respect as a proponent of "Engaged Buddhism," while living in France (see below). Since the communist North Vietnamese regime took over South Vietnam in 1975, repression has continued, but 55% of the population of the re-united country still espouse Buddhism.

During the 20th century, Buddhism has become a global religion (or group of religions) with a host of organizations, representing the original Theravada Buddhism and many of the Mahayana varieties, and operating in all continents.[10] All the world's great cities have their Buddhist Temples, Viharas or Monasteries. Notable examples include the 1000 Buddha Temple in Boston, the Chuan Yen Monastery (home of the Buddhist Association of the US), with its 10-meter tall Buddha, in Kent, NY, the Shenshin Temple in Los Angeles, focal point of the Buddhist Churches of America, and the Thai Buddhist Temple in Wimbledon, London, which welcomes the general public to walk through its landscaped gardens and meditate upon the Buddhist quotations posted along the way.

Alongside the various sects and the schools of Zen masters, there are also international ecumenical groups, such as the Buddhist Peace Fellowship,[11] the International Network of Engaged Buddhists (INEB)[12] and the Amida Trust,[13] all working to bring people together and to apply Buddhist principles in dealing with world problems of poverty, development and ecological awareness.

INEB's Sulak Sivaraksa laments that capitalist development puts profit above the welfare of the general public and believes that, "as long as development is measured in terms of material success, greed will create tension and conflict."[14] He points out that Buddhism advocates a shift of values from self-assertion and competition to cooperation and social justice, and from material acquisition to inner growth; adding that such a shift would lead to more healing developments in science and technology. He sees the greatest obstacle to universal love, the core of all faiths, as the confusion between spirituality and religion. The former is universal. When it is confused with the latter, it breeds sectarianism, hatred and destruction.

Sivaraksa criticizes those Western Buddhists who try to separate their personal quest for Nirvana from their efforts to bring about positive and meaningful social change. He points out that reducing the breeding of grain-eating animals for consumption would not only be compassionate toward the animals, but also to people who need grain to survive, and he asks:

▷ "Why are we so good at producing far too much and so bad at helping where there is far too little?"

He answers that it is our greed that leads to precious resources being wasted in the get-rich-quick fields of arms, luxury goods and drug trafficking, rather than being used in the more vital fields of basic needs, health, education and peacemaking.[15] For Sivaraksa, compassion is the key to Nirvana.

A Western Buddhist, David Brazier of the Amida Trust, is also convinced of the importance of compassion, and believes that the most compassionate act is the act of renunciation itself. He pleads, "Renounce your color. Renounce the rat race"[16] and reminds us that most of the cruelty and exploitation in the world requires the consent of many people. He rejects the view of Buddhism as an exotic pastime pursuing mystic experiences and advocates the selfless pursuit of a better world here on Earth. He accepts that capitalism and Buddhism share an acceptance of private property as an institution, but sees the race to maximize one's own material wealth as a form of self-imposed slavery. Like most Buddhists, he supports dialogue, seeing Buddhism as a non-dogmatic living religion, which, although critical of modern capitalism and consumerism, is not at odds with modern science. Indeed, he describes Buddhism as the most scientific of the great religions.

This is a view that has also been expressed by one of the greatest scientists of the last century; Albert Einstein prophesied that:

▷ The religion of the future will be a cosmic religion. It should transcend a personal God and avoid dogmas and theology. Covering both the natural and spiritual, it should be based on a religious sense arising from the experience of all things, both natural and spiritual, as a meaningful Unity. Buddhism answers this description. If there is any religion that would cope with modern scientific needs, it would be Buddhism.[17]

But, in the two and a half millennia since the Buddha originally took his vision around India, Buddhism has been subsumed within Hinduism in its home country and several other competing religions have spread around the world. These are the subjects of Chapters 6 to 9.

6
JESUS &
GOD'S LOVE

———●●●———

Jesus of Nazareth was born and raised as the son of Joseph, a carpenter and a subject of the Roman Empire, in the semi-autonomous Greco-Jewish province of Judea some 13 centuries after Moses had given God's Law to the children of Israel and a millennium after the reign of King David. Being born into the Jewish tradition, he would have been brought up to learn all the Biblical stories, including those about Abraham and his children; about Moses and the later prophets; about the Israelites' slavery in Egypt, the promised land, the rise and fall of the Kingdom of Israel, the Jews' exile in Babylon and their return to Jerusalem; and about the building, destruction and rebuilding of the temple in Jerusalem. He would have been taught of God's hand in all of these events, of the tradition that the Jews were God's chosen people and that God must be worshiped through the priests at the temple (see Chapter 2). He would also have been taught that God would soon send the Jews a Messiah or Savior, someone who would deliver them from the Roman tyranny and establish a Kingdom of God on Earth.

Growing up in Nazareth, it is unlikely that Jesus would have received any direct teaching of other approaches to God, but, during a part of his childhood spent in Egypt, he and his family may have learned more of the wisdom of the East. Persian culture and Zoroastrianism were widespread (see Chapter 1). A millennium had passed since the writing of the Upanishads (see Chapter 3). Over 500 years had passed since Lao-tzu had left us the Tao Te Ching (see Chapter 4). The teachings of the Buddha were over 400 years old and India's King Ashoka had sent Buddhist missionaries as far west as the Mediterranean coast and Alexandria in Egypt just over a century before Jesus' birth (see Chapter 5).

By Jesus' time, the mainstream Jewish tradition had already absorbed some of the Persian culture that sprang from the teaching of Zarathustra; not only the idea of universal monotheism, as opposed to that of a tribal God, but also the ideas of Satan, the Devil, an afterlife, Hell, resurrection, and the arrival of a deliverer or messiah, a savior that would appear at the end of the world prior to the day of judgment (see Chapters 1 and 2). These ideas would all provide a background to Jesus' ministry, but his ethical teaching would echo that of the Buddha much more closely than it resembled the Jewish, Greek or Roman traditions he grew up with.

Herod the Great, the Rome-appointed King of Judea, reigned from 37-4 BC. His heritage was more Greek than Jewish. He was not a religious man, and was notorious for his ruthlessness, but he was a keen builder and had temples built to various local deities in Tyre, Beirut and Rhodes. In 18 BC, he also initiated the construction of a great new Jewish temple in Jerusalem. This was eventually completed in AD 62.

Herod's death in 4 BC was followed by a time of great division in his kingdom. It was subsequently placed under direct rule from Rome. It was divided between three of Herod's sons: Herod Archelaus (Judea and Samaria), Herod Antipas (Galilee) and Herod Philip (Batanaea). The reign of Herod Archelaus in Judea was very brief and troubled. He was quickly replaced by a Roman procurator who imposed Herod the Great's grandson, Herod Agrippa I, as a puppet king.

Roman Judea was a very divided province. Alongside the Jews, the Romans ruled over Greeks, Phoenicians, Samaritans and a number of other non-Jewish communities. The Jews themselves were split into factional groups including the Saducees, Pharisees, Essenes and Zealots. The Saducees and Pharisees were orthodox Jews who worked with the Roman occupiers, but also saw themselves as guardians of Moses' Laws. They included the temple priests. The Pharisees differed from the Saducees in that they also believed in spirits, angels, life after death and resurrection. The Essenes rejected both Greek and Roman influences, holding them responsible for the urban vices that they felt had corrupted God's way. They kept to strict rules and lived in out-of-town communities in which property was held in common. They also believed in angels, and in Heaven and Hell. The Zealots were essentially political, advocating and pursuing violent resistance to the Roman occupation.

It was into this confusion that Jesus of Nazareth emerged, some 30 years after the death of Herod the Great, to be baptized in the River Jordan by John the

Baptist, near the Essene monastery of Qumran, where the Dead Sea Scrolls were discovered 1,900 years later. Following his baptism, Jesus spent 40 nights fasting in the desert. He then spent just three years in Galilee and Judea as a wandering teacher and faith healer, before being arrested, tried and crucified in Jerusalem. He left no written records. Most of what follows in the Vision section is taken from quotations attributed to Jesus in the gospel (good news) according to Matthew, the first and most detailed of the four gospels that open the New Testament. There are also some quotations from the gospels according to Mark, Luke and John, although none of these writers claim to have met Jesus or heard him speak. Matthew is the only one of these four who may have traveled with Jesus as one of his 12 disciples, but even in Matthew's case, the consensus among biblical scholars today is that the Matthew who wrote the gospel was not Matthew the disciple.[1]

THE VISION

On The Nature of God

In the beginning was the Word, and the Word was with God, and the Word was God.[2]

God causes the sun to rise on the evil and the good, and sends rain on the righteous and the unrighteous. Your heavenly Father is perfect. Your Father is unseen. Your Father sees what is done in secret. No one can see the kingdom of God, unless he is born again.[3]

On God's Purpose and Human Responsibility

Love the Lord your God with all your heart and with all your soul and with all your mind. This is the first and greatest commandment. And the second is like it: Love your neighbor as yourself. All the Law and the prophets hang on these two commandments.[7] Love your enemies and pray for those who persecute you, that you may be sons of your Father in Heaven. Do not store up for yourselves treasures on Earth, where moths and rust destroy, and where thieves break in and steal; but store up for yourselves treasures in Heaven, for where your treasure is, there your heart will be also. No one can serve two masters. Either he will hate the one and love the other, or he will be devoted to one and despise the other. You cannot serve both God and money. Do not judge, or you too will be judged; for in the same way you judge others, you too will be judged. Why do you look at the speck of sawdust in your brother's eye and pay no attention to the plank in your own eye. How can you say to your brother, "Let me take the speck out of your eye," when all the time there is a plank in your own eye? First take the plank out of your own eye then you will see clearly to remove the speck from your brother's eye. Do unto others what you would have them do to you. Watch out for false prophets. They come to you in sheep's clothing, but inwardly they are ferocious wolves. By their fruit you will recognize them. Do people pick grapes from thorn bushes? What good will it be for a man if he gains the whole world, but forfeits his soul? Give to Caesar what is Caesar's and to God what is God's.[9] Whoever wants to be great among you must be your servant, and whoever wants to be first must be your slave. Watch out! Be on your guard against all kinds of greed; a man's life does not consist of the abundance of his possessions. Be careful, or your hearts will be weighed down with dissipation, drunkenness and the anxieties of life.[10] He who has ears to hear, let him hear.[13] Any of you who does not give up everything he has, cannot be my disciple.[16]

On Worship

Get up and pray, so that you do not fall into temptation[17]. Have faith. Never give up.[18]

Prayers

Our Father in Heaven, hallowed be your name. Your kingdom come. Your will be done, on Earth as it is in Heaven. Give us this day our daily bread. Forgive us our trespasses, as we forgive them that trespass against us. Lead us not into temptation, but deliver us from evil, for yours is the kingdom, the power and the glory forever. Amen.

Prophecy

Blessed are the peacemakers, for they shall be called the sons of God.

See Chapter 10 for further highlights from the vision of Jesus.

THE LEGACY

Jesus' activities in Galilee and Judea attracted much positive interest among the common people, but also much opposition from Judea's religious elite and, perhaps, from the Roman forces of occupation. However, he left nothing in writing and there are no contemporary records of his activities, or even his crucifixion. What we do have are four biographies – the gospels – all attributed to converts to the new religion of Christianity. They were first compiled between 30 to 50 years after Jesus' death, and not finally canonized, as the first four books of the New Testament, until the Council of Carthage in AD 419.[30]

Of the four biographers, only one, Matthew, may have been one of Jesus' original disciples.[1] The others, Mark, Luke and John, came later. Mark, the first of the three, was a companion of the early Christian missionary, Saul of Tarsus (Paul), who effectively created Christianity as a new religion, rather than continuing Jesus teachings' for the reformation and globalization of Judaism. The New Testament also includes many letters from Paul to early Christians. None of them refer to any gospels or biographies of Jesus. This suggests that the gospels were written after the letters.

Mark's gospel was probably the first to be written, and is thought to have been one of Matthew's sources. Mark wrote for a Roman audience. Matthew wrote for the Jews still living around Jerusalem. Luke drew on Matthew, Mark and many others in preparing "an orderly account" for a Greek-speaking audience, addressed as "most excellent Theophilus."[31] John's gospel came later still.

All four describe Jesus' teaching on God's love and on non-violence. All four tell of his reputation as a faith healer and miracle worker. All four give accounts of his visits to the temple in Jerusalem, saying how he drove out all the traders; how he overturned the tables of the money-changers and the benches of those selling doves for sacrifice. Matthew, Mark and Luke describe such a visit taking place on Jesus' final entry into Jerusalem, while John places a similar visit at the start of his mission. Matthew and Luke both quote him as saying, "My house will be called a house of prayer, but you have made it a den of robbers."[32] Mark quotes him as saying "My house will be called a house of prayer for all nations."[33] All three are actually quoting the prophet, Isaiah.[34] In John's account of Jesus' temple visit, Jesus says simply, "Get these out of here. How dare you turn my Father's house into a market."[35]

The gospels of Matthew, Mark and Luke are all strewn with quotations from the Old Testament prophets. All three describe events in Jesus' life that appear to fulfill Old Testament prophecies. John's gospel is more of a stand-alone testament for a new religion. All four refer to Jesus as the Son of God. This claim is presented as a declaration from Heaven during Jesus' baptism at the age of about 30. The voice from Heaven is accompanied by the descent of the Spirit of God in the form of a dove.

Luke also describes Adam as the son of God and Jesus is often quoted as referring to people in general as the children of God and to peacemakers as the sons of God. Nevertheless, the description of Jesus as the Son of God was given a special meaning by Paul long before the gospels were written down:

"But now a righteousness from God, apart from law, has been made known, to which the Law and the prophets testify. This righteousness from God comes through faith in Jesus Christ to all who believe. There is no difference, for all have sinned and fall short of the glory of God, and are justified freely by His Grace through the redemption that came by Christ Jesus. God presented Him as a sacrifice of atonement through faith in his blood."[36]

Paul's interpretation made Jesus more than a teacher, more than a Jewish messiah and more, even, than Christ, the anointed one; it made him no less than the one and only Son of God, and thus a divinity in his own right. This interpretation colored much of the gospel narratives and changed Jesus from a neo-Buddhist reformer of the Mosaic faith into a new deity.

Matthew and Luke's gospels describe Jesus' immaculate conception and his birth in a manger in Bethlehem. Both provide a genealogy for Joseph. Matthew takes it back as far as Abraham; Luke goes back to "Adam, the son of God."[37] In Matthew, Jesus' mother, Mary, is found to be with child "through the Holy Spirit" and an angel appears to Joseph to explain this to him. In Luke, "the angel, Gabriel, was sent from God" to the Virgin Mary herself.

Luke also gives details of the relationships between the families of Jesus and John the Baptist, and attributes a poetic song of praise to Mary.

In Matthew, "three Magi (Zoroastrian priests) from the east" followed a star to Judea, met King Herod the Great in Jerusalem to enquire about the "one who is born to be King of the Jews", went on to present gifts to the baby Jesus in Bethlehem, then left without returning to Herod. The king subsequently massacred all the new-born children in Bethlehem to remove this potential threat to his power, but Jesus, Mary and Joseph had already left for Egypt, where they stayed until after Herod's the Great's death (4 BC).

In Luke, there is no mention of the Magi, but the baby Jesus is visited by a group of shepherds, on the advice of an angel with "a great company of the heavenly host."

The only story of Jesus' later childhood appears in Luke. Young Jesus is accidentally left behind in Jerusalem after a family pilgrimage, but found three days later, sitting in the temple with learned men who are amazed by his understanding.

The gospels according to Matthew and Luke both resume when Jesus is around 30 years old. This is also the point at which the gospels of Mark and John start. All four give accounts of Jesus' baptism followed by a 40-day fast in the desert prior to setting out on his mission. Matthew, Mark and Luke provide stories of Jesus' temptation by the Devil. Mark refers to the Devil as Satan.

Matthew and Mark also describe the imprisonment and beheading of John the Baptist on the orders of Herod Antipas, Tetrarch of Galilee. This event followed soon after Jesus' baptism. John was executed for criticizing Herod's marriage.

All the gospels describe the last supper of Jesus and his disciples prior to his arrest, trials and crucifixion: the bread and wine of the last supper are shared as the body and blood of Christ, symbols of his coming sacrifice, through which Christians of the future may be saved from eternal Hell and damnation.

The accounts of his trials differ in their details: Mark quotes Jesus as saying only "You have said so." in response to the question, "Are you the King of the Jews?" Matthew adds, "Do you not think that I can appeal to My Father and he will at once send me four legions of angels?" Luke leaves this addition out.

In the gospel according to John, Jesus is quoted very differently, saying:

"My kingship is not of this world; if my kingship were of this world, my servants would fight that I might not be handed over to the Jews; but my kingship is not from this world ... For this I was born, and for this I have come to the world to bear witness to the truth. Everyone who is sincere hears my voice."

The accounts of the crucifixion also differ in their details, particularly in the descriptions of Jesus' death. In Mark, Jesus says, "My God, My God, why have you forsaken me" then breathes his last with a loud cry and "the curtain of the temple was torn in two from top to bottom." but nothing else miraculous is mentioned.

Matthew adds that:

"The earth shook and the rocks split. The tombs broke open and the bodies of many holy people who had died were raised to life. They came out of the tombs and, after Jesus' resurrection, they went into the holy city and appeared to many people."[38]

Luke also mentions the tearing of the curtain and three hours of darkness, but nothing else miraculous, and he gives Jesus' last words as, "Father, into your hands I commit my spirit."[39]

For John, Jesus' last words were, "It is finished," and there are no references to supernatural or earth-shaking events.

Stories of Jesus' resurrection three days after his crucifixion are also included in all four gospels, but again they differ in their details. In Mark, three female followers find the stone rolled away from his tomb and are greeted by "a young man dressed in a white robe" who tells them that Jesus has risen and gone to Galilee.

In Matthew, "There was a violent earthquake, for an angel of the Lord had come down from Heaven and rolled the stone and sat on it." The angel told the women that Jesus had risen. Matthew also added that the 11 disciples subsequently saw Jesus on a mountain in Galilee and worshiped him, with the qualification that "some doubted", and a warning that people should not believe stories circulating about the disciples stealing Jesus' body in the night. Matthew's story closes with Jesus saying:

"All authority in Heaven and Earth has been given to me. Therefore go and make disciples of all nations, baptizing them in the name of the Father, the Son and the Holy Spirit, and teaching them everything I have commanded you. And surely I am with you always, to the very end of the age."

In Luke, "two men in clothes that gleamed" replace Matthew's angel and Jesus' post-resurrection exploits are expanded considerably, culminating in a blessing for his followers and his ascension into Heaven.

In John, there are "two angels in white" at the tomb and Jesus does even more after his resurrection, although he first appears to his disciples "with doors locked for fear of the Jews."[40] John also includes a dialogue between Jesus and Simon Peter in which the latter is instructed to "take care of my sheep."[41]

Other variations of these stories appeared in the gospels of the Hebrews and the Egyptians, in gospels according to Thomas and Peter, and in a book of the Acts of Paul, but none of these survived the canonization processes of the Roman Church.

The canonized version of the New Testament is completed by Luke's "Acts of the Apostles" and a number of letters written by Paul (formerly Saul of Tarsus) and James (Jesus' brother), plus letters written by Simon Peter, John and Jude, and John's "Revelation."

Paul's letters are the earliest documents expounding the new religion, being written before the gospels. They show the growing importance of Jesus' divinity and sacrifice. They also introduce the idea that the resurrection story is more important than Jesus' teaching – the idea that one can be saved from Hell by having faith in Jesus and repenting one's sins rather than by being blessed (or attaining enlightenment) through trying to follow his example.

Paul links Jesus' mission to Adam's sin: "For as in Adam all die, so in Christ all shall be made alive."[42]

Stories of changing water to wine, feeding five thousand at a rally on five loaves and two fish, and four thousand on seven loaves and a few small fish, are thus seen as supernatural miracles rather than celebrations of people being persuaded to accept water itself as "the best wine" or to share food they had originally intended to keep to themselves. These miracles become evidence of Jesus' divinity rather than illustrations of the power of his teaching.

Jesus' oral teaching was seen as a threat from the start by Jerusalem's priesthood and hierarchy. The gospels repeatedly quote his verbal lashings of the Pharisees in particular. Jesus was a rebel. His radical beliefs cost him his life. Many of his followers would also become martyrs.

The first to do so was Stephen, who was stoned to death in Jerusalem around AD 36 for continuing to preach Jesus' message. At this time, Paul, whose letters would soon be instrumental in creating the new faith of Christianity, was still known as Saul of Tarsus. He was present at Stephen's murder and even looked after the murderers' coats as they stoned him.

Saul continued to be active in the persecution of those who followed the Way of Jesus until he had a life-changing and name-changing experience. It began while Saul was leading a party from Jerusalem to Damascus to hunt down some of the Way's followers who had sought refuge there. Saul saw a flash of light, collapsed on the road and subsequently recalled hearing a voice saying "Saul, Saul, why do you persecute me?" He lost his sight and was unable to eat or drink. Three days later, after Saul's companions had led him to Damascus, Ananias, a follower of the Way, visited him. Ananias addressed Saul as "brother" and said, "The Lord Jesus, who appeared to you on the road by which you came, has sent me that you may regain your sight and be filled with the Holy Spirit." Ananias' visit led to Saul's recovery and conversion. He changed from a persecutor to an activist. A few days later, he was proclaiming Jesus as "The Son of God" in the synagogues of Damascus.[43]

Neurologists today may interpret the symptoms accompanying the start of Saul's experience as a transient ischaemic attack (mini-stroke), a nervous breakdown or an epileptic fit. Brain scans conducted recently on people having religious visions and epileptic fits have shown that both often happen concurrently and are accompanied by heightened brain activity in the temporal lobes. Such observations have given rise to the new science of neurotheology, which will be returned to in Chapter 11, but, whatever the cause of Saul's experience, it would have a profound effect on the development of Christianity, taking it a long way from the Way shown by Jesus.

Following his conversion, Saul changed his name to Paul and set about developing a new religion to be built on the stories of Jesus' death and resurrection. It would be based not only on the timelessness of Jesus' words, but also on a belief in Jesus as "The (one and only) Son of God", and in a literal interpretation of the resurrection and ascension stories.

This interpretation reduced the social challenge of Jesus' teaching, increasing its chances of general acceptance, but the new idea of a Holy Trinity of God the Father, God the Son and God the Holy Spirit would ensure that Paul's religion would be rejected within the solid monotheistic tradition of Judaism. The Trinity idea would not be a problem, however, among Judea's polytheistic neighbors in the rest of the Roman Empire. They were used to stories of the gods coming down to earth. Indeed, for them, Christianity would represent a step toward monotheism.

The new religion recognized personal devotion to Jesus, as well as right living, as a valid route to God. This would make it easier to gain converts. Paul would eventually place the importance of faith well above that of right living: "For it is by grace that you have been saved, and this not from yourselves; it is the gift of God; not by works, so that no-one can boast."[44]

Paul put his stamp on the new religion in its details as well as its essence. He overruled the idea among Jewish converts that Christians could not be saved without being circumcised. He stipulated that men should keep their hair short, but that women should have long hair: "It is her glory, for hair is given to her as a covering."[45]

He did not permit women to teach or have authority over men:

▷ She must be silent. For Adam was formed first and then Eve; and Adam was not the one deceived. It was the woman who was deceived and became a sinner, but women will be saved through childbearing – if they continue in faith, love and holiness with propriety.[46]

▷ No widow may be put on the list of widows, unless she is over 60, has been faithful to her husband, and is well known for her good deeds.[47]

He was intolerant of dissent:

▷ If anyone is preaching to you a gospel other than that you accepted, let him be eternally condemned![48]

▷ Warn a divisive person once then warn him a second time. After that, have nothing to do with him.[49]

Despite Paul's authoritarianism, some dissent survives in the New Testament. Jesus' brother, James, refused to accept that followers could be saved by faith alone, insisting that:

▷ Faith, by itself, if not accompanied by action, is dead.[50]

and that:

▷ The wisdom that comes from Heaven is first of all pure, then peace-loving, considerate, full of mercy and good fruit, impartial and sincere. Peacemakers who sow in peace raise a harvest of righteousness.[51]

Paul soon moved to Rome (see below). James led the church in Jerusalem until AD 62 when he was killed by order of the High Priest Ananias and succeeded by Matthew.

Another voice within the New Testament is provided in John's letters. This voice often echoes not only the teachings of Jesus, but also those of the Buddha before him:

▷ Do not love the world or anything in the world. If anyone loves the

world, the love of the Father is not in him. For everything in the world –
the cravings of sinful man, the lust in his eyes and the boasting of what
he has and does – comes not from the Father, but from the world. The
world and its desires pass away, but the man who does the will of God
lives forever.[52]

But it was Paul's activity that changed Christianity from a local cult in Judea
to one which spread throughout the Roman Empire. Apart from writing the
letters that make up much of the New Testament, he traveled widely as a
missionary and convened the first apostolic conference, the Council of
Jerusalem, around AD 49. Soon after this Council had met, Paul visited
Philippi, Macedonia, where he was arrested, along with Silas, a traveling
companion, following a commotion in the market place. They were both
condemned for being Jews who were throwing the city into uproar by
advocating customs unlawful for Romans to accept. They were stripped,
beaten and thrown into prison overnight, but released the following day,
having successfully protested that they were Roman citizens being detained
without trial.

Paul was later arrested again in Jerusalem for starting a riot in the temple. This
time he remained a prisoner and was transferred to Caesarea for his own
safety. At his trial there, he appealed to Caesar, and was subsequently put on a
ship to Rome. He spent three months on Malta, following a shipwreck, but
eventually made it to the capital, where he was allowed to live, with a soldier
to guard him, and to preach freely.

Paul was careful to avoid antagonizing Rome with instructions like:

▷ Everyone must submit himself to the governing authorities, for there is
no authority except that which God has established. The authorities that
exist have been established by God. He who rebels against the authority
is rebelling against what God has instituted, and those who do so will
bring judgment on themselves.[53]

Paul's Christianity spread quickly through the Empire. There were setbacks,
however, in spite of his instruction to respect Rome's authority:

▷ In AD 64 the Emperor Nero blamed Christians for a great fire in Rome
and had many executed, probably including Paul, himself, and also Peter,
a leader of the church in Rome – now acknowledged by the Roman
Catholic Church as the first Bishop of Rome and forerunner of the Popes.

▷ In 117 Ignatius of Antioch was martyred for refusing to acknowledge the divinity of Roman Emperors.

▷ In 155 Polycarp of Smyrna met the same fate.

Under Emperors Decius (249-251) and Diocletian (284-305), there were more general persecutions, but the status of Christianity was transformed under Emperor Constantine (306-337). Constantine brought temporary unity to a fading and divided Roman Empire. In 312, while he was battling in the north, a would-be Emperor, Maxentius challenged his position in Rome. Constantine invaded Italy and won battles at Verona and at the Milvian Bridge on the approach to Rome, where his rival was killed. The following year, he proclaimed equal rights for all religions and returned confiscated property to Christians and other religious groups. He subsequently decided that the Empire needed a single religion and adopted Christianity. Other popular religions and philosophies, such as Gnosticism, Mithraism, Manicheism, Platonism and Stoicism[54] were rejected. Christianity was adopted as the imperial religion and work began on an official Latin translation of the Bible. Christian leaders suddenly became politically powerful and moved quickly from being the persecuted to being the persecutors, of non-Christians and – due to theological arguments heightened by differing translations and interpretations of the Bible – of each other. The Latin translation of the Bible that was eventually adopted by the Church of Rome's hierarchy as the Word of God was written by Eusebius Hieronymous aka St Jerome (347-420) but St Jerome himself left Rome in 384 for the peace of Bethlehem, where he set up a monastic community.

Theological arguments had raged among Christians from the start. The most significant of them arose from differing interpretations of Jesus' teaching and from questions generated by the ideas of Jesus as the Son of God and of the Holy Trinity.

On Jesus' teaching, there were those who taught, as Jesus did, that believers should abandon their worldly lives for a more ascetic spiritual life. These included the Montanists, named for Montanus, who had preached as a Christian during the second century and had also accepted women among his followers. In 170, Montanus had been accused of breaking up marriages and declared an enemy of the Church of Rome, but his ideas remained popular.

On Jesus' nature, there were more serious divisions. The Docetists (from the Greek, *dokesis,* semblance) pointed out that if Jesus was divine, his body must have been an illusion. They argued that if he was God, he could not have suffered, and, if he suffered, he could not be God.

By 325, Christianity was on the point of tearing itself apart over this conundrum. The "Christ as the eternal God" position was held by Rome and championed by Alexander, Bishop of Alexandria. Alexander's priest, Arius, championed the "Christ as a man" position. He acknowledged Jesus' divinity, but could not accept that he was God's equal and co-eternal with God.

In order to settle this doctrinal argument, and other practical church matters, such as whether priests should be allowed to marry, Constantine summoned a meeting of around 300 bishops at Nicaea (now, Iznik, Turkey). On Jesus' divinity, they constructed this position:

▷ God is three Persons – God the Father, God the Son and God the Holy Spirit – and one Substance.

They also adopted a new calendar based on the year of Christ's birth, and confirmed that priests should not marry. They adopted December 25, already the feast Day of Constantine's favored Roman deity, Sol Invictus (and of Mithras), as Christ's feast day, and agreed that Constantine should be regarded as "The Holy Roman Emperor," whose rule should be seen as the earthly reflection of God's rule in Heaven. They also adopted Sol Invictus' symbol, the halo.

Despite the Bishops' unanimity over the Holy Trinity, Arius' view remained popular. It came to be known officially as the Arian heresy.

In 330, Constantine moved the Empire's capital east to Byzantium, renaming the city Constantinople. This left the Bishop of Rome (the Pope) as a key power in the western half of the empire.

In 336, Arius was executed for his views, but the arguments continued. For example, Appolinarius, Bishop of Laodicia, held that, as God, Jesus could not have had a human mind. Maron, a Syrian hermit taught that Jesus could only have one mind and founded a new church based on this principle.

Nestorius, Bishop of Constantinople, argued that Jesus must have had two completely separate natures, one human and one divine. Nestorius was particularly worried about the developing deification of the Virgin Mary as the bearer of God and held that the infant Jesus could not be regarded as the eternal God.

The bishops came together again at the Councils of Ephesus (431) and

Chalcedon (451) to thrash out these problems. The latter adopted this position:

> Christ is one substance with us with regard to his manhood; like us in all respects apart from sin; as regards the Godhead, begotten of the father before the ages; but as regards his manhood, begotten for us men and our salvation of Mary the Virgin, the Godbearer; One and the same Christ, Son, Lord, Only begotten, recognized in two natures without confusion *(sic)*, without change, without division, without separation.

Nestorius could not accept this and was deposed and banished. He died the same year, but a Nestorian church continued.

The orthodox Christian Church was also splitting, along with the Empire itself, following the sacking of Rome by Visigoth invaders in 410. For the next two centuries, the political center of the empire stayed in Constantinople (Byzantium), while Rome became a Western outpost. The old Roman Empire became the Byzantine Empire, with Greek influence in the ascendant. The Popes in Rome continued to be acknowledged as leaders of the Church, but could not maintain Roman orthodoxy throughout the Empire.

To the east, in addition to the separate Nestorian, Maronite and Egyptian Coptic Churches, the Eastern Orthodox, Greek Orthodox and Russian Orthodox Churches developed with differing interpretations of orthodoxy and different leaderships, while the Popes in Rome berated Byzantine emperors for interference in church matters.

In the seventh century, in response to the expansion of the Commonwealth of Islam to its south and east (see Chapter 7), the Byzantine court moved back to Rome in 663. It returned to Constantinople in 638. After this, its power in the West slowly began to fade: in 649, when Pope Martin I opposed the imperial doctrine that Jesus could only have one will, the court was still powerful enough to have him arrested and sent to Constantinople,[55] but by 723, when Emperor Leo III condemned image worship throughout his Empire, Pope Gregory II was able to oppose him and still remain in control in Rome with impunity – even after taking a decision to excommunicate all iconoclasts.

On the other hand, the eastern bishops supported the imperial position at the Council of Hieria (753). Monasteries were closed, Roman church property was confiscated, images were destroyed or whitewashed, and Roman monks were exiled, imprisoned or executed.

Rome's political break from Constantinople was completed just three years after Hieria when Pepin the Lombard, who already controlled most of north Italy, conquered the regions around Rome and donated them to the Pope, thus creating the Papal States as an independent entity.

Complex Christian theologies continued to be developed throughout this period. One scholar in particular, Augustine (354-430) wrote several influential treatises, including *Confessions* and *The City of God*, having converted from Manicheism to Christianity and become the Bishop of Hippo in North Africa.

Successive bishops' Councils introduced new creeds. In the sixth century, the Athanasian Creed, developing the Holy Trinity idea, was named after Athanasius, Alexander's successor, both as Bishop of Alexandria and as principle opponent of the Arian heresy. In the seventh century, the Apostles' Creed was adopted, affirming "the communion of saints, the forgiveness of sins, the resurrection of the body and the everlasting life" and accepting the use of icons in worship.

Ironically, having lost Rome in 756, the Byzantine Empire also dropped its opposition to the use of icons for worship. This was confirmed at the second Council of Nicaea held in 787.[56]

By this time, north and west Europe had descended into a political dark age, but a new feudal system was emerging and the Roman Catholic religion continued to spread through the continent. Feudal leaders were happy to benefit from Paul's instruction to the Romans to submit to authority. This instruction contributed to the emergence of the concept of the Divine Right of Kings. The concept caused power struggles between the feudal leaders and the church of the Popes in Rome, but, in 800, Charlemagne, a successful warrior king of the Franks, rose above the rest and was consecrated by Pope Leo II as Holy Roman Emperor, thus reviving Constantine's concept of Emperor as head of both state and church.

Initially, Charlemagne's compact with the Pope was not recognized by the Byzantine Empire and the Council of Constantinople (867) rejected the Pope's spiritual authority over the Byzantine Church. The total split was soon moderated, however, as the Byzantine Empire had all but collapsed in the face of advancing Islam. In response to the perceived threat of Islamic expansionism, the Byzantine court recognized the Holy Roman Empire in 869, entered a nominal union with Rome in 900 and strengthened the union in 920.

The Commonwealth of Islam had reached Asia Minor (now Turkey) by 640.

Islamic power spread across North Africa and into Spain and southern France by 732. Christian powers took a militaristic turn in response. Charles Martel, and later his grandson, Charlemagne, stopped the Islamic advance into France, but Muslims held most of Spain and kept control of the Mediterranean. When Sicily fell to a Muslim power in 827, the church itself embraced militarism and, in 847, Pope Leo IV declared that Christians who died defending the faith would receive their heavenly reward.

Islamic power remained a concern for the Holy Roman Empire and the various battling European kings, princes and warlords. In 1096, Pope Urban II was able to galvanize support for a crusade to recapture Jerusalem and the Holy Land from the infidel. This was the first of eight crusades. It started with mass eastbound migrations of peasant crusaders, usually pillaging and attacking Jewish communities as they went. Two groups got as far as Asia Minor: around 7,000 under Peter the Hermit and 5,000 under Walter the Penniless. Both groups were eventually annihilated. They were followed by a more organized army of 30,000, led by a trio of European nobles and joined, in Constantinople, by the forces of the Byzantine Empire. Their armies captured Jerusalem in 1099. They massacred its 30,000 inhabitants – Muslims, Christians and Jews; men, women and children. They destroyed all the Muslim shrines except the Dome of the Rock, which they converted to a church, and the Al-Aqsa Mosque, which became a Palace, and set up a Frankish Kingdom of Jerusalem, plus separate feudal states in Edessa, Antioch and Tripoli. Despite (or, perhaps, because of) continuing massacres and desecrations in all of these states, local resistance ensured that none of them survived for more than a few decades.

In 1145 Pope Eugenius III called for a second crusade and persuaded Conrad III of Germany and Louis VII of France to lead it. Their expeditions lasted from 1147 to 1149 and made no significant impact on the Christian/Muslim balance of power.

The Muslims recaptured Jerusalem in 1189, and a third crusade was mounted, led by the Holy Roman Emperor Frederick Barbarossa, the English King Richard I and the French King Philip II. This led to a truce with the Muslims in 1192, with the crusaders occupying a coastal strip between Acre and Jaffa and being allowed access to Jerusalem. Richard I then went his own way. He took Cyprus and sold it, and was then kidnapped while crossing Europe, held for two years and ransomed, before returning to the English throne in 1194.

The "fourth crusade" (1202-4) was, in fact an imperial adventure led by Frederick's son, Emperor Henry VI without papal support. It led not only to the crusaders' bloody capture of Constantinople from Eastern Orthodox Christians, but also to their excommunication by Pope Innocent III, who subsequently managed to promote a fifth crusade (1218-1221). This achieved marginal and temporary success in the Holy Land before ending in a truce.

The same Pope supported a separate "crusade" (1208-1226) against an austere Christian Sect, the Cathars of Albi in southern France. They were officially condemned for heresy, but their espousal of Jesus' teaching on asceticism and humility, their acceptance of women priests, their tolerance of Jews and Muslims and their opposition to corruption among the clergy and nobility were probably greater factors in precipitating their destruction at the hands of King Louis VIII. In 1209, the crusaders of the Pope and King killed over 15,000 in the Cathar town of Beziers alone.

In 1216 the Dominican Order was established to counter the Cathar heresy and, in 1233, a Papal Bull charged the Dominicans with the eradication of all heresy. They were subsequently authorized to use torture and execution to this end and became central to the inquisition (see below).

The sixth crusade (1228-9) led by Emperor Frederick II was another imperial adventure launched without papal support. The emperor gained Nazareth, Bethlehem, Jerusalem and a corridor to the coast in a truce agreement with the Egyptian Sultan, but was opposed by the Christian patriarch of Jerusalem and excommunicated by Pope Gregory IX.

When Muslims recaptured Jerusalem in 1244, King Louis IX organized a seventh crusade (1248-9). He was captured in Egypt and his army massacred. After being ransomed in 1251, Louis undertook a four-year pilgrimage to Jerusalem, then, in 1270 joined Edward of England and Charles of Anjou for the eighth crusade, which also failed miserably.

The crusaders' last outpost in the Holy Land fell to the Muslims in 1291. Its former rulers, the Knights of St John, moved west to Cyprus (1291-1310), then took over Rhodes (1310-1522) and Malta (1530-1798).

The 13th century saw several minor crusades in addition to those numbered above. They included two "children's crusades." In the first of these, the children were led to Marseilles then shipped off into slavery. In the second, the children were brought together in Germany and died while marching through Italy.

By this time, the presence of a Muslim enemy in the Holy Land had faded as a significant unifying force for Christendom. Christianity's divisions and violence began to turn inwards again. Innocent's crusade against the Cathars (1208-1226) has already been mentioned. The Roman Catholic Church also instigated a general Inquisition against heresy and, when the Muslims were finally driven from Spain in 1492, a separate Spanish Inquisition was launched. Joined by the Portuguese Inquisition in 1536, it continued until 1790, targeting heretics in general (see below) and Jews in particular (see Chapter 2).

In 1305 political instability around Rome led the Pope to move to Avignon in France, and this remained the papal center until 1378, when the installation of a new Pope in Rome led the "The Great Schism" with half the church recognizing the Roman pope and the other half staying loyal to the Avignon pope. During the schism, the two popes put their antagonism to one side for a few weeks in 1396 to support another would-be crusade led by Sigismund of Hungary when Constantinople was being besieged by the Muslim Turks. A force of 20,000 men was amassed in Buda, but, after a bloody journey down the Danube, they were overwhelmed by the Turks at Nicopolis.

In 1409 the Council of Pisa deposed both the Popes and elected a new one, effectively initiating a period of three Popes, as neither of the first two recognized the Council; then from 1414-17, the Council of Constance sat to resolve the deadlock. It restored the unity of the Roman Catholic Church, but also launched a new wave of persecution. The main targets this time were the followers of Jan Hus, a professor at the University of Prague, and follower of the English reformer, John Wycliffe (1333-84). Hus opposed the sale of indulgences, challenged the primacy of the Pope and preached that the scriptures should be regarded as the supreme authority. He challenged the Church to allow the Bible to be translated from Latin to contemporary European languages. Hus was excommunicated in 1411, but in 1415, he was granted safe conduct to Pisa by the Emperor to put his case to the Council. After giving him a hearing, however, the council arrested him, tried him and burned him to death at the stake, precipitating a series of wars between Rome and the Hussites, which continued until 1433 when a peace was negotiated at the Council of Basel.

The Council of Basel sat from 1431 to 1449. In addition to ending the Hussite wars, it addressed arguments over issues such as papal supremacy, the nature of confession, absolution and purgatory, and the conduct of the sacrament. It also sought to reunite the Roman and Greek churches. Its conclusion was celebrated by the Jubilee of 1450 in an environment of optimism.

Despite the new veneer of church unity, Italy and the rest of Europe remained politically divided. The Council's conclusions failed to carry either the Greek Church or the Roman reformers, whose protests would soon surface again (see below).

In 1453 the Turks finally took Constantinople and consolidated their control in Southeast Europe, rendering Greek and other eastern Christian rivalries to the Roman Catholic Church politically insignificant. But the printing of Gutenberg's Bible in Germany in 1456 opened a new age of challenge to papal and priestly power. With copies of the Bible becoming widely available, more and more people were now able to turn to its teaching without having to rely on the Church hierarchy as the only interpreters of its meaning. By the 16th century, the spread of the renaissance had been followed by a religious reformation that would bring upheaval and division to match anything that had occurred in Europe since the fall of Rome over a thousand years earlier, but, before the 15th century ended, a westward expansion of Christendom, which would eventually dwarf its losses in the East, was underway.

In 1492 Roman Catholicism reached the Americas with Christopher Columbus. Ironically, the faith that was having problems accommodating new approaches to Jesus' teaching at home had no such problems in embracing the introduction of both serial genocide and slavery in its New World. In 1493, Pope Alexander VI split the rights to all new lands between Spain and Portugal. The Spaniards quickly colonized the West Indies, wiping out local populations with European germs and weapons, and replacing them, from 1501, with slaves kidnapped in Africa. By 1521, Cortez had repeated the process of conquest and destruction in Aztec Mexico, from where he and his successors pushed both north and south. In the 1530s, Pizarro took Inca Peru. In the 1540s, de Valdivia destroyed the Araucanians in Chile, and by 1546 Maya resistance in the south of Mexico had also been crushed. The Spanish Inquisition was formally introduced in 1569.

In Brazil, Portuguese colonists and missionaries were more interested in converting the smaller indigenous populations than exterminating them, so their destruction was less systematic; but the introduction of slavery was a key to the new plantation economy here, just as in the Spanish West Indies.

The pattern of serial genocide and slavery would soon follow in North America too, at the hands of Catholic and Protestant colonists alike. It would continue until well into the 19th century and include the first known examples of biological warfare – the distribution of smallpox infested blankets to Native Americans.[57]

Meanwhile, back in Europe, resistance to Roman Catholic hegemony continued to develop. In 1517 a German priest, Martin Luther (1483-1546) nailed a document to the door of the court church in Wittenberg. It listed 95 arguments against the misuse of absolution and indulgences by the church. He was summoned to Augsburg by the cardinal, but refused to recant and appealed to the Pope.

The Pope responded by issuing a bull that rejected 41 of the arguments. Luther burned his copy and was excommunicated. He advocated a Protestant church that, he wrote, would be nearer to the Bible (Presbyterian) and justified by faith alone. He declared the priestly offices of the Catholics an unnecessary intermediary between the individual and God. He produced a German translation of the Bible and set up a Reformed Church under the protection of the Emperor Charles V.

In 1518 another priest, Ulrich Zwingli, started another reformed church in Zurich, Switzerland. Zwingli went further than Luther in rejecting the idea that the bread used in communion was miraculously transformed into the flesh of Christ. He argued that communion should be regarded as a purely symbolic and commemorative ritual. He died in 1531 in a war between Zurich and the Catholic cantons of Switzerland, but his view of communion, so radical and divisive then, is the most prevalent among Christians today.

In 1524, in Thuringia, Thomas Munzer led another Protestant group, the Anabaptists. This group rejected the idea of infant baptism in favor of voluntary adult baptism. Muntzer was arrested and executed the same year, but Anabaptism spread through Germany and into the Netherlands. Anabaptists established a communal theocracy at Munster, which was brutally suppressed in 1535, but their tradition lives on today in both Europe and America – notably among the Mennonites, an anabaptist group founded in the Netherlands by Menno Simons (1496-1561), which went on to pioneer many communities in the American west – but also in many of the 20,000 or more other Christian churches that have arisen since the start of the Reformation.

In 1527 Martin Cellarium, a friend of Luther, deviated further from the Roman Catholic trinitarian position, denying the deity of Jesus. This marked the birth of the Unitarian Church. At least one early Unitarian, Michael Servetus, was martyred for his views in Catholic Geneva in 1531, but the new church continued to grow slowly, building its first church in the medieval town of Kolozsvar (now Cluj, Romania) in 1568. The Unitarian Church currently has some 150,000 members, mostly in the USA.

In 1534 the English Reformation began under King Henry VIII (1509-47). Henry had been awarded the title Defender of the Faith by Pope Leo X for his opposition to Luther in 1521, but was excommunicated for divorcing his first wife in 1532. At first, the English Reformation simply recognized Henry's divorce and made the King supreme head of the Church of England, but it soon led to closures of monasteries throughout the kingdom and royal authorization for a translation of the Bible into English. In 1536 a Catholic rebellion was suppressed, but in 1539 the narrow limits of the reformation were clarified by the Statute of the Six Articles, which made it a punishable heresy to deny the current Catholic positions on transubstantiation, communion, celibacy of the priesthood, vows of chastity, mass and confession. The Statute was repealed following Henry's death in 1547 as the reformation gathered momentum and, under his son, the child-king, Edward VI (1547-1553), parliament introduced a uniform church service, a Book of Common Prayer in English (replacing its Latin predecessor) and ratified the "42 Articles of Religion" published by the leader of Edward's church, Thomas Cranmer, Archbishop of Canterbury. Then Edward became ill, died young and was succeeded by his older half-sister Mary (1553-8), a Catholic who restored the Six Articles and the old church hierarchy, executed a Protestant rival, Lady Jane Grey, along with her husband and supporters, burned Cranmer and some 300 other Protestants at the stake, and imprisoned Henry's daughter Elizabeth. All this failed to halt the Protestant juggernaut, however, and following Mary's death Elizabeth succeeded to the throne and repealed all Mary's Catholic legislation. The Church of England is now at the center of a worldwide Anglican Community of over 100 million worshipers.

The 16th-century Church of England remained intolerant, however, persecuting both Roman Catholics on the one hand and radical Protestants on the other. This led to one particular breakaway that would have far-reaching global consequences: the Pilgrim Fathers were an offshoot of a group of strict

Protestants or puritans who had split from the Anglican Church in the late 16th century. Some of these puritans left England for Holland in 1608 to avoid persecution. In 1620, a small group of them returned to England and were joined by some local puritans in assembling about 120 pioneers, the Pilgrim Fathers, to sail from Plymouth to North America aboard *The Mayflower* in search of religious freedom. They founded the Plymouth Colony near Cape Cod and drafted the Mayflower Compact as a constitution for the organization of their church and state. During their first winter, half of them died, but others soon joined them and more new settlements were founded, including Salem (1626) and Boston (1630). Unlike the Spaniards in South & Central America and the English in Virginia, the puritan colonists managed to live in peace and to trade fairly with the indigenous populations during their first 10 years, but as their numbers increased, war and genocide became the norm here too. The Pequots were among the first tribes to be decimated, losing 600 men, women and children to an attack on their main village in 1636. In common with other tribes, they also lost many more of their numbers to the smallpox epidemics that the colonists had inadvertently introduced.

One colonist, Roger Williams, opposed taking Indian land by force and also advocated the separation of church and state. At his trial in 1635, he said: "I do affirm it to be against the testimony of Christ Jesus for the civil state to impose upon the soul of the people a religion, a worship, a ministry. The state should give free and absolute permission of conscience to all men in what is spiritual alone. Ye have lost yourselves. Your breath blows out the candle of liberty in this land."

Williams was banished from the colony. He moved south with some followers and set up a new colony at Providence in which church and state were kept separate. This principle was subsequently incorporated in the constitution of the USA.

In 1691 the puritan settlements of the Cape Cod area were united as the province of Massachusetts, but by the following year the original ideal of freedom from persecution had suffered a further setback: a witchcraft scare in Salem led to the trial and execution of 19 "witches" and some of their defenders. This religious lunacy led to a decline in the credibility and political importance of religion in Massachusetts, which subsequently became a center of revolutionary opposition to British colonialism and a creative power in the birth of the United States of America. However, despite the fact that the United

States' Constitution still separates church and state, the country continues to be dominated by its own collection of Christian dogmas, some of which are reviewed later in this section.

But first let us return to the 16th century in Europe and the story of Old World Christianity. A key move in the Catholic counter-reformation came in 1540: Pope Paul III recognized Ignatius Loyola's Society of Jesus, founding the Jesuit Order. The Order was organized with militaristic discipline under papal control in defense of the Roman Church, but the following year, Protestant power was also given another boost: John Calvin (1509-64), a Protestant since 1533, who had moved to Geneva to avoid persecution, became Head of State in Geneva for the second time and introduced a far-reaching reformation there. Like Luther, Calvin rejected papal authority in favor of the Bible, but he also referred to the writings of Augustine, and stressed the concept of predestination and the need to subordinate the state to the church. Geneva was turned into a theocratic Calvinist republic. It became part of the Swiss Confederation in 1648 and part of modern Switzerland in 1815, but Calvinism became important in Germany, Holland, Scotland and Massachusetts, and also spawned and influenced other Protestant churches, such as the Huguenots in France and the Orangemen in Northern Ireland.

From 1562 to 1598 religious wars between Catholics and Huguenots racked France. These ended April 1598, by Edict of Nantes, which gave Huguenots limited but acceptable political rights.

In 1608 a Protestant Union was formed in Germany under Palatine Elector Frederick IV. In 1609 a rival Catholic Union was formed under Duke Maximilian of Bavaria.

This soon led to the Thirty Years War (1618-48) that racked most of Europe until the Treaties of Westphalia formalized the division of Europe into Protestant and Catholic countries and secured some rights for religious minorities.

While the war was raging, the church shot itself in the foot on another front. Galileo, the famous renaissance physicist and astronomer, was brought before the Roman Inquisition for the heresy of agreeing with the theory of Copernicus (1473-1543) that the Earth is not the center of the universe, but just one of several planets orbiting the sun. He was forced to recant to avoid losing his life to his inquisitors.

Once the war ended, however, most of Europe experienced a period of unprecedented progress in science and industry. The Church faded as a cause of persecution and war across most of the continent. Increasing numbers of educated Europeans rejected more and more of its bizarre dogmas, and the political significance of Christianity faded, giving way to nationalism and economics as the main issues.

The British Isles were a little late in reaching a similar situation. The uneasy peace that followed the accession of Elizabeth I (1558-1603) had become more fraught under her successors. The Church of England continued persecuting Roman Catholics on the one hand, and many of the new Protestant groups, including Baptists, Anabaptists, Calvinists, Congregationalists, Presbyterians, Puritans, and Unitarians on the other. In 1605, a Catholic plot to blow up the Houses of Parliament on November 5 was foiled, and its perpetrators, including one Guy Fawkes, were arrested, tried and executed. The English still burn Guy Fawkes in effigy on bonfires up and down the country every year on November 5.

By 1642 divisions between the Catholic-leaning King Charles I and his puritan-leaning parliament led to the English Civil War (1642-6 and 1648-9). The king lost and was beheaded in January 1649 and replaced by a puritan Commonwealth.

The Commonwealth put down royalist and Catholic rebellions in Scotland and Ireland in its first year, massacring garrisons at Drogheda and Wexford in Ireland, but gave way to the restoration of the monarchy under Charles II in 1660.

The restoration was intended to provide a balance of power between king and parliament – between Catholic and Protestant forces. The latter intent was formalized in the Declaration of Liberty and Conscience of 1687. Opposition to the king's anti-protestantism continued, however, and led to his replacement by William and Mary in the "Glorious Revolution" of 1689.

The deposed king managed to rally Roman Catholic forces for an invasion via Ireland in 1690. He was defeated at the Battle of the Boyne on July 1. This battle is still celebrated every July by Orangemen in Northern Ireland in a series of provocative marches designed to antagonize the Catholics of their province, who were separated from the rest of Ireland when the country achieved independence from Great Britain in 1922. This little corner of Ireland is still home to handfuls of psychopaths and political retards, for whom

Protestant ascendancy remains more important than peace or justice, and for whom Europe's 17th-century religious wars continue into the 21st.

The victory of Parliament in the English Civil War boosted the new religious thinking of the reformation, but not all new views were tolerated. One group, the Friends in the Truth, founded by George Fox (1624-91) was persecuted for its pacifism and its claim that there is "that of God in everyone." Fox was arrested and tried for blasphemy in 1650. His taunt from the dock that the judge should "quake at the word of the Lord" led to the group being referred to as Quakers, a name they adopted without apology and still use today, although their official title is now The Religious Society of Friends.

The Quakers taught that the spontaneous experience of God had been smothered by the institutionalism of the church and resolved to practice their religion without recourse to either priests or ministers. Between 1650 and 1687, 338 died for their beliefs. Most of these were victims of the Roman Inquisition, but their number also includes four hanged on Boston Common between 1659 and 1661. Another 198 were transported from Europe and some 13,000 imprisoned. Nevertheless, the Quakers continued to spread their message, even attempting to reach the Popes in Rome, and at least one, Mary Fisher (1623-98), went further still and took the Quaker message to the Sultan in Constantinople in 1657.

There are now some 200,000 Quakers around the world and, in spite of their pacifism, egalitarianism and still-small numbers, they have produced some notable leaders: William Penn (1644-1718) founded the Quaker colony of Pennsylvania and the city of Philadelphia, and acted as a mediator between non-pacifist colonists and indigenous populations there. John Bellers (1654-1725) was a social reformer whose ideas would influence Robert Owen and Karl Marx. John Woolman (1720-72) pioneered the movement for the abolition of slavery in America; and Quaker businessmen founded Barclays and Lloyds banks, and the chocolate manufacturers, Cadburys and Rowntrees.

Ironically, the work of a pacifist Quaker, Abraham Darby (1677-1717), facilitated both the genocidal westward expansion of the USA and the European imperialism of the 19th century: Darby's invention of the coke-fired blast furnace, further developed by his son, led to the mass production of steel, crucial to the industrial revolution and the age of big ships, big guns and railways. In general, however, Quakers continue to be a force for world peace and sustainable development: many were imprisoned as conscientious objectors during World War I (1914-18); two Quaker organizations, the British Friends Service Council and the American Friends Service Committee, shared the 1947 Nobel Peace Prize, and many other Friends' Committees continue to sponsor and organize peace and development programs around the world.[58]

Many other groups broke away from existing churches between the 17th and 19th centuries. Some of these – the Amish (1693), Church of the New Jerusalem (1758), Shakers (1774), Episcopalians (1776), Methodist Episcopals (1784), Wesleyan Methodists (1795), Mormons (1830), Plymouth Brethren (1831), Adventists (1831), Jehovah's Witnesses (1870), Reformed Episcopalians (1873), Christian Scientists (1879), Pentecostalists (1880) and Unity School (1889) – are discussed briefly here. There were thousands of other breakaway churches during this period, but these examples cover much of the range of reformed beliefs and practices and, each for their own reasons, such as their current numbers and/or influence, warrant a mention.

The Amish were a group of Swiss anabaptist Mennonites, who followed Jakob Ammann (1645-1730) in breaking away from their main church to follow their Christian principles more faithfully and conservatively. In the 1720s, many followed other puritans to North America to establish their own small agricultural communities. Some of these still survive in the USA and Canada, working the land, wearing plain home-made clothes, rejecting many of the trappings of the modern world, such as cars and phones, and practicing non-cooperation with the state authorities.

The Church of the New Jerusalem is a breakaway from the Protestant church in Sweden. It was founded by Emmanuel Swedenborg. He was born in Stockholm in 1688 and enjoyed an illustrious career as a metallurgist, mining engineer and writer on science and philosophy. In 1745, he gave this up to develop and propagate his own version of Christianity, having received revelations of "the spiritual truth" which rejected the ideas of "three Gods" and vicarious atonement. He wrote extensively on these errors and other revealed truths before he died in London in 1772. His Church currently claims about 50,000 members, mostly in Scandinavia, England and the USA.

The Shakers, or United Society of Believers in Christ's Second Appearing, were founded as a breakaway from the Quakers in England in 1774. In addition to the Quaker teachings outlined above, they also practiced celibacy, emphasized the dual male/female nature of God, and accepted one of their number, Mother Ann Lee (d1784), as a reincarnation of God. In 1774 Ann Lee and eight of her followers emigrated to New York to found a commune. Within 100 years, there were around 6,000 Shakers in 18 communes in the USA. Shakers were given their nickname on the basis of the fervor of their worship, but their key legacy is the peaceful simplicity of their lifestyle, recalled particularly through the style of furniture they produced in the 19th century, which is currently enjoying renewed attention.

The Episcopalian Church was born as a result of the American Revolution. The Episcopalians were the Anglicans who broke away from the Church of England after the declaration of independence in 1776. The new church was formally established with its own constitution and its own Book of Common Prayer in 1789, just two years after the signing of the US Constitution. It is now one of the main Protestant churches in the USA, with around 2.4 million members. It remains part of the worldwide Anglican Community, although this community is currently under renewed threat over the acceptability of gay clergy. Many of its members and leaders do not share the view of Gene Robinson, gay Bishop of New Hampshire, that "our perception of what God wants is expanding."

Another breakaway church founded in the USA soon after independence is The Methodist Episcopal Church. The Methodists' split from the original Episcopalians mirrored a another division that was about to happen in the Church of England under the influence of an evangelical movement founded by John Wesley (1703-91) and benefiting from the prolific hymn-writing of his younger brother, Charles (1707-88).

The Wesleyan Methodist Church was formally established in England in 1795. Although the Wesleys had been active evangelists within the Anglican Church since 1729, it was only after the death of John Wesley that his followers in England broke away to form a separate church. The split resulted from a dispute over the power of Anglican bishops. They soon split further, forming the Methodist New Connection (1797) and Primitive Methodists (1811). Ongoing splits and reunions, plus combinations with other Protestant groups, make it difficult to keep track of the total number of Methodist churches at any given time, but overall Methodist churches worldwide claim a membership in excess of 50 million. In November 2003 the main Methodist Church entered into a Covenant of Cooperation with the Anglican Church.

The next group on our list, the Mormons, are a product of a much more dramatic break. Their church, the Church of Jesus Christ of Latter Day Saints, was founded as The Church of Christ in Manchester, New York, in 1830. Ten years earlier, God the Father and God the Son had appeared to Joseph Smith (1805-1844) in a vision and charged him with restoring the true Christianity. Smith, whose own father was a mystic, a treasure hunter and an alleged counterfeiter,[59] subsequently discovered material support and further guidance for his mission in the form of *The Book of Mormon*, written in a cuneiform script similar to those of the ancient Middle East, etched into gold plates and buried near Palmyra, New York. Smith was able to translate this script and produce the document that would become a Bible for his new church. Converts were baptized and set about building a new community based on the teaching of Jesus and Mormon, and preparing for the Kingdom of Heaven. Early attempts to build their communities in Ohio, Missouri and Illinois all met with opposition from other settlers and failed. Smith was murdered by a mob while being held in gaol in Carthage, Illinois. He was succeeded by Brigham Young (1801-77) who led a migration further west to Utah, founded Salt Lake City in 1847 and became governor of Utah (1850-57). The Mormons reject tobacco and alcohol. They once adopted polygamy temporarily as an aid to the community's survival in their harsh pioneering environments of 19th-century Illinois and Utah. In 1857, they protected their new Utah community by massacring a wagon-train of over 100 non-Mormon would-be immigrants at Mountain Meadows, Utah. Nowadays, they are much more secure and non-Mormons can visit the state in relative safety. They even produced a whole family of pop icons, the Osmonds, in the 1970s, and Salt Lake City played host to the 2002 Winter Olympics. It is a booming city with a population of 170,000, including a significant non-Mormon minority and, with its magnificent temple and Brigham Young University, remains the world center of Mormonism. The Mormons are actively evangelical. They have missionaries all over the world and it is estimated that there are over 10 million Mormons worldwide (albeit divided into some 200 different denominations). The original Church of Jesus Christ of Latter Day Saints claims a membership of 9.5 million.

The Plymouth Brethren arose from another 1820's revelation – received in Ireland by an Anglican priest, J N Darby. It moved him to start a new breakaway evangelical community based on a return to true Christian values. Unlike some of his predecessors, he did so without the help of a new reincarnation of God, a host of new hymns, or newly discovered scriptures on gold plates. Nevertheless, he managed to found a lasting community in Plymouth, England, in 1831, and this has since generated many new puritan breakaway groups of varying exclusiveness or openness. Indeed, the groups include one officially known as the Open Brethren and another known as the Exclusive Brethren. All these groups share a requirement for austere living, and their combined numbers remain in thousands rather than millions.

The Adventists are another group of churches that date back to 1831. William Miller (1782-1849) founded the first in the USA. The common belief of the Adventist churches is the imminent return of Christ, so, not surprisingly, many of them fall apart if they get too specific about a date and then it passes without any sign of the return. Indeed, this was the fate of Miller's original Adventist Church.

However, one Adventist church, that of the Seventh Day Adventists, has become a worldwide movement by predicting Christ's absolute destruction of the wicked when he does return, but avoiding the naming of a specific date. This church was also helped by the phenomenon of Ellen White (1827-90). Ellen was hit on the head at the age of nine and spent three weeks in a coma. She never returned to school. During her teens, she experienced dramatic episodes during which she experienced religious visions that supported her Seventh Day Adventism. These visions were given wide publicity and generated many conversions. Modern neurotheologists analyzing the Ellen White phenomenon suggest that this is a classical example of visions generated by post-brain injury epilepsy.[60]

As the 19th century progressed, the wider Christian civilization, having learned from the Catholic Church's mistake over Galileo's support for the Copernican theory that the Earth could not be the fixed center of the universe, was generally able to look at the proliferation of new scientific discoveries fairly objectively. When geologists and biologists showed that the age of the Earth was almost a million times greater than that calculated from Biblical history, that life appeared on Earth billions of years ago, and that humans appeared billions of years later – a mere several million or so years ago – by a process of evolution; and when medics demystified much of the workings of our bodies, most Christians made an effort to get their heads round this new information. The Bible became a series of symbolic stories for them, rather than a literal history. There were some, however, who could not cope with this, and continued to believe in the literal truth of the entire Bible as the Word of God. These were the fodder for many of the new breakaway churches that emerged toward the end of the century. The USA was the most fertile breeding ground for these new churches – and for splits among its older churches.

In 1870 Charles Taze Russell (1852-1916), a Congregationalist from Pittsburgh, Pennsylvania, preached in support of biblical certainty and against existing organized religion at bible classes. He went on to spawn the Jehovah's Witnesses. In 1879, he founded a magazine, *The Herald of the Morning* with a print run of 6,000. Its successor, *The Watchtower (announcing Jehovah's Kingdom)* now has a circulation of 20 million in 110 languages. Jehovah's Witnesses of the Watchtower Bible and Tract Society, with its headquarters now in New York, claim a membership of 600,000 missionary volunteers around the world. They teach that the Bible is the Word of God (Jehovah), that it is the literal truth throughout, that Satan was a great angel who challenged Jehovah, that Jesus Christ was a man (not God) who has been resurrected as a divine spirit, that the doctrines of Hell and the Trinity are falsehoods invented by the church without biblical foundation, and that a theocratic millennial Kingdom of Jehovah is at hand and will bring salvation here on Earth to all believers.

In 1873 divisions between modernizers and traditionalists among the Episcopalians caused a split, which led to the foundation of a new Reformed Episcopalian Church alongside the old unreformed one.

In 1879 Mary Baker Eddy (1821-1910), a Congregationalist from Bow, New Hampshire, founded the Church of Christ Scientist, whose followers reject medical treatment and believe that both moral and physical problems should only be dealt with through spiritual and mental activity. Like Jehovah's Witnesses and some of the earlier breakaways, Christian Scientists also reject the Trinity concept as polytheistic.

In 1880 Charles Mason (d1961), the son of a former slave, who was suffering from tuberculosis, saw "the radiant presence of God" and quickly recovered. He went on to become an evangelical preacher,[61] relating his experience to that of Jesus' disciples at Pentecost[62] and preaching to revivalist meetings that all his followers could experience baptism in the holy spirit – thus giving birth to Pentecostalism. Mason founded The Church of God in Christ in Los Angeles in 1897. Although this church was nominally multiracial, it remained a primarily black phenomenon. A separate white Pentecostal movement was subsequently founded in Topeka, Kansas in 1901. Both groups shared a belief in the literal truth of the Bible, but differed with respect to lifestyle. White Pentecostalists shunned alcohol, tobacco, dancing and other pleasures, cast doubt on Mason's "miracle cure" and accused him of introducing voodoo into Christianity. The Church of God in Christ continued to grow, however, and now has congregations of over 1,000 in all of the USA's major cities (13,000 members and 155 staff in Los Angeles).[63] At a meeting in Memphis in 1994, white Pentecostalist leaders sought forgiveness for having excluded the Church of God in Christ from their fellowship. The combined Pentecostalist churches now claim a worldwide membership of 450 million, including around seven million members of the Church of God in Christ.

Another late 19th-century breakaway, the Unity School of Christianity, differed from the rest in that it arose from an attempt to link Christianity with another religious system, Hinduism. Its roots go back to a meeting in Kansas City, Missouri, in 1889, led by Charles and Myrtle Fillmore. Myrtle had been a Methodist, then a Christian Scientist. Charles had studied other religions, including Hinduism. They subsequently launched a magazine, initially called *Modern Thought*, then *Christian Science Thought*, then just *Thought* (following complaints from Mary Baker Eddy). They adopted the Unity name in 1891 and their Unity School of Christianity now claims a worldwide membership of 1.5 million. Although small, Unity's significance is that it was the first modern attempt at a syncretist religion to emerge from the Christian tradition.

A final 19th-century development that also deserves a mention is the formation of the Salvation Army. William Booth (1829-1912), a Methodist evangelist, founded the Christian Revival Association in London, England, in 1865, and changed the association's name to the Salvation Army in 1878. He also introduced a distinctive uniform for its members and gave himself the title of General. The Salvation Army is now an international church of over a million members. It concentrates on evangelistic and social work among the poor.

The 20th century saw a continuing proliferation of new churches around the world, again mostly in the USA, but also including significant new breakaways beginning in Asia and Africa: the Unification Church and the Celestial Church of Christ. The USA itself was more notable for the arrival of a pair of overlapping new Christian phenomena – fundamentalism and tele-evangelism, which we will return to at the end of this chapter.

The Unification Church was founded by the Reverend Sun Myung Moon (Shining Sun and Moon) in South Korea in 1954. Born Yong Myung Moon (Shining Dragon Moon) in the north of Japanese Korea in 1920, Moon experienced a vision of Jesus in 1936 telling him that he had been chosen to usher in the Kingdom of Heaven and another in 1945 telling him that he had been elevated to the position of God's True Son. Moon was imprisoned by the new communist regime in North Korea and, on his release, moved to South Korea, joined the Pentecostalist movement in Seoul, then founded his own church, The Holy Spirit Association for the Unification of World Christianity. With its rejection of the Trinity concept, its elevation of Moon to the same status as Jesus, its advocacy of universal love and world unity, its evangelism, and its mass marriage and blessing ceremonies, the church has attracted a worldwide membership of several million "Moonies."

The Celestial Church of Christ was founded by Samuel Oschoffa (d1985), a Roman Catholic carpenter born in French West Africa. The spiritual experiences that led Oschoffa to found his own church followed an eclipse that happened while he was on a canoe trip to buy wood. He was deserted by his frightened guide and spent three months lost in the wilderness with only a voice saying "Grace of God" for company. On reaching a village, he found that dead children could be brought back to life by the touch of his hand. Then, while he was praying on his return home, an angel spoke to him saying "The son of man, we want to send you into the world because so many believers are worshiping gods and Mammon ... warn them to worship only Christ" and "I am giving you powers to wake the dead and perform all kinds of miracles in the name of God."[64]

Oschoffa taught that any of his followers could receive revelations during their church services. Their visions are recorded, interpreted by their leaders, and acted upon. The Church is now the largest in West Africa and has churches in cities on every continent, including one in Moscow and eight in Washington DC.

Despite the original Roman Catholic Christianity's split into some 20,000 denominations – its losses to the Orthodox Churches in the first millennium, to Protestantism since the 16th century and to the Moonies, Oschoffans etc on the one hand, and to agnosticism or atheism on the other, in the 20th – the Roman Catholic Church remains the world's largest Christian denomination, claiming 600 million followers worldwide.

Roman Catholic political influence has risen again since hitting an all-time low at the end of the 18th century when Napoleon set up a Roman Republic (1798) and sent the Pope to France, where he died in 1799. It rose a little during the 19th and early 20th centuries, but was not helped by the re-establishment of the Inquisition following the new Pope's return to Rome (1814), by Pius IX's rejection of "progress, liberalism and modern civilization" (1864) and his Decree of Papal Infallibility (1870) – still used in formalizing doctrine, such as that of the Assumption that the body of Mary was taken into Heaven and reunited with her soul being confirmed in an infallible declaration by Pius XII (1950). The Church's reputation also suffered in retrospect as a result of its support for fascist regimes in Italy (1922-43), Spain (1923-75) and Portugal (1930-74) and its failure to oppose the rise of the Nazis in Germany.

However, the Second Vatican Council (1962-65) acknowledged some of the church's previous errors and announced some key changes, including the introduction of local languages to replace Latin in its liturgy.

The 20th century also saw the emergence of a new force within the Catholic Church: liberation theology. This is an interpretation of the scriptures that has inspired priests and lay people to campaign for human rights and to oppose unjust regimes, which are often still supported by the church hierarchy, particularly in Latin America. One of them, the Brazilian sculptor Adolfo Perez Esquivel, won the 1980 Nobel Peace Prize for his human rights work. He describes liberation theology as protesting against poverty and struggling to abolish it by unmasking the anti-Christian elements that can be discovered in Christian society. As an example, he questions the morality of rich kids being flown over the favelas from their gated communities in Sao Paolo, and on to Disney World in Florida, while the poor kids down below them don't even have access to safe drinking water.[65]

This brings us back to modern Christianity in today's rich West.

Among Western Europe's Christians, ecumenicalism is on the rise – despite some resistance from so-called evangelists – but Christianity's political significance in its secular democracies continues to fall despite this. In the USA, on the other hand, religion remains a significant force, but ecumenical developments have to compete with the fundamentalism and tele-evangelism of the religious right (see below).

Christianity's crisis in Europe is poignantly encapsulated in the personal crisis of one man in particular: David Jenkins, the former Bishop of Durham. David was plucked from the ivory towers of Leeds University in 1984 and elevated to the third most senior position in the Church of England. He soon found that the reasoned views of an academic theologian would not always please all the grassroots activists in the declining membership of his church:[66]

▷ The ministry of openness and exploration to which I had committed myself so enthusiastically plunged me into more controversy and angry confrontation than I had ever dreamed of.

▷ I was sincerely shocked by the argument circulated by several respectable and even learned critics that it was quite in order for me to hold – and even to express – my views as a scholar and professor, but that the same views were inappropriate from the mouth of a bishop. Now that I had become a bishop, I was expected to lie for the sake of the faithful.

▷ Institutional Christianity in all its guises seems determined to live in the past and to draw its directions from there, from the worlds of the Old Testament, the New Testament, the early church and the patriarchal society of the medieval Mediterranean. Yet all these are worlds apart from the interlinked and globalized earth as we now experience it.

▷ While the controversy around me was at its height, I soldiered on in faith. Now, in retirement, the question is: "How did I ever come to believe in all this?"

▷ The petty prejudices displayed by religious people about beliefs, morals and actions are a far stronger obstacle to reviving widespread belief in a living God than are the more metaphysical, logical and philosophical arguments claiming to demonstrate the impossibility of the existence of God.

▷ The common assumption is that authority is granted to a bishop only as he confirms the faithful in the various details of belief that they firmly hold to be right. I would observe that atheists certainly welcome – and expect – such firmness and clarity from bishops. It clarifies precisely what they are rejecting when they dismiss the possibility of the existence of God.

▷ The suggestion that I should keep quiet about truths I [have] discovered through a life of academic study – that I should suppress and modify what I would share with students [and] "the ordinary man and woman in the pew" – is frankly blasphemous. If God cannot cope with the pursuit of truth, then religion is a sham and the professed concern for those "in the pew" nothing more than an exploitative fraud.

▷ The Gospels were written down by human beings, couched in the terms of their times. As the writers are no longer available for direct interview,

* cf. exoteric/esoteric views of Leo Strauss).

it is only through painstaking scholarship and archaeology that we reconstruct a sense of the cultural language that shapes the way they communicated [their faith]. Thus the advances of a century of faithful scholarship cannot be so summarily dismissed.

▷ To traditionalists, it is essential that [Christianity's] "historical claims" be defended from any investigation that might lead to their interpretation in the light of modern realities. They have to be guaranteed as literally true because they were stated in certain biblical texts and were thereby authenticated by divine scriptural warrant as revealed truths handed on by the God-granted authorities of the church. I am convinced that the traditionalists' view involves an untenable idea of God; one that it is impossible to hold or commend if one takes seriously advances in modern thought since at least the middle of the 17th century.

▷ The aggressive complaints with which the traditionalists meet any missionary attempt to reach out into modern secular reality characterize a neurotic quarrelling church which at every point makes Christianity ever more unbelievable to the wider world.

▷ Christians who demand certainties as essential to belief must be exclusive. Demanding certainty about faith is essentially schismatic – as is illustrated by the wretched history of Christian quarrelling. The central question for the future of the Christian faith is whether it is possible to attain sufficient assurances of faith to sustain realistic hope while at the same time deepening humility and opening us up to deeper truth.

▷ If religious faith must be tied to authoritarian rejections of human development since the 17th century, then it is hopelessly outmoded bigotry – superstition constructed to shelter our religious fantasies of hope and sustain the material power of our religious organizations.

▷ Our humane mission now is not primarily to convert, but to share; not to conflict, but to collaborate. We are not called to write off our neighbors, but to seek to understand and to contribute some sharable insights into our mission, our hopes and our enjoyment.

By the time Jenkins retired in 1995 Anglican Christianity had moved a long way toward sharing his views. Since 2002, with the appointment of Rowan Williams, a like-minded bishop, to its top position – Archbishop of Canterbury – the Anglican Church seems set to strengthen its engagement with rationality and with its secular environment. The vociferous traditionalists who opposed Williams' appointment represent only a dwindling and largely irrelevant minority. The Church of England is now finding its niche in our multicultural world as part of the global Anglican Community, although it still remains painfully divided over the issue of the acceptability of gay clergy.

In America, Christianity remains stronger than in Europe in terms of both its numbers and its continuing espousal of traditional "certainties" (if not values). In the USA today 85% of the population espouse Christianity in one form or another and 40% are regular churchgoers. These figures are similar to those for the UK fifty years ago. The figures for the UK today are 70% and 7% respectively.[67] But the more significant difference is that most American versions of Christianity remain much more fundamentalist. Sadly, the success of the fundamentalists combines with America's shortsighted material acquisitiveness and its military might to threaten the world with a new dark age.

American fundamentalism has its roots in the Christian reaction against scientific advances of the 19th century in general and against Darwin's theory of evolution in particular. It became a movement with a name in the early 20th century, following the publication of a series of twelve tracts, *The Fundamentals* (1909-15), by a group of US evangelical leaders.

Their main fundamentals were beliefs in the divine origins, literal truth and infallibility of the Bible, the divinity and virgin birth of Christ, Christ's bringing of salvation for all by his atonement on the cross, the resurrection, the Prophecy of Christ's second coming and redemption through faith and repentance. The idea of making any sincere attempt to live according to Jesus' teaching is not one of the fundamentals of this fundamentalism. The movement was backed by much of America's business and political leadership from the start. It soon became an important reactionary force within the Protestant churches and throughout American society. In 1925, it suffered a setback with the Scopes "monkey trial," but has since been boosted by the advent of tele-evangelism.

When moveable metallic-type printing brought Christendom mass access to the Bible, it facilitated a radical revolution in interpretation and in wider moral philosophy. The advent of television, on the other hand, empowered only those rich enough to exploit it. Corporate control of the medium has tended to stifle individual thought at the grass-roots level, generating passive acceptance of reactionary viewpoints instead. Although this is a global phenomenon, nowhere is it more significant than in the USA, where specifically fundamentalist broadcasters such as Pat Robertson's Christian Broadcast Network complement the three big networks. Although Robertson is no more than "a paranoid pinhead with a deep distrust of democracy" according to the Wall Street Journal, millions of Americans believe he has "a hot-line to God" and are prepared to send him all the money he asks for.[68] Robertson is just one of many radio and television evangelists who grow fat on "widows' mites", getting away with a message that is little more than "Send me your money so that I can use it to persuade other suckers to send me their money too."[69]

In spite of continually mounting scientific evidence and a series of financial and sexual scandals among tele-evangelist leaders, the combination of fundamentalism and tele-evangelism has played a large part in creating today's USA. To many observers outside the States – and to some within – modern American society seems to be run by an accidental coalition of two camps:

▷ The cynical manipulators, who use faith, fundamentalism and narrow-minded nationalism for their own greedy and short-sighted ends.

▷ The gullible masses of churchgoers and TV viewers who are falling for, or participating in, their deceptions.

There are, of course, many Americans who oppose this coalition, but there are also many good, sincere Christians who have been drawn into its web. If this were not so, the US would not be the troubled, divided society and threat to the world that it is today.

When it entered the TV age, having risen to great wealth and power through genocide, slavery, and massive immigration and inward investment, the USA was already the world's most powerful nation with its corporations exploiting lands and people on every continent. With less than 5% of the world's population, its corporations now control over 50% of the world's resources and produce over 50% of the world's pollution. Its mass media and telecommunications industries dominate the soul of its own people and many others beyond its shores.

But what for? This superpower can claim the highest percentage of Christians and church-goers in the West, but it is also home to the West's most unequal society, with the highest numbers of drug addicts, rapes, deaths caused by obesity, violent deaths (15-20,000 murders + >40,000 road deaths per year); the highest numbers of people in prison, of people on death row, of people executed, of people exonerated after execution; of child mothers, child executions, child suicides and child deaths from gunshot wounds.[70] Its self-styled Christian leaders and its predatory corporations have produced a culture that seems to be sliding inexorably down the road to soulless bigotry and junk materialism.

To "protect" this society, the US spends more on its military than the next 19 countries combined. It has troops in 140 countries. It refuses to recognize decisions of the International Court of Peace and Justice in The Hague. It refuses to ratify the UN Convention on the Rights of the Child and international agreements on combating global warming and on banning germ warfare and land mines. It refuses to abide by the international agreement establishing the International Criminal Court and has threatened at least 78 countries with trade and aid withdrawal to bully them in to signing deals granting its troops immunity from possible prosecution in this Court (by the end of 2003, 43 had complied; the rest preferring to live with the adverse consequences of trying to treat the US like any other country) and, in its approach to the invasion and occupation of Iraq, the US failed to recognize the United Nations as our greatest (albeit flawed and faltering) step so far toward world peace and a global democratic order, and sacrificed legality for expediency without regard for the negative effects of this action on the future of global stability.

The George W Bush administration tapped the phones of six UN Security Council delegations (Angola, Cameroon, Chile, Bulgaria, Guinea and Pakistan) in its attempts to control the Council's decisions,[71] then wrote off the UN – the nearest thing the world has to a barrier against chaos and terror – as "an ineffective and irrelevant debating society" when the Security Council still sought to find a peaceful solution to a serious problem in the face of a US rush to war. It was able to do this on behalf of 200 million American voters, even though 154 million of them did not vote for Bush in the last presidential election; even though more of those who did so voted for his main rival; and even though the events surrounding the presidential election in Florida were subsequently exposed as racist and corrupt.[72] Bush's presidential candidacy did have the support of Pat Robertson and his million-strong Christian Coalition, however, as does his terror crusade.

The crusade is, in fact, not a radically new approach to US foreign policy. Following the Atom-bombing of Hiroshima and Nagasaki in 1945, but before the terrorist attacks on the World Trade Center and the Pentagon in 2001, the US attacked, occupied, or otherwise intervened in not only Japan, the last country to actually attack the US (Pearl Harbor, Hawaii, 1941) but also North and South Korea, China (twice), Cuba, Haiti, The Dominican Republic, Peru, Chile (where "9/11" recalls the date in 1973 when an elected president and thousands of others were killed in a US-supported military coup), Guatemala (3 times), Indonesia (where over a million civilians died while the US supported the dictator, Suharto), Congo, Somalia, Mauritius (where the total population of the Chagos Islands were forcibly evicted to make way for a US military base), the Philippines, Vietnam, Laos, Cambodia, Afghanistan (where the 1979 Soviet invasion was preceded by $5m US aid to Islamic anti-government warlords, soon to be joined by Osama Bin Laden), Lebanon, Libya, Grenada, Nicaragua, Panama, Brazil, Colombia, Ecuador, El Salvador, Albania, Bulgaria, Iraq, Iran, Sudan, Italy, Greece and Yugoslavia (bombing Belgrade), even though none of these 35 countries (or any other) ever attacked or threatened the US.[73]

Apart from the war in Korea (1950-53) triggered by its division following World War II, this list of US overseas adventures consists of illegal operations not sanctioned by the UN.[74] Korea is included in the list because UN sanction was obtained only by default: the Soviet Union's UN delegation, which would have vetoed the US resolution to send troops to Korea, was boycotting the Security Council at the time. US action to support South Korea in resisting an invasion from North Korea subsequently brought China in to protect the North against invasion by a US-led UN coalition. After three years of war and over a million deaths, the active war was ended with an armistice agreement, but no negotiated peace. Thus Korea remains dangerously divided and the North's fear of another US invasion has enabled a military dictatorship to hold on to power there for over 50 years and to justify a nuclear weapons program under the ultimate control of its "Dear Leader," Kim Jong Il, son of the "Great Leader," Kim Il Sung, still revered by the North Koreans as their liberator following the Japanese occupation.

Although the US had a UN resolution for the Korean War and varying levels of international support for some of its other operations of this period, the general picture is that the political ambition of the US leadership took a heavy toll in foreign civilian lives. Many of its post-1945 and pre-2001/9/11 actions fit well within the internationally accepted definition of terrorism: "the intentional use of or threat of violence against civilians or against civilian targets in order to attain political aims."

Derisory offers of compensation to the dispossessed Chagos Islanders and casual apologies for collateral damage elsewhere in the world are inadequate responses to the global criticism faced by the USA. Although most Americans support their country as the world's last bastion of Christian values, much of the rest of the world identifies it as a terrorist state.

So, when George W Bush proclaimed his "crusade" or "war on terror" in September 2001, he was not starting something new, but simply announcing that US terror was about to be moved up a gear, as his subsequent invasions of Afghanistan and Iraq have shown. His statement that "either you are with us or you are with the terrorists" insults the vast majority of the world's population – of all religions and none. Most actually just want peace and justice. Most oppose all terrorist actions, not just selected anti-American terrorist actions. This was the clear message of most of the world leaders on the "irrelevant" Security Council when they sought to give the UN weapons inspectors enough time to finish their work in Iraq in March 2003.

The American belief in the USA as God's own country with a monopoly of truth on its side is a travesty of logic, even in terms the Christian story, in which Jesus died for all mankind, not just for the fundamentalists and manipulators currently controlling the US administration and bent on world domination in their "New American Century". Modern American Christianity has little, if anything, to do with the teaching of Jesus; and US foreign policy has much more to do with the abuse of economic and military might than with the freedom and democracy it claims to cherish.

There can be no doubting the evil of the recently deposed Afghan and Iraqi regimes (see Chapter 7). We may even believe that Afghans and Iraqis may one day enjoy net benefits as a result of the US invasions. But there is little sign of this yet; either in Afghanistan, where over 3,000 have died and only 3% of the $10 billion+ the US has spent there has gone on development aid, or in Iraq (see below and Chapter 7).

The benefits are similarly hard to spot in countries the US "liberated" earlier, like their neighbors, Nicaragua, Haiti, and the Dominican Republic. But any faint hopes for the liberated countries must be secondary to the damage US "certainties" are doing to peace and order in the wider world, and to global perceptions of American humanity. This applies particularly to Iraq. No one outside America – and only the most gullible TV viewers inside – believed there was a link between the godless Saddam Hussain and the Islamic fundamentalists of Al-Qaeda. There were no real logical or evidential connections. Indeed, Saddam was closer to Donald Rumsfeld, who twice visited Iraq to support the dictator in the 1980s. By 2003, few really believed that Saddam's weapons threatened the USA: after 12 years of UN sanctions and inspections, his Baathist regime, evil though it was, could no longer threaten even the Kurds of North Iraq. He was "unable to project conventional power against his neighbors" (Colin Powell, February, 2001) and his forces had not been rebuilt following his 1991 defeat: "We [the US] are able to keep arms from him." (Condoleeza Rice, July, 2001).[75]

When Iraq was invaded, no weapons of mass destruction were used in its defense, and none have been found since the overthrow of the Baathist regime. On the other hand, more innocent Iraqi lives were taken in 2003 (current estimates vary between 4,000 and 7,000 civilians plus 12,000 soldiers, mostly unwilling conscripts) than in any year since the regime's US-supported war against Iran (1980-88) and the 1991 Gulf War and its aftermath (see Chapter 7).

In the words of the Nuremberg Judgment: "to initiate a war of aggression is not only an international crime; it is the supreme international crime differing from other war crimes only in that it contains the accumulated evil of the whole."[76] And in the words of an ordinary Iraqi victim of the bombing of Baghdad: "What sort of Christians are they? Who can do this to us?"[77] The answer to these questions: American Christians could do this to you; American Christians following their fundamentalist leaders and their president, George W Bush, who, in turn, was listening the American Enterprise Institute and to a very different Christian God from the one heard by the Pope, the Archbishop of Canterbury and over 90% of Christians polled outside the USA.[78]

Jesus was a teacher of peace and love. Christianity was founded as a religion of peace and love. It has strayed a long way from these ideals over the last two millennia, but, thankfully, in most of the world, and even to a small extent in the USA, many Christians are rejecting the bigotry and militarism that has corrupted American (and Western) culture, and are returning to the promotion of the Way Jesus taught.

To quote one American singer/songwriter "on the side of the rebel

Jesus"[79]:

"You might ask what it takes to remember, when you know that you've
seen it before
Where a government lies to its people and a country is drifting to war
And there's a shadow on the faces of the men who send the guns
To the wars that are fought in places where their business interest runs.
There's a shadow on the faces of the men who fan the flames
Of the wars that are fought in places where we can't even say the names.
They sell us the president the same way they sell us our clothes and our
cars.
They sell us everything from youth to religion. The same time they sell
us our wars.
I want to know who the men in the shadows are.
I want to hear someone asking them why
They can be counted on to tell us who our enemies are
But they are never the ones to fight or to die."

Jackson Browne[80]

Some American theologians are also aware of the problem of the arrogance of
US power and its religious underpinning. Two are quoted below:

"Judaism and Christianity have nurtured millions of people to live deep,
passionate lives in awareness of the ultimate meaning that we call God and in
commitment to compassionate engagement in the world in the service of
others, [but] to insist on the cultural hegemony of western patterns of
understanding and faith is to run the constant risk of losing credibility. To
pretend that biblical ideas map the entire world is to miss the fact – apparent
to almost everyone else – that the [ancient] Mediterranean World is but one
source of culture and faith. To insist upon the uniqueness of western revelation
or western metaphysics is arrogantly to impose western norms on other people.
May we all learn to engage the pluralistic age of our present and our future in
such a way that we each may be ready to die for our faith, but never to kill for
it."

John P Keenan, Vicar of St Nicholas Episcopal Church,
Scarborough, Maine[81]

"American greed, especially our craving for cheap oil, [has] fostered anger
around the world. How should we work with ignorance, whether the broad
ideological brush that paints the West as Satan, or the rationalizations and

denials offered by Americans pursuing economic gain in the guise of promoting freedom and democracy, and in this way denying moral culpability for the uglier dimensions of our foreign policy and international business dealings? How can we overcome the widespread ignorance of these issues that results from corporate influence on the media?"

Christopher Ives, Dept of Religious Studies,
Stonehill College, Massachusetts[82]

The big question for the world now is whether or not significant numbers of American Christians will ever return to recognizing the difference between the Way of Jesus and the way of their self-serving fundamentalist leadership. Will enough of them join the still-small minority of American peace-lovers and internationalists in time to reject a leadership that would risk taking the world to Armageddon or a new dark age on the basis of the patently false claim that it is seeking only to defend Christian values and democracy?

7

Muhammad & God's Unity Reclaimed

————— •●• —————

M uhammad bin Abdullah bin Abdul-Muttalib was born into the clan of Hashim of the tribe of the Quraysh of Mecca, Arabia in 570 – some two millennia behind the births of Zarathustra (see Chapter 1) and Moses (see Chapter 2), half a millennium after the Romans had expelled the Jews from Jerusalem (Chapter 2 again) and a quarter of a millennium after Christianity had become the official religion of the Roman Empire (see Chapter 6). Arabia was peopled largely by warring polytheistic desert nomads and Mecca was one of its first permanent settlements. To the northeast, the Persian Empire, which reached the fringes of the desert, was still a home to the traditions that grew out of Zarathustra's monotheism. To the northwest, the Byzantine inheritors of the Roman Empire still professed Christianity. In the wild border regions of these neighboring empires, the Arabs' battles to protect their territorial and water rights were complicated by the permanent conflict between these empires and their competing religions.

Judaism was also widespread, surviving in both empires and in the desert. Many of the Jews of the diaspora had clung on to their religion and their self-styled identity as God's chosen people. The settlement of Yathrib, growing up to the north of Mecca, contained a major Jewish colony and was becoming known as Medina, their Aramaic word for the city.

Mecca, on the other hand, was already an established center for the local polytheistic cults, housing the sacred spring of Zamzam and a cube-shaped temple called the Kaba. This temple was filled with idols surrounding a large black meteorite, the Kaba Stone, which was believed to possess mystical powers. Mecca's Kaba was the focal point for a religious pilgrimage, the *hajj*, and a rivalry was developing between Mecca and Medina, both situated on the trade routes between the Byzantine and Persian empires to the north and the kingdoms of Abyssinia and Yemen to the south.

In the sixth century King Yusuf of Yemen had converted to Judaism. Soon after this Christian Abyssinians conquered his kingdom with Byzantine support. The Abyssinians had gone on to threaten Mecca with an army that included elephants. Their failure is referred to in the Koran[1] as an example of God's intervention in military matters. The Abyssinians were subsequently driven out of Arabia by Zoroastrian Persians.

Meanwhile in Mecca, Muhammad's father died before he was born and the boy became an orphan at the age of six when his mother, Aminah, also died. He was raised by his grandfather, then his uncle, Abu Talib, the chief of the Hashim clan. In 595, he married Khadija, a rich widow, who bore him six children – two sons and four daughters. Both his sons died in infancy, but the family later adopted two other boys – Muhammad's nephew, Ali ibn Ali Zayd, and ibn Harith Talib. Each of them would soon play a part in the Muhammadan legacy (see below).

Muhammad worked as a trader, traveling as far north as Syria and learning much from the monotheistic traditions of the Jews and the Christians. By the age of 40, he was convinced that there must be something better than his local polytheistic religions, but also better than the big three prevailing versions of monotheism – the dualist corruption of Zorastrianism in the Persian Empire, the racist arrogance of Judaism in Medina, and the replacement of simple monotheism by the deification of an earthly being in the Christianity of the Byzantine Empire.

Like many ascetic *hanifs*[2] before him, Muhammad retreated to the desert. He found a cave on Mount Hira overlooking Mecca, in which to meditate. On the 17th night in the month of Ramadhan, 610, he experienced a vision – described in the Koran as seeing and hearing the angel Gabriel – commanding him to recite the word of the Lord.[3] Muhammad accepted this divine instruction, and continued to recite until his death. As he was illiterate, the recitals had to be recorded by scribes. Some of them edited Muhammad's words as they received them, but none of them compiled or maintained a chronological record. The recitals were written and kept in a wide variety of forms on materials as diverse as stones and palm leaves, and their chronology was soon lost.

During the years following Muhammad's death, the first Caliph, Abu Bakr collated the surviving recitals. They were subsequently re-edited and arranged by a committee appointed by the third Caliph to produce the canonized version of the Koran. The Exordium (see Chapter 10) was chosen as the obvious opening chapter, but the remaining chapters were all arranged in order of length – longest first, shortest last – without regard to chronology. Many of the longer chapters can be seen by their references to historical events to date from long after Muhammad's original recitals.

Islam is also based on lesser sources, or traditions, attributed to Muhammad, but not canonized in the Koran. These are known as the *Hadith* and, together with the Koran, have been used to develop or justify Islamic law (*Sharia law*) with its lashing for alcohol consumption, stoning for adultery and amputation of hands and feet for theft.

Selections from the Koran are presented in this book's standard sub-sections: On The Nature of God, On God's Purpose and Human Responsibility, On Worship, and on Prayer and Prophecy. Many of the words chosen here are frequently repeated in the Koran, in either identical or similar form in a variety of contexts. They include re-worked biblical stories and references to contemporary situations. Some highlights follow below. Other selections appear in Chapter 10. The selections generally follow the Koranic sequence within each of the sub-sections, but there are occasional minor rearrangements to aid the continuity. All selections show the Koranic chapter and verse numbers. The Koran is also quoted in the Legacy section of this chapter to illustrate Muhammad's responses to local polytheism, to Judaism and Christianity, to other contemporary cultural realities and to specific historical events.

THE VISION – SELECTED HIGHLIGHTS

On The Nature of God

2.115 God is omnipresent and all-knowing. 2.120 The guidance of God is the only guidance. 2.255 God knows what is before and behind us. We can grasp only the part of God's knowledge that God wills. God's throne is as vast as the heavens and the Earth, and the preservation of both does not weary God, the Exalted, the Immense One. 2.256 God is the patron of the righteous and leads them from darkness into light. 8.24 God stands between man and his desires.

8.46 God is with those who are patient. 10.5 God makes his revelation plain to those of understanding. 13.16 God is the Creator of all things – the One, the Almighty. 13.31 All things are subject to God's will. 16.9 God alone can show the right path. 16.128 God is with those who keep from evil and do good works. 27.65 No-one in the heavens or on the Earth has knowledge of what is hidden, except God. 29.7 God has no need of his creatures' help. 35.38 God knows the mysteries of Heaven and Earth, the hidden thoughts of men. 38.61 God is the Lord of the heavens and the Earth and all that lies between them, the illustrious, the benign One. 47.19 Know that there is no god but God. 112.1 God is One; the eternal God begat no man, nor was begotten. No one is equal to God.

On God's Purpose and Human Responsibility

47.38 You are called upon to give to the cause of God. Some of you are ungenerous, yet whoever is ungenerous to this cause is ungenerous to himself. Indeed, God does not need you. It is you who need God. 2.190 Fight for the sake of God those who fight against you, but do not attack them first. God does not love the aggressors. 2.195 Be charitable. God loves the charitable. 2.271 To be charitable in public is good, but to give alms to the poor in private is better. 2.213 Mankind was once one nation. 4.86 If a man greets you, return his greeting. 4.114 Enjoin charity, kindness and peace among men. 8.25 Guard yourselves against temptation. 8.27 Your worldly goods are but a temptation. 8.46 Have patience. God is with those who are patient. 8.61 If your enemies incline to peace, make peace with them, and put your trust in God. 8.73 Give aid to one another. If you do not, there will be persecution in the land and great corruption. 10.24 God invites you to the Home of Peace. 16.50 You shall not serve two gods, for God is but one God. Revere none but God.

16.124 Call men to the path of your Lord with wisdom and kindly exhortation. Reason with them in the most courteous manner. 17.37 Do not walk proudly on the Earth. You cannot cleave the Earth nor rival the mountains in stature. 30.33 Do not split up religion into sects, each exulting in its own beliefs. 39.56 Follow the best of what is revealed to you without arrogance. 39.72 The dwelling place of the arrogant is evil. 76.29 Let those that will take the right path to the Lord. 42.43 To endure with fortitude and to forgive is incumbent on all.

On Worship

2.46 Fortify yourselves with patience and prayer.

Prayer

1.1 Guide us to the straight path, the path of those whom You have favored, not of those who have incurred your wrath, nor of those who have gone astray.

Prophecy

13.29 Blessed are those who have faith and do good works; blissful is their end.

42.15 God will bring us all together. To God we shall return. 45.28 You shall see all the nations on their knees. 91.7 Blessed are those that keep the soul pure and ruined are those that corrupt it.

See Chapter 10 for further highlights from the Vision of Muhammad.

THE LEGACY

On returning from his mountain retreat, Muhammad told his wife, Khadija, of his vision and of his decision to follow his calling as a messenger of God – to preach God's Unity as opposed to the polytheism of his countrymen, to explain God's purpose to them and to expose the errors of the Jews and Christians. Khadija supported his decision from the start and thus became Muhammad's first convert to Islam.[16] In one way, this made Muhammad and Khadija the first Muslims. But the Koran acknowledges Abraham, the biblical father of Ishmael and Isaac, as the first Muslim on the basis of his devotion to the one God.[17]

The Koran also acknowledges Abraham as the forefather of all Arabs and Jews, through his sons, Ishmael and Isaac. Other biblical characters mentioned in the Koran include Adam,[18] Cain,[19] Noah,[20] Lot,[21] Jacob/Israel,[22] Joseph and his brothers,[23] Moses and the Pharaoh,[24] Saul,[25] David,[26] Goliath,[27] Solomon,[28] Sheba,[29] Job,[30] Jonah,[31] Elisha,[32] John the baptist,[33] Mary,[34] Jesus[35] and Satan.[36] There are also numerous references to the six days creation, to angels, the Torah, the Gospels, the Psalms,[37] to the People of the Book (Jews and Christians), and to Judgment Day.[38]

Muhammad gave much credit to Judaism through the Koran's extensive borrowing from Jewish scriptures. But the Jews of Medina would soon become his enemies (see below).

Muhammad's first enemies, however, were members of his own tribe, the Quraysh of Mecca, particularly leaders of the more powerful clans – the priests of the Kaba and the chiefs of the business establishment, all with vested interests in the status quo.

The Kaba was a shrine for the god, *Hubal*, whose idol had a predominant position. *Al-Lah*, the high god of the Arabs was also among the deities worshipped there, along with the goddesses, *Al-Lat, Al-Uzza* and *Manat* – the daughters of *Al-Lah*. Even before Muhammad, many Arabs identified *Al-Lah* with the God worshiped by Jews and Christians, and his name lives on in Islam as the Arabic word for the universal God.

From 610 to 612, having been warned that prophets are generally ridiculed by most of their neighbors, Muhammad did not publicize his visions beyond his immediate family.[39] But his repeated visions increased his self-confidence until he was ready to extend his mission. He saw that a malaise had descended on Mecca as its settled communities prospered materially. He saw the decline of the tribal values of communalism and sharing; the rise of selfishness, individual pride and ungodly hedonism, and divisions between rich and poor. He knew that there was a need for something to combat this malaise, and he identified it as a fresh dissemination of God's Will, as communicated to him through his visions. His first task was to convince his fellow Meccans of the power and the singularity of God.

From 612 to 615 he remained cautious. He spoke to private meetings and his converts spread the word quietly. The first Muslims met for prayer each morning and evening. They were drawn largely from his own clan, from the young and dispossessed of other clans and from foreign slaves. An Abyssinian slave, Bilal, has the distinction of being the first Muslim to be given the job of calling fellow Muslims to prayer.

Muhammad's uncle, Abu Talib, and the other leaders of the Hashim clan were not among the early converts to Islam, but remained protective of Muhammad as hostility developed among the other clans. This hostility became widespread in 616 when the priests of the Kaba realized that Muslims had stopped worshiping the daughters of *Al-Lah*. Muslims were no longer welcome at the Kaba and their numbers dropped dramatically. Even when those remaining retreated to spots outside Mecca to pray, they were followed and beaten. Muhammad's attempts to deal with this problem have given rise to the legend of the Satanic Verses, recitals in which idolatry becomes acceptable. But no such verses were ever collated in the Koran, which is very clear in rejecting idolatry in general and the worship of the daughters of *Al-Lah* in particular (Koran, Chapter 53). None of the accepted records suggest that Muhammad was prepared to compromise on the principle of monotheism.

Muhammad's personal safety was assured as long as he retained the protection of Abu Talib, but less privileged Muslims, particularly slaves, were suffering. Bilal, the Abyssinian, remained devout despite being regularly tied up and left exposed to the sun by his owner, Ummayah bin Khalaf. He was eventually bought and given his freedom by Abu Bakr, a powerful merchant of the Taym clan who had accepted Islam.

The new religion was now dividing the clans and even splitting families. Before the end of 616, 83 Muslims, including Abu Talib's son, Jafar, and Muhammad's daughter, Ruqayyah, left Mecca with their families and sought refuge across the Red Sea in the Christian kingdom of Abyssinia. The Muslims who remained in Mecca continued to suffer from verbal abuse and a general boycott. Muhammad was also a victim of physical abuse when he visited the Kaba.

The miracle of the Koran, and the way the Muslims held on to their faith despite the abuse, impressed many. Muslim numbers soon started to increase again, both among the Quraysh of Mecca and among pilgrims to the Kaba. One pilgrim, Tufayl ibn Amr, a poet of the Daws tribe, was so impressed by what he heard from the Koran, that he overcame his initial hostility to Islam and returned to his tribe as an inspired and successful Muslim missionary.

But within Mecca the persecution of Muslims continued under the leadership of Abu Al-Hakam, referred to by Muslims as Abu Jahl, the father of lies. He was able to persuade all the clan leaders except Abu Talib to sign an anti-Muslim treaty to reinforce the boycott.

But the boycott was not successful in starving the Muslims into submission to the majority will and in 619 the treaty imposing it was revoked. Following this good news, most of the refugees returned from Abyssinia, believing that a new dawn was at hand.

But this was not yet to be. The small band of Muslims suffered new reverses. Soon after being reunited with her returning daughter, Muhammad's wife, Khadija, died. This loss was quickly followed by the death of Muhammad's uncle and protector, the Hashim leader, Abu Talib. He was succeeded by his half-brother Abu Lahab, a man with far less sympathy for Islam.

Although no longer victims of an organized boycott, the Muslims became far more vulnerable to their enemies. Incidents of verbal and physical abuse rose again. Even Abu Bakr, the once-influential merchant who had bought the Muslim slave Bilal to rescue him from Ummayah bin Khalaf was taken by Ummayah and subjected to the same abuse that Bilal had suffered. Abu Bakr was forced to leave Mecca to join the small Muslim community that had remained in Abyssinia. He subsequently returned to Mecca in safety under the newfound protection of Ibn Dughumma, a powerful chief of the nomadic Ahabish tribe – but only for as long as he promised the Quraysh that he would not pray in public.

This was typical of the choice Muslims were facing in Mecca during the year of 619: keep the faith in private or risk physical abuse. Abu Lahab could not and would not protect the Muslims as Abu Talib had, so Muhammad decided to seek a new protector. He left Mecca for Taif, a nearby oasis settlement. Taif was a popular summer retreat for wealthy Meccans. Muhammad hoped that he could persuade local clan leaders to offer protection to the Muslims. But Taif also housed a shrine to the goddess, *Al-Lat*, so this was a risky endeavor. Muhammad suffered several refusals and was chased through the streets of Taif before finally winning the personal protection of a chief: Mutim of the Nawfal.

The following year Muhammad returned to Mecca to visit relatives. While there, he entered the Kaba one night to recite and pray. He fell asleep and experienced another vision, which is referred to in the Koran (Chapter 17: The Night Journey): Muhammad met the angel Gabriel again and was transported to the temple in Jerusalem. From there, he ascended to seven levels of Heaven, meeting biblical prophets at each level, including Abraham, who inhabited the seventh level. This vision marked a turning point in Muhammad's confidence and in the spread of Islam. He now saw himself as God's messenger for the world; not just for the Quraysh of Mecca.

He visited the valley of Mina, where pilgrims on the *hajj* to the Kaba traditionally camped. There he met and impressed six polytheistic pagans from Medina, convincing them that he was the prophet the Jews were waiting for. In Medina, there was mounting tension between the Jews – mostly agriculturalists – and the formerly nomadic Arab tribes, who were also beginning to settle around this fertile oasis. Medina needed a leader who could unite its inhabitants and these pilgrims saw just such a leader in Muhammad. Like them, he was an Arab, but they also saw him as the prophet awaited by the Jews. They adopted Islam immediately and when they returned to Mecca for the 621 *hajj* representatives of several of the tribes accompanied them. They sought to replace the old tribal collectivism of their nomadic past, which was not working in their current more settled environment, with the ideals of the Koran. They saw Islam as a force that could unite the warring tribes of Medina and also improve the moral climate there. Muhammad chose one of his closest followers, Musab Ibn Umayr, to return to Medina with them to help prepare the way for Islam's move from Mecca. Musab's recitals of the Koran attracted more and more converts to Islam. Decisions to incorporate more Jewish practices, such as praying at mid-day as well as in the morning and evening, and facing Jerusalem (the site of Muhammad's ascent to heaven) during prayer, were also welcomed as bridging the gap between the Jews and the Arabs. The adoption of the Jewish name, Medina, for Yathrib was also helpful in this respect. Musab's mission was so successful that, within a year, the scene was set for the Muslims of Mecca to move to Medina. This exodus, or *hijra*, marks the official start of the Muslim era.

By August 622 virtually all the Muslims (around 70 households) had left Mecca and were being housed by converts or other sympathizers in Medina. Muhammad and Abu Bakr remained in Mecca to oversee the final departures, which were becoming more precarious as the Muslims became a smaller and smaller minority there, and as the disappearance of the Muslims had left the city with so many empty houses and all-too-visible signs of desertion and depression. When his protector, Mutim of the Nawfal, died, Muhammad faced real danger in Mecca. He and Abu Bakr escaped under the cover of the night, leaving Ali – Muhammad's nephew and adopted son – behind as a decoy. The Quraysh then let Ali go too, but offered a reward of 100 camels for the capture of Muhammad – dead or alive.

After hiding in desert caves and traveling by night, Muhammad and Abu Bakr made it to Medina on September 4, 622 and were welcomed as heroes. Muhammad was recognized as a neutral arbiter by all the tribes, and the people of Medina – Muslims, Jews, Christians and pagans – would live as one community (*umma*) under God. A mosque was built at Quba to the south of the city, the nearest center to the point at which Muhammad had reached the oasis. Bilal would call the faithful to prayer three times a day. They would pray facing Jerusalem. More and more of Medina's citizens quickly became Muslims.

Islam's honeymoon in Medina was short-lived, however. Some of the Arabs, both pagans and Christians, and most of the Jews, while accepting much of the still embryonic Koran, began to criticize many of its details. Muhammad, in turn, produced further recitals. Some of these were aimed specifically at the desert Arabs, mostly pagans, but potentially new converts and allies. Some were aimed at Jews and Christians. Some of the recitals attempted to accommodate the pagans and other critics, but most sought to persuade, threaten or condemn them. Many of these recitals found their way into the official Koran, as canonized after Muhammad's death. An illustrative selection follows.

For the poor of Medina and the nomadic desert Arabs, the strict dietary laws adopted from Judaism were relaxed:

▷ 5.3 He that is constrained by hunger to eat what is forbidden will find God forgiving and merciful.

For the misogynist, slave-owning society he was part of, Muhammad was prepared to allow the denigration of women and slaves:

▷ 2.223 Women are your fields. Go, then, into you fields as you please.

▷ 2.228 Men are a degree above women.

▷ 2.229 Divorce may be pronounced twice then a woman must be retained with honor or allowed to go with kindness.

▷ 2.233 Mothers shall suckle their children for two whole years if the father wishes the suckling to be completed.

▷ 4.3 You may marry women who seem good to you: two, three or four of them, but if you feel that you cannot maintain equality among them, marry one only, or any slave girls you may own.

▷ 4.15 If any of your women commit fornication ... confine them to their houses until death overtakes them or until God finds another way for them.

▷ 4.24 You are forbidden to marry women who are already married – except captives whom you own as slaves.

▷ 4.34 Men have authority over women because God has made one superior to the other and because they spend their wealth to maintain them. Good women are obedient. As for those from whom you fear disobedience, admonish them and send them to beds apart and beat them.

The injunctions allowing polygamy and slavery were subtly tempered, however:

▷ 4.129 Try as you may, you cannot treat all your wives impartially.

This has been interpreted as an injunction to ordinary Muslims to remain monogamous.

Pagans from the desert were also given clear advice on monotheism:

▷ 41.37 Do not prostrate yourselves before the sun or the moon; prostrate yourselves before God who created them both.

▷ 49.14 The Arabs of the desert declare: "We are the true believers." Say: "You are not."

Rather say: "We profess Islam," for faith has not found its way in to their hearts.

▷ 9.97 The desert Arabs surpass the townspeople in disbelief and hypocrisy – they have more of an excuse for their ignorance of the laws which God has revealed to His Apostle.

Jews that questioned the Koran were also addressed directly:

▷ 2.91 [The Koran] is the truth, corroborating your own scriptures.

Koranic references to the Torah and the Bible were also used to persuade both Jews and Christians of the need to embrace Islam:

▷ 33.8 God made a covenant with Muhammad as with the other prophets:

Noah, Abraham, Moses and Jesus, the son of Mary.

▷ 61.6 Jesus said to the Israelites: "I am sent forth to you by God to confirm the Torah already revealed and to give news that an apostle called Ahmed[40] will come after me."

▷ 61.15 Some of the Israelites believed him [Jesus] while others did not.

▷ 2.87 God gave Jesus the son of Mary veritable signs and strengthened him with the Holy Spirit. Will you [Jews] scorn each apostle whose message does not suit your fancies?

Those that weren't persuaded were subjected to scornful recitals:

▷ 62.5 Those with whom the burden of the Torah was entrusted and yet refused to bear it are like a donkey laden with books.

▷ 62.6 Say to the Jews: "If your claim be true that you alone are God's friends, then you should wish for death," but because of what their hands have done, they will never wish for death. God knows the wrongdoers.

▷ 5.13 Because they [the Jews] broke their covenant, God laid his curse on them and hardened their hearts. They have perverted the words of the scriptures and forgotten much of what they were taught. You will always find most of them deceitful.

▷ 5.14 With those who say they are Christians, God made a covenant also, but they too have forgotten much of what they were taught, so God stirred enmity and hatred among them, which shall endure until the Day of Resurrection.

▷ 5.73 Those that say God is one of three shall be sternly punished.

▷ 16.42 The apostles that God sent before Muhammad were no more than mortals who God inspired with revelations and with writings. Ask the People of the Book if you doubt this.

▷ 18.2 Admonish those that say God has begotten a son.

▷ 21.25 They say, "The Merciful has begotten children." God forbid! The prophets are but God's honored servants. They do not speak until He has spoken. They act by His command.

▷ 43.60 Jesus was no more than a mortal who God favored and gave as an example to the Israelites.

▷ 19.30-38 Jesus, the son of Mary said, "I am the servant of God. He has given me the Word and ordained me a prophet. His blessing is upon me wherever I go." God forbid that the Lord, Himself, should beget a son. God is my Lord and your Lord. Serve only God. That is the right path. Yet the sects are divided concerning Jesus.

▷ 19.67 From every sect, God will carry off its stoutest rebels and cast them down to the fires of Hell.

▷ 19.88 Those who say, "The Lord of Mercy has begotten a son," preach a monstrous falsehood at which the very heavens might crack, the Earth break asunder and the mountains crumble to dust.

▷ 23.90 Never has God begotten a son, nor is there any god besides God.

▷ 9.32-34 They [Jews and Christians] worship their rabbis and their monks, and the Messiah, the son of Mary, as gods beside God. They would extinguish the light of God with their mouths. Many are the rabbis and the monks who defraud men of their possessions and debar them from the path of God. Proclaim a woeful punishment to those that hoard gold and silver and do not spend it in God's cause.

▷ 3.68 Abraham was neither Jew nor Christian. He was an upright man. One who surrendered himself to God.

▷ 3.70 People of the Book, why do you deny God's revelations when you know that they are true?

▷ 4.18 God will not forgive those who do evil all their lives and, when death comes to them, say, "Now we repent."

As his power in Medina grew, Muhammad also sought to isolate those who questioned his vision, and drew on Biblical ideas such as Satan, Judgment Day and Hell, with which to threaten them:

▷ 4.145 Believers, do not choose infidels rather than the faithful for your friends.

▷ 5.50 Believers, take neither Jews nor Christians for your friends.

▷ 5.55-56 Your only friends are God, His Apostle and the faithful: those who attend to their prayers, pay their alms tax and kneel down in worship. God's followers are sure to triumph.

▷ 2.113 The Jews say the Christians are misguided and the Christians say the Jews are misguided. The pagans say the same of both. God will judge their disputes on the Day of Resurrection.

▷ 98.7 The pagans and the unbelievers among the People of the Book shall burn forever in the fires of Hell. They are the vilest of all creatures.

▷ 47.15 They shall abide in Hell forever and drink scalding water which will tear their bowels.

▷ 83.35 The faithful will mock the unbelievers as they recline upon their couches.

Once his power in Medina was supreme, Muhammad and his followers set about attacking traders traveling to and from Mecca, and this led to battles with Quraysh armies from Mecca. It was probably during this period that the Arabic word, *jihad,* was given a new meaning. Originally meaning simply effort, or struggle, with the higher struggle being the spiritual struggle (a concept common to other religions such as Buddhism or Christianity) the *jihad* now became associated with the concept of Holy War. More recitals were produced to support these developments:

▷ 9.5 When the sacred months are over, slay the idolaters wherever you find them. Arrest them, besiege them, and lie in ambush everywhere for them. If they repent and take to prayer and pay the alms tax, let them go on their way.

▷ 8.65 Prophet, rouse the faithful to arms. If there are twenty steadfast men among you, they shall vanquish two hundred; and if there are a hundred, they shall rout a thousand unbelievers, for they are devoid of understanding.

▷ 2.190 Fight for the sake of God those who fight against you. Kill them wherever you find them. Drive them out of the places from which they drove you.

▷ 66.9 Prophet, make war on the unbelievers and the hypocrites and deal sternly with them.

▷ 47.4 When you meet unbelievers in the battlefield, strike off their heads and, when you have laid them low, bind your captives firmly.

▷ 48.29 Muhammad is God's apostle; those who follow him are hard to the unbelievers, but merciful to one another.

▷ 49.15 True believers are those who fight for God's cause with their wealth and persons.

Following Muslim successes in battle, more verses were added commenting on their victories:

▷ 8.9 When you prayed to your Lord for help [at the Battle of Badr, 624] (see below) He answered, "I am sending to your aid a thousand angels."

▷ 8.11 You were overcome by sleep, a token of His protection. He sent down water from the sky to cleanse you and purify you of Satan's filth, to strengthen your hearts and to steady your footsteps.

▷ 8.12 God revealed His will to the angels, saying, "I shall be with you. Give courage to the believers. I shall cast terror into the hearts of the infidels. Strike off their heads! Maim them in every limb!"

▷ 8.17 It was not you but God who slew them.

▷ 48.20 God has promised you rich booty and has given you this with all promptness. (eg following the massacres of the Jews of Qurayza and Khaybar, 627 and 629 – see below)

Verses on Muslim losses were also added:

▷ 22.58 As for those who have fled their homes for the cause of God and have died or been slain, God will make generous provision for them.

▷ 47.8 As for those who are slain in the cause of God, He will admit them to the Paradise he has made known to them.

▷ 2.154 Do not say that those who were slain in God's cause are dead. They are alive, although you are not aware of them.

▷ 9.25 God has been with you on many a battlefield. In the Battle of Hunayn [630] (see below) you set great store by your numbers, but they availed you nothing. The Earth, despite its vastness, seemed to close in upon you and you turned your backs and fled; then God caused His Presence to descend upon his apostle and the faithful. He sent invisible warriors to your aid and sternly punished the unbelievers.

From the tone of these illustrations, we can see that the recitals no longer seem universally holy or prophetic words. They become more like the rantings of a local demigod, intoxicated by power. Was Muhammad allowing himself to be corrupted by political realities in order to survive as a temporal leader?

In addition to deviating from the spirit of his own earlier visions, Muhammad also changed the direction for prayer from facing Jerusalem to facing Mecca.[41] He accepted the pre-existing importance of the Arabs' traditional *hajj*. This importance was now justified in the new religion by new stories associating the Kaba with the biblical Ishmael and his father, Abraham. Ishmael was now rediscovered in Mecca after disappearing from the Bible. Abraham had visited him there and helped him build a temple. Mecca's House of the Kaba thus became older than Solomon's Temple in Jerusalem, notwithstanding the sanctity previously achieved by the latter through its association with Muhammad's Night Journey of 620:

> ▷ 2.127 Abraham and Ishmael built the House and dedicated it saying: "Accept this from us, Lord. You hear all and You know all. Lord, make us submissive to you. Make our descendants a nation that will submit to you."

> ▷ 5.97 God has made the Sacred House of the Kaba, the sacred month, and the sacrificial offerings with their ornaments, eternal values for mankind.

> ▷ 2.125 God made the House a resort and a sanctuary for mankind, saying: "Make the place where Abraham stood a house of worship."

> ▷ 2.196 Make the pilgrimage and visit the Sacred House for God's sake. If you cannot, send such offerings as you can afford and do not shave your heads until the offerings have reached their destination.

While Muhammad's strategy, despite a number of reverses during his lifetime, would consolidate Islam's early local gains, and pave the way for its eventual success as both a continental religion (albeit divided into the sects that he so abhorred) and as a vehicle for temporary imperialist triumphs and for political manipulation of the masses under its control, it would also ensure its inevitable failure as a force for world peace and unity. The pure monotheism of Islam was clearly an advance on its competing religions. But the intolerance, opportunism and lack of spirituality in so many of the verses of the Koran (mainly the post-*hijra* ones) would inevitably assure its rejection as the Word of God by the vast majority of mankind.

Initially, however, the Muslims were buoyed up by their successes in banditry and by a victory over the Quraysh, against the odds, in the Battle of Badr (624). But this was followed by the massacre of up to fifty Muslim missionaries by neighboring Arab tribes and defeat by the Quraysh in the Battle of Uhud (625), in which around 70 Muslims were killed. The Jews of Medina, particularly members of the Jewish tribe of Nadir, were accused of collaborating with the Quraysh in this battle and expelled from the city. Some traveled north to Syria, but others sought refuge in the nearby Jewish settlement of Khaybar, which was subsequently destroyed and looted by the Muslims in 629 after a month-long siege.

By March 627 the Quraysh of Mecca had raised an army of around 10,000 Arabs and Jews. They marched on Medina under the command of Abu Sufyan and Abu Jahl's son, Ikrimah. But the Muslims of Medina had dug an impressive defensive trench and were able to withstand the siege that followed and then to repel the invaders in the Battle of the Trench.

The Muslims subsequently marched on the Jewish fort and village of Qurayza, which they entered after a 25-day siege. They beheaded all but one of the 800 defeated men and sold all the women and children into slavery. All the property of the Jews of Qurayza was divided among their Muslim conquerors, and the remaining Jews of Medina were caught up in a massacre in the souk the following May. Muhammad did, however, make a covenant with the surviving Jews of Medina. They were allowed to live in peace without further reprisals as long as they promised not to collaborate with the enemies of Islam.

By March 628 Muhammad felt secure enough to lead a party of a thousand Muslim men on a *hajj* to Mecca. Because the Muslims were going as pilgrims, the Quraysh should be duty-bound to let them in. But, as Muslims rejected the polytheistic religion of the Quraysh and remained their enemies, the Quraysh may instead be honor-bound to bar their entry. A new battle would be a strong possibility. The pilgrims therefore stopped short of Mecca, camping at Hudaybiyah. Battle was avoided by negotiations leading to a treaty which established a 10-year truce between the Muslims and the Quraysh, and by which Muhammad and the pilgrims would go back to Medina and stop raiding Quraysh caravans, but would be allowed to make the *hajj* the following year. The Quraysh agreed to vacate Mecca before the pilgrims entered, and not return until the Muslims had finished their circumambulations of the Kaba.

Immediately after agreeing to the Treaty of Hudaybiyah and during the year that followed, Muhammad's leadership of the Muslims came under pressure from those who saw it as an unacceptable climb-down. But appropriate recitals helped him to maintain his power and the success of a *hajj* of 2,600 pilgrims in 629, held under the terms of the treaty, enhanced his prestige so dramatically, that, on the pretext of an attack by one desert clan allied to the Quraysh upon another clan allied to Medina, Muhammad was able to respond by raising an army of 10,000 to march on Mecca.

This action is, of course, justified in the Koran:

▷9.12 If, after coming to terms with you, they break their oaths and revile your faith, make war on the leaders of disbelief.

The breach of the truce happened in November 629. By January 630 Muhammad's army was at the gates of Mecca. He entered the city without resistance, destroyed all the idols in the Kaba, and obliterated all but one of the frescoes. The fresco that was spared depicted Jesus and Mary. It was obliterated later.[42] The citizens of Mecca, on the other hand, were granted a general amnesty. Only a handful of anti-Muslim propagandists, including Abu Jahl, Ikrimah and Ummayah ibn Khalaf, the tormentor of Bilal and Abu Bakr, were condemned. Even these were given the opportunity to embrace Islam and be spared. This they did, and the descendents of Ummayah would subsequentually become the leaders of the Muslim world during the Ummayad Dynasty of 661-749 (see below).

During the years between the loss of his first wife, Khadija, in 619 and his triumphal return to Mecca in 630, Muhammad re-married – many times. In addition to seeking the usual comforts of marriage, he helped to consolidate his power by making a number of astute political marriages. This was not particularly unusual for tribal leaders of these or earlier times. Indeed, Muhammad's harem never exceeded nine wives (plus slave girls). It was modest in comparison with those of many of his contemporaries or even Biblical heroes such as King Solomon. In 620, while still in Mecca, he married Sawdah, a widowed daughter-in-law of Kuzaymah, the chief of the Amir tribe; he was also betrothed to Aisha, the six-year-old daughter of Abu Bakr, marrying her three years later. In 625, once established in Medina, he added Hafsah, widowed daughter of Umar ibn Al-Khattab – a once-powerful opponent from Mecca who had now embraced Islam – and Zaynab bint Kuzaymah, a daughter of the Amir chief, widowed when her first husband was killed at the Battle of Badr. In 626 Zaynab died and Muhammad married Hind bint Al-Mughira of the aristocratic Makhzum clan of Mecca and widow of his cousin, Abu Salamah, but he also had an affair with Zaynab bint Jahsh, the wife of his adopted son, Zayd ibn Harith. Zayd was persuaded to divorce Zaynab, so that she could marry Muhammad, but this violated a taboo against fathers marrying their children's wives, and would also make Zaynab Muhammad's fifth concurrent wife – violating the Koran's limit of four. Fortunately for Muhammad, he received suitable new revelations from God:

▷ 33.36-38 It is not for true believers to make their own choices in their affairs if God and His Apostle decree otherwise. He that disobeys God and His Apostle strays far indeed. You said to the man whom God and yourself have favored [Zayd], "Keep your wife and fear God," but you sought to hide in your heart what God was to reveal. You feared men, but you should have feared God, and when Zayd divorced his wife, God gave her to you in marriage, so that it should become legitimate for true believers to marry the wives of their adopted sons if they divorce them.

▷ 33.50-51 Prophet, God has made lawful unto you the wives to whom you have granted dowries and the slave girls God has given you as booty; the daughters of your uncles and aunts who fled with you and the other women who gave themselves to you and whom you wish to take in marriage. This privilege is yours alone, being granted to no other believer. You may put off any of your wives you please and take to your bed any of them you please, nor is it unlawful for you to receive any of those whom you have temporarily set aside.

▷ 33.57 Those who speak ill of God and His Apostle shall be cursed by God in this life and the life to come.

▷ 33.60 If the hypocrites, tainted-hearts and scandal-mongers of Medina do not desist, God will rouse you against them and their days in the city will be numbered. Cursed wherever they are found, they will be seized and put to death.

Muhammad also received these further revelations regarding his wives – and women in general – at the same time:

▷ 33.6 The Prophet has a greater claim on the faithful than they have on each other. His wives are their mothers.

▷ 33.31-33 Wives of the Prophet. Those of you who commit a sin shall be doubly punished. This is not difficult for God. You are not like other women. Do not be too complaisant in your speech, lest the lecherous should lust after you. Show discretion in what you say. Stay in your homes and do not display your finery as women used to in the days of ignorance.

▷ 33.53 If you ask Muhammad's wives for anything, speak to them from behind a curtain. This is more chaste for your hearts and their hearts.

These new revelations should be seen in the context of other (probably earlier) Koranic revelations regarding sex and women:

▷ 24.2 The adulterer and the adulteress shall each be given a hundred lashes and their punishment be witnessed by a number of believers.

▷ 24.3 The adulterer may only marry an adulteress or an idolatress. The adulteress may only marry an adulterer or an idolater.

▷ 24.5 Those that defame honorable women and cannot produce four witnesses shall be given eighty lashes.

▷ 58.3 Those that divorce their wives by so saying, and then retract, shall free a slave as a penalty before touching their wives again. He that has no slave shall fast for two months or feed sixty of the poor. Such are the laws of God.

In 629 Muhammad, now 58 years old, married Safiyah, the 17-year-old daughter of Huyay ibn Akhtab, defeated chief of the Jewish Nadir tribe, after her first husband had been killed during the Muslim victory over the Jews of Khaybar. The same year, he married Maryam, a Coptic Christian slave girl sent to him as a gift from the king of Egypt. Maryam bore him a son, Ibrahim, his first since Khadifa's two sons had died in infancy in his pre-visionary days.

By this time, Muhammad was sending messengers on missions to all the known world's great leaders – to the Byzantine Emperor, Heraclius, and to the kings of Abyssinia, Yemen and Persia – inviting them to embrace Islam. He was also sending armies across Arabia inviting the tribes to do the same. Following his triumphant re-entry into Mecca and the Kaba in 630, he became the most powerful man in Arabia. And Islam became the most powerful religion.

Muhammad sent armies to destroy the shrines to *Al-Uzzah* at Naklah, *Manat* at Hudhayl and *Al-Lat* at Taif. The Hawazin tribe amassed an army of 20,000 to defend Taif and held off a similar sized Muslim army at the Battle of Hunayn, but they were eventually defeated by the combined forces of the Muslims and the Quraysh. This new alliance laid siege to Taif, which surrendered one year later, accepting the Muhammad as ruler of Arabia.

Muhammad was thus able to raise an army of 30,000 to march north to challenge the power of the Byzantine Empire, conquering the border kingdom of Eilat and its neighboring Jewish settlements of Jarba, Adruh and Maqna. Muhammad himself returned to Medina to live out his old age, and died there in 632, shortly after returning from his final *hajj* to Mecca. Along with those already quoted, the following selections from the Koran give a flavor of the new Mecca-based theocracy:

▷ 59.6 God gives his apostles authority over whom He will. He has power over all things.

▷ 59.8 A share of the spoils shall go to the poor who fled Mecca for Medina.

▷ 60.9 God forbids you to make friends with those who have fought against you on account of your religion and driven you from your homes or abetted others so to do. Those that make friends with them are wrongdoers.

▷ 49.8 If two parties of believers take up arms against one another, make peace between them. If either of them commits aggression against the other, fight against the aggressors until they submit to God's judgment, then make peace between them in equity and justice.

▷ 16.63 God sent apostles before you [Muhammad] to other nations, but Satan made their foul deeds seem fair to them and to this day he is their patron.

▷ 22.52 Never has God sent a single prophet or apostle before you with whose wishes Satan did not tamper.

A terrible irony in these verses referring to Satan is that Muhammad too was going the way of the prophets or apostles they warn against. And the following verses do little for Islam's potential relevance to the progress of science, spirituality or international understanding:

▷ 5.101 Believers, do not ask questions about things that, if made known to you, would only pain you.

▷ 109.1-6 Say: "Unbelievers, I do not serve what you worship, nor do you serve what I worship. I shall never serve what you worship, nor shall you ever serve what I worship. You have your own religion and I have mine."

On the other hand, the Five Pillars of Islam (listed below) that emerged as the requirement for embracing the new religion remain spiritually beneficial as an individual life option.

1 Declare faith in the unity of God and accept Muhammad as a messenger of God.

2 Pray five times a day to develop a personal relationship with God.

3 Fast during the daylight hours of the holy month of Ramadan to

reinforce your effort to remember God.

4 Give alms for the benefit of the poor and needy.

5 Make at least one pilgrimage to Mecca during the 12th month of the Islamic calendar (The *hajj*).

After Muhammad's death, a problem of succession arose. His closest lieutenant, Abu Bakr, was elected as his representative and God's steward on Earth (*Khalifa* or Caliph), but many believed that Ali ibn Abi Talib, Muhammad's nephew and adopted son, who had also become his son-in-law by marrying his daughter, Fatimah, was the rightful heir to the leadership of the faithful. The legacy of this split lives on today in the division between Sunni and Shia Muslims (*Sunni*, traditional majority, and *Shiah-I Ali*, partisans of Ali). The Shia still recognize Ali as their first Imam (leader), but the groups on both sides of this early division have since split further into a wide variety of sects (see below).

Abu Bakr carried the day initially and managed, during his short Caliphate, to subdue a revolt of secessionist tribes and re-unite Arabia. Although he was successful in military campaigns, he is also remembered for taking his role of stewardship of the Earth seriously and quoting Muhammad from the *Hadith* in support of his approach:

▷ Do not cut down a tree. Do not abuse a river. Do not harm animals; and always be kind and humane to God's creation, even your enemies.[43]

Abu Bakr died in 634, and was succeeded by Umar ibn Al-Khatib, whose Muslim armies invaded Iraq, Syria and Egypt, conquered Jerusalem, and garrisoned the towns of Kufah and Basra in southern Iraq and Fustat in Egypt. The crumbling empires of Byzantium and Persia were easily driven out of these imperial borderlands. Umar was assassinated by a Persian prisoner of war in 644. His successor, Utman ibn Affan conquered Cyprus and much of North Africa, Iran, Afghanistan and Sind. In 656, Utman was also assassinated. Utman's assassins were some of his own troops who accused him of failing to live up to the standards of Islam.

This finally made way for Ali ibn Abi Talib, the Shias' first Imam. He became the Fourth Caliph. Many of the Sunni still rejected Ali, however, including the Prophet's influential widow, Aisha. He was deposed within a year by Muawiya, the governor of Syria, who was proclaimed the Fifth Caliph in Jerusalem, founded the Ummayad Dynasty, and moved the capital of the

Caliphate from Medina to Damascus.

In 661 Ali was murdered by a *khariji* (secessionist) and his eldest son, Hasan (the Second Imam), was persuaded to renounce any claim to the Caliphate and to remain in Medina, where he died in 669. Caliph Muawiya I died in 680 and was succeeded by his son, Yazid I. He was challenged by a group of Shias. They claimed the caliphate for Ali's second son, Husain – the Third Imam – and marched on Damascus from Kufah with a small Shia army. The Shias were annihilated by Yazid's troops on the plain of Karbala in what is now Iraq. Husain was among the dead. His death is still marked by an annual Shia pilgrimage to Karbala, banned in Saddam Hussain's Iraq, but revived following Saddam's fall in 2003, only to be targeted by terrorists in 2004. The fourth Imam, Husain ibn Ali's son, Ali Zayn Al Ibidin eschewed politics to live quietly in Medina.

Meanwhile, in Damascus, Yazid I died in 683 and was succeeded by his infant son Muawiya II, who also died the same year. Muawiya II was then succeeded by Marwan I, who had to contend with *kharaji* rebellions in Iraq and Persia and a separate Shia uprising in Kufah. Marwan died in 685. He was succeeded by Abd Al Malik, who, by 691 had defeated all the rebels and presided over the completion of the construction of the Dome of the Rock in Jerusalem. Although Sunni/Shia divisions continued, succeeding Caliphs consolidated Muslim rule in North Africa, conquered Spain, and even sent expeditionary forces into France, where they were defeated by Charles Martel in the Battle of Poitiers (732).

In 743 a new Shia faction, led by Abu Al Abbas, rose to power in Persia and by 749 its army was able to take Kufah and overthrow the Ummayad Dynasty. In 750, they massacred all members of the Ummayad family and founded the Abbasid Dynasty as an absolute monarchy. Abu Al Abbas was succeeded in 755 by Abu Jaffar, who consolidated Abbasid power by means of further massacres.

In 756 Spain seceded from the Caliphate, but Muslim rule continued there under a succession of dynasties until the last of them were driven out in 1492.

In the 760s the Abbasids built a new capital in Baghdad and the Shias' Sixth Imam, Jafar As-Sidiq, advocated the separation of religion and politics. This idea was endorsed by the Abbasid Caliph, Al Mahdi, and welcomed by the Sunni majority, but it split the Shias into a number of sects.

Jafar appointed his elder son, Ismail, as the Seventh Imam. He is still considered to be the last true Imam by some sects (Ismaili Muslims or Seveners), while Jafar's younger son, Musa Al Kazim, is recognized as the seventh in a continuing line of Imams by most Shia Muslims. The seventh, eighth and ninth Imams of the main Shia sect were either unwilling or unable to impose their wills on politics, but Shia uprisings and *kharaji* revolts continued into the ninth century, and there were further splits within both Shia and Sunni factions.

In 833 Caliph Al Mutazim moved his capital to Samara. From 848, the Shias' Tenth Imam was imprisoned there for life. In 868, when the Tenth Imam died, his son and successor was also arrested and imprisoned. When he also died in custody in 874, his son, Abu Al Qasim Muhammad, the Twelfth Imam, fearing the same fate, went into hiding. The authorities never found him and the Shias accepted no successor. Instead, in 974, they announced that he had been miraculously concealed by God and that he would return as the Mahdi (Messiah, or rightly guided one) shortly before the Last Judgment. He would then destroy the enemies of Islam and usher in a golden age of peace and justice.

There have since been many claimants to the Messianic role of a resurrected Twelfth Imam within Islam, but two of the most notable of them both emerged in the 1880s: in Sudan in 1881 and in India in 1882.

In Sudan, Muhammad Ahmad (1844-85) was accepted by enough followers to lead a successful revolt against British imperialism. He took Khartoum in 1885 and set up an independent Islamic state that survived beyond his death and held out against the British until 1898.

In India, Mirza Ghulam Ahmad (1835-1908) revealed himself as the true Mahdi in 1882 and founded the Ahmadiyya Muslim Association in 1889. The Association soon became an international phenomenon. It has built over 8,000 mosques around the world, including London's first (Southfields, 1924) and latest (Morden, 2003). It claims a worldwide membership of 200 million, despite being rejected by mainstream Islam (see below).

Like the Shia majority "Twelvers," the Shia minority "Seveners" or Ismailis, suffered from many further schisms over the years. One sect, the Nizari Ismailis was born in violence, but has survived to become an influential peace-loving international community today. In late 11th century Egypt, the Nizari Ismailis rejected the Cairo Caliphate, itself a breakaway from the Baghdad/Samara

Caliphate, in protest at their lapse from Islamic values. As a persecuted minority, the early Nizaris turned to violence against their enemies, sending killers to take out their leaders. It was rumored the killers got high on hashish prior to their missions. This accusation gave birth to the word, assassin.

Although their founding imam, Nizar, was executed in 1095, his followers managed to set up a small independent state in Persia. When this state was destroyed by the Mongols, their communities were fragmented and many moved further east. In 1835, a Nizari Ismaili army joined the British in the siege of Kandahar in Afghanistan. They were rewarded with recognition by the Raj, and a pension and royal title, Aga Khan, for their leader. Many Nizari Ismailis settled in Bombay and became successful in business. Sultan Aga Khan III served as President of the League of Nations Assembly in 1937. His younger son, Sadruddin Aga Khan, spent 40 years working for the UN – 12 of them as High Commissioner for Refugees. The Nizari community is now a global one and has founded such institutions as:

▷ The Aga Khan Development Network (1967), which disburses around $100 million a year on health, housing and education projects in Asia and Africa.

▷ The Aga Khan Award for Architecture and the Institute for Ismaili Studies, London (1977).

▷ The Aga Khan Program for Islamic Architecture at Harvard University and the Massachusetts Institute of Technology (1979).

▷ The Aga Khan University in Karachi (1985).

▷ The Aga Khan Trust for Culture in Geneva (1988).[44]

A different division of political significance – a doctrinal division – also emerged at around the time of the early Shia splits. This was a split between the groups called *Al Hadith* and *Al Mutazilah*. The leaders of *Al Hadith* accepted only the Koran and the Hadith (the canon of reported pronouncements of the prophet). They insisted on the literal truth of every word to support their policies. On the other hand, *Al Mutazilah* (the withdrawn) were followers of Wasil ibn Ata (d748) who also accepted the Koran, but sought to apply logic and reason in its interpretation. Wasil was forced to withdraw from the *umma* at Basra, hence the name given to his followers. This division also continues to the present day, overlaying the Sunni/Shia splits.[45]

Like Messianic Shias and the Mutazilah, Sufi mystics are another group within Islam that first appeared during its second century (eighth century AD). Alongside the new material might of Islam, with its imperial conquests, its construction of magnificent forts, palaces and mosques, and its emphasis on Sharia law, there were always Muslims who chose more ascetic, peaceful, contemplative and/or spiritual ways of life.

An ascetic woman, Rabia (d801), preached about a personal search for God's love. She was followed by others who introduced a range of techniques for conducting this search, including Abu Yazid Al Bistami (d874) who advocated fasting, breathing exercises and chanting, and found union with God through ecstatic enlightenment, hearing God saying "I am you. There is no God but you." Husain Al Mansur was another "Drunken Sufi," his cries of "*Ana al-haq!* (I am the truth)" and claim that the *hajj* could be a spiritual journey conducted at home, rather than a trip to the Kaba in Mecca, led to his execution in Aleppo in 922.

Junaid of Baghdad (d910), on the other hand, advocated quiet meditation as a means of finding union with God. His followers, the "Sober Sufis," believe that enlightenment achieved this way transcends that of the drunken sufis. Other notable Sufis include Hamid Al-Ghazali (1058-1111),[46] Jalal al-din Rumi (1207-75), founder of the Mawlani Order, or "whirling dervishes", and Muhammad ibn Ali Al-Sanusi (d1832), whose Sanusiya movement is still significant in Libya.[47]

The Islamic world has also produced a number of influential philosophers from as early as the ninth century: Al-Razi (b *circa* 865), a physician and administrator, wrote two books (*Spiritual Medicine* and *Philosophic Life*) showing how his studies and contemplation led him to the view that the essence of truth is pure universal love that manifests itself in just behavior to others, irrespective of their labels. He was followed by others including Ibn Sina (Avicenna) and Ibn Rushd (Averroes) whose influence would eventually spread beyond the Islamic world to inform the Renaissance in Europe. Ibn Sina interpreted heaven and hell as inner feelings experienced during life as a result of our moral choices, rather than physical destinations for the dead. Ibn Rushd argued that scientific inquiry should not be hampered by religious dogma, that the scriptures should be interpreted allegorically and that natural beauty, dialectical argument, art and literature were equally valid as sources of inspiration and enlightenment.

The 10th century saw the collapse of the Caliphate, starting in 909 with the secession of Tunisia, where a group of Shias established the Fatimid Dynasty. Reduced and competing middle-eastern "Caliphates" survived into the second millennium, but the Caliphate concept was finished irrevocably with the Mongol invasions of the 13th century.

Islam continued to spread, however, under local and imperial leaders, especially in the East. There were also signs of reunification near the center – around the Holy Land – in response to the Crusades (see Chapter 6). Indeed, regional Muslim imperialism continued for much of the millennium. The most notable imperialists were:

▷ The Seljuk Turks (990-1118) in the Middle East and Asia Minor (now eastern Turkey).

▷ Saladin and the Kurdish Ayyubid Dynasty in the Middle East (1187-1250),

▷ The Ottomans in Turkey, South-East Europe, the Middle East and North Africa (1326-1918).

▷ The Safavids in Iran and Iraq (1500-1722).

▷ The Moguls in India (1526-1707).

The final defeat of the Ottoman Empire in World War I marked a low point in the political status of Islam. Turkey was reconstituted as a secular state and its empire followed the rest of the Islamic world into the hands of Western imperialism. This nadir in Muslim fortunes was seen by many as not only political, but also spiritual and cultural; and, except for the oil-exporting states of the Middle East, it was soon to usher in economic collapse too. It was to mark the start of a desperate period of Islamic revivalism.

The fightback can be traced back to the 19th century. A key activist was called Al-Afghani. Born in Iran, he traveled from Russia to Egypt and from Turkey to India advocating Islamic resistance to western influence before dying of cancer while on the run from the Iranian authorities. Al-Afghani supported modern science, citing its roots in early Islamic culture, but rejected Western morality and imperialism.

The first political victories of the fightback came, naturally enough, in Arabia. They were achieved by Abd al-Aziz ibn Saud, a leader who had adopted Wahabism, an extreme medieval brand of Sunni Islam named after Muhammad ibn Abd al-Wahab (1703-92). Saud was able, with the support of

Wahabi clerics, to re-unite the tribes of most of the Arabian Peninsula, founding the Kingdom of Saudi Arabia in 1932. The Wahabis had been powerful in Mecca since 1803, and ibn Saud conquered much of eastern Arabia in the early 20th century. He was a key leader of the Arab Revolt against the Turks during World War 1, having made a treaty of friendship with Britain in 1915. He conquered Taif and Mecca in the west in 1924, and Jeddah in 1925. After seven more years, he had consolidated his conquests throughout Arabia and gave his name to his newly re-unified and independent country.

The Kingdom of Saudi Arabia is still an absolute monarchy, enforcing a strict Wahabi version of the Sharia code on its 16 million subjects, around 99% of whom are Sunni Muslims. Enriched by the discovery of oil in 1936 and supported by the USA as an anti-communist ally during the Cold War, the House of Saud has managed to hang on to power with the support of a US-equipped military machine on the one hand and the Wahabi clerics on the other. Although the immense royal family is largely immune from Wahabi Sharia control, the general population and foreign workers remain subject to all its restrictions, even down to a prohibition on women driving. In addition to oil, the *hajj* is a significant part of the Saudi economy, but the numbers of Muslims visiting Mecca have also brought problems. Some 400 pilgrims were killed in 1979 when a group of revolutionary anti-monarchy fundamentalist students tried to take over the Kaba. Another 400 were killed in a similar demonstration in 1987. Hundreds more have died there since, simply crushed by the sheer weight of numbers when the traditional walks around the shrine have turned into stampedes, notably in 1990 (1,400 killed), 1994 (270), 1997 (350, following a fire), 1998 (180), 2001 (35) and 2002 (14). Although Mecca remains the geographical and spiritual center of Islam, the Saudi Arabian state, with its continuing dependence on American weapons and its continuing subservience to American pressures regarding oil production (notwithstanding the brief boycott in 1973) has long ago lost its claim to either political or spiritual leadership of the Islamic world.

Between 1921 and 1996, most of the Muslim world beyond Arabia also emerged from the colonial yoke, the most significant exception being Palestine (see Chapter 2), but the need to overcome the post-colonial domination of Western cultural imperialism, global capitalism and American military power (not least in creating and sustaining the State of Israel) remains significant in fostering widespread antipathy to the West in many Muslim countries – and allowing virulently anti-Western pockets of Islamic fundamentalism to flourish within some of them. This has recently been exacerbated by the 2002 & 2003 US-led invasions and occupations of Afghanistan and Iraq (see below) and US threats against Syria and Iran.

In 1921 following World War I, British and Russian forces withdrew from oil-rich Iran (now 60 million people, 99% Shia Muslim), leaving a secularizing puppet dynasty (the Pahlavis) in place. This was briefly overthrown in 1951, by a regime that sought to nationalize the oil. The Pahlavi Shah fled, but was re-instated in 1953 by a UK/US-led coup, so that – in the words of the UK foreign office – "the oil question could be settled on reasonable terms." With the help of American and Israeli intelligence, the Pahlavis were kept in power until 1978, when the dynasty was finally overthrown and replaced by an Islamic republic under the Ayatollah Khomeini (d1989).

In 1928 Jordan (now four million people, 50% Palestinian, 93% Muslim) achieved independence from Britain, albeit as a British-sponsored kingdom. In 1967 the kingdom lost control of the west bank of the Jordan when it was occupied by Israel.

In 1932 Iraq (now 20 million people, 96% Muslim) achieved a similar independence deal, but without the oil-rich sheikhdom of Kuwait, which remained the property of Sheikh Al Sabah, under British protection up to and beyond the granting of "independence" (ie handing over to the Al-Sabahs and the oil companies) in 1961. Kuwait was re-incorporated into Iraq briefly in 1990, but an American-led UN force quickly reversed this situation in the Gulf War of 1991.

Iraq had been liberated from Turkish control in 1918. But, with its central Baghdad area populated by Sunnis, its oil-rich north by Kurds and its oil-rich south by Shias, the new country has been kept under effective Western control for most of the last century and been given little chance to enjoy any real independence or stability – or its oil-wealth.

Occupied by UK forces in 1919, it was placed under UK mandate in 1920. The resulting "Great Arab Insurrection" was put down by the use of overwhelming UK military superiority, including the use of gas. The British installed a king in 1921 and put down a Kurdish insurrection in 1922-3, again using gas. They kept the oilfields under UK control and split Kurdistan between Iraq and Turkey. Iraqi "independence" under the UK-installed king was agreed in 1927. But the British remained in control of Kuwait (see above) and British forces also remained in Iraq to train its army. There were further Kurdish insurrections before the agreement was implemented in 1932 and further post-implementation reactions which included a massacre of Assyrian Christians in 1933, several more Arab revolts, and a coup under General Bakr Sidqi in 1936. The following year, Sidqi was assassinated by a Kurd. In 1939 the British consul was stoned to death amid allegations that he was involved in the death of the king in a car crash. This was followed by a full British re-occupation from 1941-47 and continuing UK control of the new child-king, Faisal II, and his government. In 1952, martial law was introduced in order to deal with anti-British rioting. In 1953 Faisal II, now 18, was crowned, parliamentary elections were held, and Iraq was linked to the UK, Turkey and Pakistan through the Baghdad Pact. In 1958, the king proclaimed a confederation with Jordan, but he was subsequently assassinated in a coup led by General Al Kassem, who jettisoned the monarchy, the confederation and the Baghdad Pact, to join Nasser's Egypt (see below) in a United Arab Republic – finally freeing Iraq from the direct control of the UK and its oil interests, but managing to substitute only further chaos and confusion.

In 1961 Al Kassem revived the Iraqi claim to Kuwait, now nominally independent of the UK, but subject to a continuing defense agreement. He failed to press this claim, however, and was subsequently killed in 1963 during an air-force coup that brought the Baathist Party into government for the first time. The new president, A S Arif, was then killed in a helicopter crash in 1964 and succeeded by his brother, A R Arif, who also failed to act on Kuwait, but did join the coalition that was humiliated in the six-day war with Israel in 1967. A R Arif was then overthrown and killed, along with thousands of others, by the Baathists in 1968.

The Baathists promised Arab nationalism, political stability through strength, and economic justice through socialism. Their resistance to Western imperialism was secular rather than Islamic and they responded to continuing Kurdish revolts with the launch of a full-blown war in the north.

Our brief review of Iraq's long struggle against Western Imperialism, and of the Kurds' long struggle against Iraqi (and Turkish) imperialism, continues below. Although fairly central to the overall struggle to liberate the world of Islam from Western control, Iraq is only a part of the whole. To trace the continuing struggle elsewhere, we must backtrack 30 years, when World War II and its aftermath gave a major boost to the liberation of the Islamic world from the old European colonial control:

▷ In 1942 Indonesia (now 200 million people, 87% Muslim) was liberated from Dutch control by the Japanese and achieved full political independence after Japan's World War II defeat in 1945.

▷ In 1944 Syria (now 13 million people, 90% Muslim) achieved independence from France.

▷ In 1945 Lebanon (now three million people, 60% Muslim) followed.

▷ In 1947 Pakistan (now 140 million people, 97% Muslim) achieved independence from Britain (see Chapter 3).

▷ In 1951 Libya (now five million people, over 99% Muslim) achieved independence, via six years of UN administration, from Italy.

▷ In 1953 Egypt (now 56 million people, 94% Muslim), nominally independent since 1922, achieved full independence from Britain, replacing a puppet king with a secular military dictatorship under Gamel Abdul Nasser (1918-1970) and forming the short-lived United Arab Republic with Syria and Iraq (1958-63).

▷ In 1956 Tunisia (now 8.5 million people, 98% Muslim) achieved independence from France, and the Kingdom of Morocco (now 27 million people, over 99% Muslim) achieved independence from France and Spain, although Spain still holds on to the enclaves of Ceuta and Melilla plus several small offshore islands, while the status of one more island (Perejil/Toura) remains confused.

▷ Also in 1956 Sudan (now 27 million people, 70% Muslim) achieved independence from Britain and Egypt, but the Muslim north continues to maintain colonial control over the Christian south, where civil wars have claimed tens of thousands of lives.

▷ In 1957 most of Malaysia (now 18 million people, 53% Muslim) achieved independence from Britain. The rest of the current country, plus Singapore, joined the Federation of Malaysia in 1963, but non-Muslim Singapore seceded in 1965.

▷ In 1958 Guinea (now six million, 85% Muslim) voted for independence from France and in 1960 Somalia (now 10 million, 90% Muslim) and Nigeria (now 90 million, 45% Muslim) achieved independence from Britain, as did Mali (10 million, 90% Muslim), Mauritania (two million,

90% Muslim), Niger (eight million, 90% Muslim), Senegal (eight million, 94% Muslim) and Chad (six million, 40% Muslim), although Chad, split between a Muslim north and a Christian south, has endured several civil wars, with Libya and France supporting client leaders on opposite sides.

▷ In 1961 Sierra Leone, (4.5 million, 40% Muslim) also achieved independence from Britain, only to be plagued by decades of civil war.

▷ Also in 1961 Kuwait (1.5 million, 99% Muslim) followed the rest of Iraq in achieving independence from Britain, but joined the UN as a separate Sheikhdom. Since the failure of Iraq to regain Kuwait in 1990/1, the oil-rich Kuwaiti royal family have enjoyed increased Western support, and in 2002-3 hosted the build-up of US and UK forces for the invasion and re-occupation of Iraq.

▷ In 1962 Algeria (now 27 million people, 97% Sunni Muslim) achieved independence from France, at a cost of around 250,000 lives.

▷ In 1965 Gambia (one million, 95% Muslim) achieved independence from Britain.

▷ In 1971 oil-rich Bahrain, Qatar and the United Arab Emirates (around three million people, 99% Muslim) achieved independence from Britain, and poverty-stricken Bangladesh (now 120 million, 87% Muslim) achieved independence from Pakistan, with military assistance from India, at a cost of over a million lives.

▷ In 1989 Afghanistan (23 million, 90% Muslim), with support from the USA and Saudi Arabia among others, drove out the Russian forces who had been supporting a communist regime there, but remained divided between tribal groups, Sunni and Shia factions, liberals and fundamentalists. Civil war continued, with the fundamentalist Taliban dominant from 1996 to 2001. The Taliban were ousted by an American-led coalition following attacks by the Afghan-based terrorist organization, Al-Qaida, led by Saudi dissident, Osama bin Laden, on the World Trade Center in New York and the Pentagon in Washington, on September 11, 2001. These attacks cost around 3,000 lives. Many more thousands have died in US bombing raids since then and, in July 2002, the post-Taliban coalition's newly-installed interim president replaced his Afghan bodyguard with a US army team.[48]

▷ In 1990 Yemen (now 12 million people, over 90% Muslim) was formed by the merger of the former British protectorate of South Yemen with North Yemen.

▷ In 1991 Azerbaijan (seven million, 90% Shia Muslim), Kazakhstan (70 million, 90% Muslim), Kyrgyzstan (five million, 90% Muslim), Tajikistan (5.5 million, 90% muslim), Turkmenistan (four million, 90% Muslim) and Uzbekistan (21 million, 90% muslim) all achieved independence following the collapse of the Soviet Union.

▷ In 1993 Eritrea (four million people, 60% Muslim and, as the coast of Abyssinia, the refuge of the first Muslim refugee community that fled persecution in Mecca at the time of the Muhammad) achieved independence from Christian Ethiopia following a 30-year war.

The 1990s also saw the collapse of the former communist federation of Yugoslavia, with civil wars in Bosnia (five million people, 50% Muslim) and Kosovo (two million people, 80% Albanian, 20% Serb; 60% Muslim). Bosnia became a federated state in 1995 and Kosovo remains an autonomous province of Serbia under NATO protection. Neighboring Albania (four million people, 60% Muslim) was liberated from communist control by an indigenous revolution in 1996.

The most significant Muslim majority areas still under foreign non-Muslim control are Kashmir, Mindanao, Chechnya, Oman, Palestine and, since April 2003, Iraq again.

▷ Kashmir (seven million people, 80% Muslim) was incorporated into India in 1948, precipitating a war between India and Pakistan. The cease-fire line left most of the state under Indian control. A promised referendum on self-determination never materialized, and this failure has generated endemic terrorism, further Indo-Pakistan wars, and a dangerous stand-off between these now nuclear powers (see Chapter 3).

▷ Mindanao (15 million people, 50% Muslim), the impoverished southern island of the Philippines also suffers from civil war between the authorities and Islamic separatists, as does

▷ Chechnya (1.5 million, 60% Muslim). Civil wars and atrocities on both sides here have taken the death toll to around 100,000 since 1990. Russia clearly sees Chechnya's location between the Caspian oil fields and the Black Sea ports as giving it a strategic importance that overrides any desire for self-determination.

▷ Oman (two million, 90% Muslim) has been nominally independent and ruled by sultans of the Said Dynasty since 1748, but the sultans have relied on British protection for most of that time and, since the discovery of oil in 1964, the British military presence has increased.

▷ Palestine is discussed in Chapter 2.[49]

▷ Iraq's pre-Baathist struggle is reviewed above and its Baathist regime and post-Baathist US/UK-led occupation are discussed below.

Although the late 20th century saw a widespread revival in the political status of Muslim-majority states (except Palestine and now Iraq), with their people escaping from colonial domination, most are still prisoners of either poverty or despotic regimes, or both. Their situations still serve as breeding grounds for disaffection and violence. This is countered by repression, which leads, in turn, to increased disaffection. Thus a vicious spiral is fuelled until the regime collapses, usually to be replaced by another despotic regime, or, post 2001 (9/11), by US occupation.

These spirals continue for a variety of reasons:

▷ anti-fundamentalist self-justification (eg Egypt and Algeria)

▷ acceptance of fundamentalism (eg Iran)

▷ imperialist support (eg Turkey, Jordan, Saudi Arabia and the Gulf States)

▷ anti-imperialist self-justification (eg Syria and Lebanon)

▷ some mix of the above (eg Pakistan)

▷ renewed Western occupation (eg Iraq)

In Egypt, conflict with the Muslim Brotherhood is the principal excuse for the continuation of repressive government. Founded Al Banna in 1928 as a benevolent social movement building schools, clinics, hospitals and factories, The Brotherhood was subsequently organized into "families" and "battalions" by Sayyid Qutb. It adopted an ideology that condemned all modernizing or secularizing Arab governments as corrupt, and advocated their overthrow and replacement by Islamic rule and Sharia Law. It was banned in Egypt during Nasser's dictatorship and has now metamorphosed into a pan-Arab terror organization. It has been implicated in the 1981 assassination of Egypt's President Anwar Sadat, the 1997 killing of 70 tourists in Luxor, and a number of more recent terrorist attacks at tourist sites around Egypt.

In Algeria, the failure of the National Liberation Front to implement effective welfare programs led the people to vote en masse for the opposition Islamic Salvation Front in its 1991 elections, only to have the result ignored and the party banned. The civil war that followed (1992-7) cost 100,000 lives and the society is still torn by violence.

Iran has remained an Islamic Republic since the 1978-9 revolution (see above), but despite losing 500,000 lives in the 1980-88 war with Iraq and being implicated in international terrorism (eg support for Hizbollah in Lebanon and the 1994 bombing of the Jewish Mutual Association in Buenos Aires, Argentina, which killed 85 people and injured hundreds more – Argentina's worst ever terrorist outrage), Iran now seems to be turning away from fundamentalism and terror in favor of more democracy and diplomacy. A big step in this direction came with the election of President Hojjat Khatemi in 1997, but the residual theocratic power of Ayatollah Khomeini's successor, Ayatollah Khameini, and the mullahs still leaves the country delicately balanced on the edge of stability.

Turkey held its first democratic elections in 1950 and has been a NATO member since 1952. It suffered a military coup in 1960 and, since 1984, has been waging a US-aided war against Kurdish separatists, in which over 3,000 towns and villages have been destroyed, tens of thousands of people have been killed and millions more turned into refugees.

Jordan remains a less than democratic kingdom, and in 1970-71 waged a US-aided war against the Palestinian refugees that made up half its population, killing thousands and forcing thousands more to flee for fresh refuge.

Saudi Arabia continues to survive as an iniquitous so-called Islamic regime. But it is still condemned by the Muslim Brotherhood (see under Egypt, above), not only for its dependence on US military aid and its willingness to kowtow to US demands on oil production – even to the extent of cajoling other OPEC members on behalf of the US – but also for its medieval interpretation and application of Sharia Law. A recent example showing the absurdities of Saudi Sharia occurred at a girls' school in Mutawwa in March, 2002. There was a fire in the school, and in the name of gender separation and dress decency, Saudi police kept out male rescuers and sent would-be escapees back inside because their heads were not covered. Fourteen of them died.

Syria lost land (the Golan heights) to an Israeli invasion in 1967 and has been in the grip of a repressive Baathist dictatorship since a coup in 1970. The dictatorship justifies itself on the basis of perceived threats of Israeli and/or American invasion.

Lebanon has suffered a series of civil wars[50] and an Israeli invasion in 1980 (see Chapter 2). It is now virtually controlled by the Syrian dictatorship.

Pakistan has oscillated between westernizing and Islamic regimes ever since independence. Repression and terrorism are endemic. Poverty, the dispute with India over Kashmir, and the tensions thrown up by the proximity of Afghanistan and the US war on terror only serve to aggravate the instability of this nuclear power.

Iraq's Baathist coup in 1968 led to war with the Kurds and tension with the Shah's Iran. The war was ended with the granting of limited autonomy to the Kurds in 1969, but continuing divisions within the Baathist Party led to purges in 1970 (including 44 executions) and again in 1979 (hundreds of executions and disappearances) and the emergence of Saddam Hussein as Iraq's all-powerful dictator. With US support, Saddam immediately sought to take advantage of the revolutionary confusion in the new (Shia) Islamic Republic of Iran and occupy disputed oil-rich lands to the east of Basra. This plan backfired, however, and his invasion led to an eight-year war that cost a million lives and revived Kurdish aspirations for independence. These aspirations were quashed by major operations in 1988, including the use of gas, following the UK examples of the 1920s (see above) on the Kurdish town of Halabja and 40 surrounding villages, killing many thousands of civilians.

Having finally made a peace with Iran that recognized the pre-war boundary, Saddam revived the old Iraqi claim to Kuwait, the oil-rich, UK-created mini-state to the west of Basra. His 1990 occupation of this tiny artificial sheikhdom was achieved in hours with virtually no resistance. But the action triggered the formation of a US-led UN liberation coalition that easily forced Saddam's army back in 1991. He was left in power in Iraq, subject to agreements limiting his regime's right to possess or develop weapons of mass destruction. His defeat encouraged uprisings by the Shias in South Iraq and the Kurds in the North; revolts that were crushed with a cost of further 300,000 lives. US-enforced no-fly zones north and south of Baghdad allowed the Kurds to maintain a small autonomous area in the north and increased the security of Kuwait, but left ordinary Iraqis at the mercy of the Baathists, who responded to their situation by increasing repression on the ground and limiting their co-operation with UN weapons inspectors. The UN responded to this non-cooperation with economic sanctions against Iraq that cost the lives of 60,000 children a year between 1991 and 2001, weakening the country, but not the dictatorship of Saddam Hussein.[51] In 1998, the inspectors withdrew. In 2002, following the US invasion of Afghanistan and increased UN pressure, the inspectors were invited back with promises of improved cooperation. But by this time, the US regime had decided to invade and occupy Iraq anyway. In March, 2003, a US/UK invasion deposed Saddam at a cost of a further 14-17,000 lives (10,000 Iraqi troops, 4-7,000 Iraqi civilians, 105 US troops, 32 UK troops, 10 visiting civilians), liberating Iraqis from the repressive dictator the Americans had supported in the 1980s, but returning them to a state of subjection recalling the UK occupations and colonial control of the 1920s to 1950s. The re-occupation of Iraq has certainly exacerbated bad relations between the West and the world of Islam and continues to cost more lives on a daily basis and to fan the flames of fundamentalist resistance, not only in Iraq, but throughout the Islamic world.

While the foreign, economic and environmental policies of the US make it enemy number one – the "Great Satan" – for the world of Islam, the US, itself, is a country of some 10 million Muslims, around half immigrants and half indigenous. In the main, the immigrant Muslims are professional and business people who have entered the US as students or economic migrants and have managed to develop lifestyles which allow them to combine the best of Western and Islamic values. Along with their children, they are becoming a significant part of the cultural mosaic that makes up the US community, and their integration into American society and contribution to American culture could be an important factor in avoiding the horrors of Huntington's "Clash of Civilizations" scenario.[52] This is certainly how they see themselves, expressing sentiments such as "parents should not confuse ethnic habits with the Islamic religion"[53] and "There is no place for the Sunni-Shia division for Muslims in America. Whatever happened 1,400 years ago in the Middle East is not relevant to the future of Islam in America."[54]

Organized Islam in America dates back at least as far as 1910, when Hazrat Inayat Khan introduced his Sufi Order International. Now led by his son, Vilayat Inayat Khan, the Order has around a hundred centers in the US and sponsors regular Dances of Universal Peace in major cities.[55] However, following 9/11, many Muslims have been unfairly ostracized in the US, along with Sikhs; the Sikhs' dress code serves to distinguish them from Muslims in India (see Chapter 8), but in the US the same dress code leads them to be confused with Muslims!

Indigenous versions of American Islam are almost as old as the imported versions. Timothy Drew (Noble Drew Ali) founded the first Moorish Science Temple in Newark, NJ, in 1913.[56] The Moorish Science Temples of America are now headquartered in Chicago, but they have been overtaken in significance by newer American Islamic organizations: the Nation of Islam and its successors. The original Nation of Islam was founded as a black separatist movement by Wali Fard in Detroit in 1930. Fard was joined by Elijah Poole (1897-1975) in the early 30s and subsequently disappeared. Poole took over the movement, claimed that Fard had been an incarnation of God and that he, now calling himself Elijah Muhammad, was God's messenger. The message had little to do with the Koran. It held that white people were the creation of the Devil and inherently evil.

The Nation promoted black self-sufficiency and racial segregation. It became popular among black Americans in the 60s, thanks to the charismatic leadership of Malcolm X (1925-65). But X was assassinated when he rejected the movement and converted to Sunni Islam, having been impressed by the multiracial brotherhood he experienced on a *hajj* to Mecca. The American Muslim Mission, founded by Malcolm X, became a part of the world of Islam, while the Nation of Islam, now led by Louis Farrakhan, remained separate. The Nation of Islam condemns the racism and misogyny it still sees in world Islam and cites Mecca, with its Saudi elite and immigrant African servant classes as a prime example of this. In 2000, the Nation also defied world Islam by appointing the first woman Imam to head the Atlanta Mosque, but it has also entered into dialogue on unity with the American Muslim Mission, now the Muslim American Society, led by Malcolm X's successor, W D Mohammed.

Internationally, Islamic unity is fostered by the Islamic Conference Organization, established in 1971. It represents, through its 50 member states and other associated organizations, more than a billion Muslims, 80% of them Sunni. It regularly votes to reject terror in the pursuit of political objectives. In 1989, 48 of its then 49 member states voted to condemn Ayatollah Khomeini's *fatwa* against Salman Rushdie for the alleged blasphemy in his novel, *The Satanic Verses*. Iran, which once supported the *fatwa*, withdrew its support in 1998, making the opposition unanimous. In September 2001, the Conference met in Qatar immediately after the terrorist attacks on New York and Washington and was again unanimous in its wholehearted condemnation of terrorism.

On the fringes of mainstream Islam and rejected by much of it, the Ahmadiyya Muslim Community continues its world-wide peace mission, aided, since 1994, by its own satellite TV station. Ahmadiyyas are legally barred from calling themselves Muslims in Pakistan and are boycotted by the Muslim Council in the UK, but the community claims 200 million members in 174 countries. In Africa, they supply water, distribute sewing machines and set up internet cafes. In the UK, they provide important support to the Save the Children Fund and London's Great Ormond Street Children's Hospital, and their new mosque, built to accommodate 10,000 worshipers, in Morden, South London rivals London's main mosque in Regent's Park in its grandeur. Some of the Ahmadiyyas' teaching (eg that Jesus didn't die on the cross, but was revived and traveled east to continue his mission among the lost tribes of Israel, died in 120 and was buried in Srinagar, Kashmir, where his tomb can be visited) may seem a little romantically far-fetched to many, but their emphasis on the peaceful and non-misogynist aspects of Islam clearly has appeal.

While we can be reasonably sure that certain parts of the Koran, some of them discussed above, will forever disqualify it from being accepted by the majority of the world's population, we should remember that the Arabic word, *islam,* means *being at peace with God.* Given this definition, *islam* must be seen as a positive condition. The clashes between Islamic and Christian (or Western) civilizations can surely be transcended if both sides avoid dogmatism and intolerance, but are guided by their higher moral values – if the West can conquer the short-sightedness and greed that manifests itself in imperialistic exploitation of the weak and the environment, and if Islam can escape from the medievalism of the more questionable parts of the Koran.

In the words of three respected Muslim academics:

▷ The West has once before liberated itself from the Dark Ages of its religious tradition ... It may now once again through a better understanding of Islam liberate itself from the religious racism engendered by the doctrine of "The Chosen People" and from the narrow view of God and man. At the same time, the Arabs (and Muslims) must liberate themselves from the legalistic view of Islam by learning, from the experience of the West, the art of translating the principles of Islam's view of the human being into the proper social, political and educational orders.[57]

▷ One's *islam* to the Creator is total and complete when one becomes finally and fully liberated from all the divisive identifications and loyalties of gender, race, color and language.[58]

▷ The sharing of experience, exchange of views, debate and dialogue and the comparing of notes on a civilizational scale can only proceed on the basis of equality and mutual respect.[59]

▷ The answers to the problems of Muslim societies are not hard to find – merely difficult to initiate. Political freedom, open debate, the liberation of society to be civil, plural and humane – these are obvious remedies, but the [fundamentalist] Islamic movements have become a barrier to them.[60]

▷ Islam teaches that the more we embrace diversity in God's creation, the closer we are to acknowledging the unity of God. It is essentially this creative paradox that escapes Muslim extremists.[61]

Muhammad's initial motivation was the need to promote the Oneness (*Tawhid*) of God, a rational spirituality and a just world society. These goals and many of his teachings were close to the best of those of his predecessors presented in "The Vision" sections of Chapters 1 to 6. The Koran, however, especially with its later absurdities, cannot realistically be claimed as the Last Word of God, nor can the religion it spawned ever bring peace and unity to the world – at least, not until the spirit of *islam* transcends the medieval dogma of Islam.

The next two chapters look at two more recent presentations of "divine guidance" to promote this elusive unity, both of them born, in 16th century India and 19th century Iran respectively, as a result of Islam's failure to do so.

8
NANAK DEV & GOD'S UNITY RECLAIMED 2

————————•●●————————

Nanak Dev was born into the Kshatrya caste of a Hindu community in the Punjabi village of Talwandi (now Nanka Sahib), 40 miles west of Lahore (now in Pakistan), on April 15, 1469. Although his community was heir to the teachings of Atharva and Siddhartha Gautama (see Chapters 3 and 5), the ideas of a single God and the way of the Buddha had long ago been lost in the polytheistic religions of his forbears. Buddhist political influence had been driven from its home in North India hundreds of years earlier and the fertile valleys of the Punjab had been a Hindu-Muslim battleground for centuries. The name, Hindu, had, in fact, been coined by Muslims as a generic term for all the infidels of the various religions of India.

The first successful Muslim invasion of the region led to the conquest of Lahore by the military leader, Subaktagin, in 977. He founded the Ghaznavid Dynasty there and it survived until 1186. Hundreds of Hindu temples were destroyed as the conquerors set about converting their subjects to Islam and as Hindus resisted the Muslim occupation. Many lower caste Hindus, attempting to escape from the iniquities of the caste system and to curry favor with their new masters, did convert to Islam, but the majority of Hindus, under the leadership of the higher caste Brahmins (priests) and Kshatryas (warriors), continued to resist throughout the Ghaznavid period. Incursions of other Muslim imperialists from the northwest also continued, and the Ghaznavid dynasty eventually fell to Muhammad of Ghar (1125-1206) in 1186. The conquest of Delhi followed in 1193 and, further east, the vestigial Buddhist community in Bihar was finally extinguished in 1197. The Punjab continued to be ruled by Muslim kings from Delhi during the 13th and 14th centuries, but the 1390s saw the region overrun by the armies of Tamerlane, who destroyed Delhi itself in 1398-9. In the years that followed, competing armies of Muslim invaders and Hindu hill princes trampled the Punjab until a period of relative calm dawned under the Lodhi Dynasty (1450-1526) founded by an Afghan invader, Bahlol Khan Lodhi. It was during this period that Nanak Dev was born.

Although he was born into a Hindu family, Nanak had at least one Muslim schoolteacher and his early interest in poetry and literature led him to the works of a number of Sufi mystics, and to one in particular: Kabir (1440-1518). Kabir was born a Muslim, but developed an interpretation of Islam that, while never abandoning monotheism, allowed him to worship alongside Hindus and to respect their approach to spirituality. Kabir's teaching impressed young Nanak, but Nanak's early life was subject to more mundane preoccupations. He was betrothed at 12 and married at 19. He fathered two sons and spent his time in various occupations in order to support his family, eventually moving to the city of Sultanpur to join his brother-in-law in the service of the local governor, Nawab Daulat Khan Lodhi. In 1496, after several years in Sultanpur, Nanak took to traveling east, south, north and west in search of religious enlightenment. He visited Benares, Jagganath, South India, Ceylon, Tibet, Kabul, Baghdad and possibly even Mecca. Following his travels and encounters, he experienced a spiritual vision that would change his life: it was a vision that embraced the Islamic views of God's unity and the brotherhood of mankind, but one that rejected the Muslims' temple-smashing, their misogyny and their dogmatism over the details of the Koran; Nanak's vision also embraced Hinduism's spiritual depth, its tolerance and its pacifism, but eschewed its rituals and idolatry and the doctrine of *ahimsa*, and totally rejected the caste system.

Nanak soon began to share this vision in an attempt to synergize Muslims and Hindus in an improved relationship with God. Such synergy was not to be, however, and instead of uniting Muslims and Hindus, the followers of Nanak and his successors became a third major religious force in a region that remains horribly divided to this day.

Nanak's endeavors made him the first guru (teacher) of the Sikhs (followers). The selected highlights of Sikhism below and the extended highlights in Chapter 10 are Nanak's words taken from the Sikh holy book, the Granth Sahib (respected compilation).

The Granth Sahib also includes hymns and teachings of earlier Muslim Sufi mystics and of some of the Sikh Gurus who succeeded Nanak. A few of the later Gurus' writings are quoted in the Legacy section at the end of this chapter, but are not included in the Vision sections.

THE VISION – SELECTED HIGHLIGHTS

On The Nature of God

There is but one God. God is all that is. God is the Creator of all things and is all-pervasive.

God is without fear and without enmity. God is timeless, unborn and self-existent. God is the enlightener and can be realized by grace alone. God was in the beginning and in all ages. The true One is, was, and forever shall be.[1] God's seat is everywhere. God's treasure houses are in all places.[2] The one Lord made us all.[3] The Lord is true, plainly known, His loving kindness infinite. To those who crave and seek, God gives with full abandon.[4] God's state is beyond description. One who undertakes description will regret it afterwards. No use of pen or paper is availing. One knows God in his heart on due reflection.[5]

On God's Purpose and Human Responsibility

If we remember God, we live. If we forget God, we die.[7] Let no man be proud because of his caste. The man who has God in his heart, he, no other, is the true Brahmin, so, O fool, do not be vainglorious about your caste, for vainglory leads to most of the mind's evils. Though they say there are four castes, one God created us all; all of us are molded of the same clay. The Great Potter has merely varied our shapes. All of us are made of the same elements. No one can reduce an element in one or increase it in another.[8]

Let compassion be your mosque. Let faith be your prayer mat. Let honest living be your Koran. Let modesty be the rule of observance. Let piety be the fast you keep. In such wisdom try to become a muslim [ie one who is at peace with God, rather than a traditional Muslim]. Let right conduct be your Kaba. Let submission to God's will be your rosary. If you do these things, the Lord will be your protector.[10] Pilgrimages, penances, compassion and alms-giving bring a little merit, the size of a sesame seed, but one who hears and believes and loves God shall bathe and be made clean in a place of pilgrimage within.[11]

On Worship

Devotion leads to happiness. Sins and sorrow are destroyed by harkening. Death itself is overcome by harkening. Truth, knowledge and contentment come by harkening. By harkening one knows the avatars, the role of saints, prelates and rulers. The blind find their own paths by harkening. By harkening, impassable streams are forded. One knows God in one's heart on due reflection. Wisdom and understanding come by reflection. Slights and slaps are brought to nothing by reflection. Death's ties are cut asunder by reflection. One's path is rid of hindrance by reflection. Let good deeds be your prayers.[17] Put on the garb of deeds and salvation's way is open.[18]

Prayers

Words are vain, but teach me the mystery, O Lord, such wisdom may I cherish.[20]

Prophecy

There is no Hindu. There is no Muslim.[22] Whoever sings and listens, heart-felt praise retaining, his sorrows fade and he will dwell in blessing.[23]

See Chapter 10 for further highlights from the Vision of Nanak Dev.

THE LEGACY

From around 1500, as Nanak continued with his travels, he began preaching his new vision – sometimes out in the open, sometimes inside mosques and temples. He demonstrated his rejection of the caste system by accepting the hospitality of people of the lower castes in preference to those of higher castes. When questioned about this apparent perversity by a higher caste official, he is said to have replied, "Your food reeks of blood, while that of Lalo, the carpenter, tastes of honey and milk. Lalo earns with the sweat of his brow and offers what little he can to the wayfarer, the poor and the holy, so it tastes sweet and wholesome, but you squeeze blood out of the people through bribery, tyranny and a show of authority."[24]

Most of Nanak's early converts were Hindus of his own or lower castes, but he also attracted followers from Muslim communities, including one, Mardana, who became his constant traveling companion. When a group of people accepted Nanak's message, he would leave an organized community behind before traveling on. Members of these communities were known as Nanakpanthis. The name, Sikh (follower), came later.

During the early 1500s the stability provided by the Lodhi dynasty was under threat and traveling was becoming more dangerous. The armies of Babur (1483-1530), a descendant of Tamerlane, were driving in to India from the northwest. Having conquered Kabul in 1504, Babur took Lahore in 1524. Nanak, now 55 years old, decided to curtail his travels through this war-torn region and settle 90 miles east of Lahore on a piece of land he had been given on the right bank of the River Ravi.

Babur went on to defeat Ibrahim Shah Lodhi at the battle of Panipat in 1526, taking Delhi and founding the Mogul Empire (1526-1707).[25] In the same year, Nanak founded the village of Kartapur on the River Ravi. He lived there peacefully among the followers that joined him until his death in 1539. The Nanakpanthi community at Kartapur welcomed all comers, regardless of gender, caste or religion. They lived communally, with no priests. They were all expected to take care of themselves and contribute to the general welfare of the community to the best of their ability. One notable feature of the community was the *langar* (free canteen) that was open to all and served to emphasize the inclusivity of the group. This feature remains a key part of Sikhism, as I recently found to my pleasure when invited to share lunch while visiting a magnificent new Sikh temple in Southall, West London.

Nanak participated in the agricultural and domestic chores. The role of leading religious activity was shared as widely as possible among all members of the community. Just before his death, however, Nanak did choose one particular follower, Lehna (1504-52), to replace him as the community's guru (teacher).

The 35-year-old Lehna was given the name Angad Dev (inseparable part) and is recognized by all Sikhs as the second of 10 personal Gurus of the faith. He devised a new script, *Gurmakhi*, for recording Nanak's teaching and began a written compilation of the hundreds of hymns that the community used, adding 62 of his own. This was the beginning of the Granth Sahib.

A wealthy follower called Gobind Angad Dev donated land between Kartapur and Lahore on the River Beas near Khadur (now a suburb of Amritsar) to the Sikh community. This land was used for the development of a new village, Gobindwal (now Goindal). Although surrounded by Mogul/Afghan violence, the Sikh community continued to grow rapidly under the Mogul Emperor, Babur and his successor, his son Humayun (1530-56). Humayun was preoccupied with the threat from the Afghan leader, Sher Shah, and spent most of his reign as a refugee in Persia while rival armies fought for control of Northwest India, but Kartapur and Gobindwal remained separate from the surrounding convulsions and Angad Dev passed away peacefully in 1552. Shortly before his death, he named the 73-year-old elder, Amar Das as his chosen successor.

Amar Das (1479-1574) was very active as the Third Guru. He formalized the *langar*. He introduced Sikh ceremonies for birth, marriage and death. He condemned *suttee*, the practice of requiring widows to commit suicide on their dead husbands' funeral pyres, as a Hindu ritual that the Sikhs must reject. He added 907 new hymns to the Granth Sahib and he made Gobindwal a center for Sikh pilgrimage. He also organized the wider Sikh community into local congregations (*sangats*), grouped together in 22 districts (*manjis*), some of them led by women, thus giving the Sikh religion a formal structure that survives to this day.

In 1556, four years into Amar Das' term as Guru, the Mogul Emperor, Humayun, died and was succeeded by his son, Akbar, who defeated the Afghans decisively at Panipat, consolidating Mogul control over the region. Akbar visited Amar Das at Gobinwal in 1567 and granted him more land and permission to build a Sikh shrine. A key leader of the project to build the shrine was Amar Das's son-in law, Jeva. The Guru chose this son-in-law as his successor, re-naming him Ram Das (servant of the Lord).

Ram Das (1534-81) became the Fourth Guru in 1574 following Amar Das' death at the age of 95. The new Guru completed the construction of the Sikh shrine and a holy lake (*amrit sarawar*). The city of Amritsar quickly grew up around them. Ram Das continued to live communally, as his predecessors had done, but, during his 7-year tenure, the role of Guru became more ruler than teacher and, when he named his youngest son, Arjan Dev, as his successor, the Sikh Gurus became a hereditary dynasty that would survive until the death of the Tenth Guru in 1708.

Arjan Dev (1563-1606) became the Fifth Guru on his father's death in 1581. During his rule, the holy lake was improved and a golden temple was built alongside it. The ground around the temple was leveled, facilitating the introduction of circumambulation for pilgrims, a ritual already practiced (around the Kaba) by Muslim pilgrims to Mecca, but not a part of Guru Nanak's vision, which had equated the value of such rituals with the value of a sesame seed (see the Vision section), preferring his followers to embark upon "a pilgrimage within."

Arjan Dev also developed the Granth Sahib, adding 3,384 new hymns. In 1604, he had an authorized version, the *Adi Granth*, placed in the Golden Temple.

The following year the Mogul Emperor, Akbar, died and was succeeded by his son, Jahangir (1605-27). Worried about the still-growing influence of the Sikhs, and with the support of both Muslim leaders and Hindu Brahmins, Jahangir set about persecuting the new religion. In 1606, Arjan Dev was arrested and ordered to remove all passages critical of Islam from the Granth. When he refused, his property was confiscated and he was tortured to death, being burned with hot irons and sand, then immersed in near-boiling water. Before dying he was able to deliver his final words through a Sufi mystic: "I bear all this torture in order to set an example to the teachers of the true God, that they may not lose patience or rail at God in their affliction."[26] He was also able to warn his young son, Hargobind, to leave Amritsar, surround himself with bodyguards and prepare to defend the faith: "not to mourn or indulge in unmanly lamentations, but to sing God's praises."[27]

Hargobind (1595-1644) became the Sixth Guru at 11 years old 1606. He was arrested by Jahangir, but released after a few months detention and returned to Amritsar, where he was advised by a group of Sikh elders. They prepared him to assume political and military command as well as spiritual authority. His advisors regularly assembled on an embankment across the lake from the Golden Temple in a place they called *Akal Takht* (God's throne), now the site of an impressive domed building. Another institution that dates back to Hargobind's reign is the construction of *Gurdwaras* (Guru's doors) as meeting places for Sikh communities around the world.

Hargobind outlived Jahangir, who died in 1627, but the latter's successor, Shah

Jahan (1627-57) renewed the Mogul persecution of Sikhs in 1628, following a dispute over hunting in which one of Hargobind's men killed an imperial official. Hargobind fled Amritsar again. After several years of wandering, and after surviving battles with imperial troops at Lahira (1631) and Kartapur (1634), he settled in and fortified the Himalayan village of Kiratpur (now Anandpur), where he died in 1644.

Hargobind was succeeded as Seventh Guru by his teenage grandson, Har Rai (1630-1661), who was born and raised in Kiratpur. The new Guru led the spiritual life of a wandering teacher, extolling the virtues of Nanak's vision and the Granth Sahib. He was once summoned to Delhi by Shah Jahan, but refused to go, sending his eldest son, Ram Rai, instead. Although Ram Rai was able to convince Shah Jahan that the Sikhs presented no threat, Har Rai was unhappy with tales of Ram's willingness to doctor the message of the Granth Sahib to please the emperor. He subsequently disowned his eldest son and named his second son, Har Krishan (1656-64) as his successor.

Meanwhile in Delhi the Mogul Emperor, Shah Jahan, now old and sick, was imprisoned in 1657 by his third son, Aurangzeb, who also killed his elder brothers in order to claim the Mogul throne.

When Har Rai died in 1661, Har Krishan became the Eighth Guru at only five years old. He died of smallpox three years later leaving a leadership vacuum. This was filled when the Sikh elders named Tegh Bahadur as the Ninth Guru.

Tegh Bahadur (1621-75) was the youngest son of Hargobind, the Sixth Guru, and Har Krishan's great-uncle. He had been born in Amritsar, but had left as a child for his mother's village of Bakala after his father had been forced to flee the city. He grew up a stranger to both Amritsar and Kiratpur. On becoming the Ninth Guru, in 1664, he did not move to the Sikh stronghold at Kiratpur, but left the Punjab altogether, moved his family to safety in Patna, then travelled to Bengal and Assam, where he preached among the hill tribes and initiated work on gurdwaras, notably the Damdama Gurdwara in Dhubri, and lived for several years among the Sikhs of Dacca (now capital of Bangladesh). He also visited various places of pilgrimage in North India, including Bodh-Gaya, the site of the Buddha's enlightenment. Eventually, when he felt it safe to do so, he even visited Delhi to meet the Emperor Aurangzeb and arrange for his family's safe return to the Punjab. On their return, they settled in the fortified Sikh hill village of Kiratpur.

Tegh rejoined them there in 1672, but when the tide of Mogul oppression of non-Muslims began to rise again, he set off, in July 1675, for Delhi, for another meeting with Aurangzeb. But he was arrested *en route* and finished his journey to Delhi in an iron cage. His advice to Aurangzeb, that "the prophet of Mecca could not impose one religion on the world, so how can you? It is not God's will"[28] cut no ice with the emperor, and the latter's decision to torture and kill Tegh's companions in front of him did not convince Tegh to adopt Islam, so he was publicly beheaded in November, 1675.

Tegh was succeeded by the tenth and last personal Guru, his nine-year-old son, Gobind (1666-1708). Gobind had been born in Patna then safely ensconced in Kiratpur, where he grew up with a siege mentality and a determination that the Sikhs should continue to defend their religion against all odds. By the late 1680s and early 1690s, he was leading the Sikhs in successful battles against other hill rajahs, while Aurangzeb was away campaigning in South India. Gobind formalized Sikh militarism and identity with the institution of the *Khalsa* (pure ones). Members of the Khalsa would be required to die for their religion and to identify themselves by always wearing "the five Ks": *kesh* (unshorn hair), *kanga* (a comb in the hair), *kara* (a steel wristband), *kachh* (short breeches) and a *kirpan* (short sword). They would adopt the name Singh (lion) and their women would be called Kaur (princess). They would be led by the *panjpiyare* (the first "beloved" five among equals). A religion that had been formed in the hope of achieving a peace and unity that would transcend the caste system had now effectively transformed itself into a militaristic caste in its own right. The ethos of the Khalsa was what the Sikhs of Gobind's time wanted, but it was the antithesis of the pacifism of Guru Nanak's Nanakpanthis. A religion that had emerged as a holy quest to establish universal peace in a divided world had effectively become a separate club centered on violence for identity preservation.

At the start of the 1700s some 50,000 Sikhs were baptized into the Khalsa. Gobind Singh was ready to challenge the Mogul Empire. But the emperor had a different agenda. He sent his imperial army, augmented by troops of the hill rajahs, to take Kiratpur (now called Anandpur). The fortress was besieged for several months. In December 1704, the Sikhs, on the verge of starvation, were granted safe passage to leave. But this was not honored. The refugees were massacred in battle at nearby Chamkaur within days of leaving. Gobind survived the battle at Chamkaur and another at Dina, south of Amritsar, before escaping east to Assam. He spent three years in Damdama, where he gave instructions that there should be no more personal Sikh Gurus, but that the Granth Sahib should be referred to directly for future guidance. He added some of his father's writings to the existing Granth Sahib before canonizing it as the Guru Granth Sahib. Gobind's Tegh Bahadur additions include the following:

▷ The truly enlightened ones are those who neither incite fear in others nor fear anyone themselves.[29]

Gobind Singh also left writings of his own, including:

▷ Recognize all mankind as one, whether Hindus or Muslims.
The same Lord is the creator and nourisher of all.
Recognize no distinctions between them.
The monastery and the mosque are the same,
so is Hindu worship and Muslim prayer.
We are all one![30]

In 1707 he arranged a meeting with the Emperor Aurangzeb, who was still engaged in border wars in South India, but Aurengzeb died before the meeting could happen. Gobind then met and made an alliance with Aurangzeb's son and heir, Bahadur Shah, but was assassinated while traveling with him the following year, bringing an end to the age of Sikh Gurus.

Gobind's traveling companions of the Khalsa elected a Kashmiri, Banda Singh, to succeed him. Banda Singh was a farmer turned soldier and yogi, and a recent convert to Sikhism. He and a band of 25 returned to the Punjab. Fellow Sikhs joined them to attack the towns of Samana and Lohgar, which they took at a cost of around 10,000 lives in 1709. The Sikhs were subsequently besieged in Lohgar by around 60,000 imperial troops, but Banda escaped to the hills as the town capitulated.

The Mogul Emperor, Bahadur Shah, died in 1712 and his already crumbling empire was further divided by a new war of succession, which left a power vacuum in the Punjab. Banda Singh returned from his Himalayan hideaway to recapture Lohgar. He soon made it the capital of a new Sikh state. He introduced land reforms that empowered the farmers at the expense of the landlords. He minted his own coins and set up a relatively stable and popular administration. Within three years, however, Mogul forces were able to break his power, and take him in a cage to Delhi. Some 300 Sikhs were beheaded in Delhi during 1715 and Banda met the same fate in 1716. The Khalsa became bandits and terrorists during the years that followed, until they were offered their own small state around Amritsar in 1733.

They accepted this offer and set up a new state under Supreme Commander Kapur Singh, only to have it re-occupied by Mogul forces in 1734. But Mogul power continued to fade. India was invaded from Persia by the armies of Nadir Shah. In 1739, Shah took absolute power in the region after killing some 100,000 people and sacking Delhi.

When the Golden Temple in Amritsar was requisitioned to provide government offices for the new regime, the governor was assassinated. Thousands of Sikhs were massacred on the spot as a reprisal for this assassination and 3,000 more were executed in Lahore. The Sikhs fought back under a new commander, Jassa Singh, retook Amritsar by 1748, re-excavated the holy pool that had been filled in, and re-established the Sikh state. In 1753, the Khalsa claimed the whole Punjab. In 1758, a combined Sikh and Maratha force occupied Lahore briefly and, in 1761, the Sikhs occupied it without the Marathas, but again only briefly. In 1762, Afghan invaders defeated them and went on to capture and sack Amritsar.

The Sikhs recaptured the Amritsar in 1763, only to lose it to the Afghans again in 1764. Then, in 1765, the Sikhs recaptured Lahore and managed not only to keep it, but also to establish their power throughout the Punjab and to take and re-build their capital at Amritsar.

In 1783, they went on to take Delhi briefly and in 1785, they took it again for a little longer. In 1800, the Khalsa marched on Lahore and, in 1801 they crowned their leader, Ranjit Singh, Maharajah of the Punjab.

In 1809 Ranjit Singh signed the Treaty of Amritsar with the British, defining the Punjab's southeastern border as the River Sutlej. He then expanded his empire north into Kashmir and west beyond Multan and Peshawar (now in Pakistan). By the end of his reign, he ruled over a population of around 20 million (7% Sikh, 42% Hindu and 50% Muslim).

A power struggle followed his death in 1839 and in 1845 the British crossed the Sutlej and took two villages they accused of harboring criminals. This precipitated the Anglo-Sikh Wars (1845-8) that led to the Punjab being annexed by the British Empire and Kashmir being given to a Hindu prince. The Khalsa subsequently became loyal to the British and many Sikh soldiers went on to win respect as valuable members of the army of the British Raj right up to its withdrawal in 1947. Many Sikhs still retain similar respect in the post-independence Indian Army.

But Sikhs were always involved in India's struggle for independence. Many took part in a peaceful 20,000-strong anti-colonialist demonstration in the Jallianwallah Bagh in Amritsar on a Spring Sunday in 1919 and were caught up in a massacre by the Raj army, which killed between 379 (the official British figure) and 500 demonstrators, and wounded over a thousand more. Others, under the leadership of the newly formed *Akali Dal* (God's Party), were involved in a rural uprising in the Punjab in 1921, and still others in the all-India independence struggles of the Congress Party and the Indian National Army.

When British India was partitioned at independence in August 1947, to give birth to the secular Indian republic and the Islamic Republic of Pakistan, the Punjab was divided between the two new states, with the west going to Pakistan and the east to India. The Sikhs were caught up in the carnage and ethnic cleansing that surrounded partition. Some 2,000 Sikhs were massacred by Muslims in east Punjab in the months before independence, and, by the end of the year, several million Sikhs and Hindus had moved east to the Indian side of the new border and as many Muslims had moved west into Pakistan. Some 600,000 people were killed in the violence that accompanied this upheaval.

Today, most of India's 12 million Sikhs live in the small state around Amritsar that retains the name of the Punjab, but the majority religion of the Punjab is, nevertheless, Hindu, and the Sikhs make up just 43% of the state's population. There are some Sikhs, however, notably those of the Akali Dal, who are pursuing the goal of establishing an independent theocratic Sikh republic (Kalistan). During the 1970s and 80s, their activities led to a state of emergency in the Punjab, and in 1984 the Indian Army was used to attack the Golden Temple Complex in Amritsar, where one group of rebels was taking refuge. The rebel leader, Sant Jarnail Singh Bhindranwale, and up to 5,000 civilians were killed in the action and, soon afterwards, the Indian prime minister, Indira Gandhi, was assassinated in Delhi by two Sikh soldiers of her personal bodyguard. This, in turn, led to communal violence in both Delhi and the Punjab that cost another 3,000 lives, and on June 23, 1985, an Air India flight from Montreal to New Delhi was blown up over the Atlantic with the loss of 329 lives. In 2003, two Sikhs went on trial in Vancouver in connection with this disaster.

Since the events of 1984-5, the Akali Dal has lost much of its influence and modern Sikhism is gradually returning toward prioritizing the universalist and pacifist values contained in the teachings of Guru Nanak and the Guru Granth Sahib rather than the militaristic values expressed in the 18th century activities of Gobind Singh, Banda Singh and their successors, and the 20th century activities of the Akali Dal.

This progressive approach to Sikhism is particularly notable among the seven million people of the global Sikh diaspora, almost half of whom now live in the West, with around 300,000 in the US alone, including those of the Sikh/Spanish community of California. It can be summarized in the words of N Muthu Mohan, Guru Nanak Devji Chair of Religious Studies at Madurai Kamaraj University in South India:

▷ Religion is the spiritual weapon of suffering people. It helps to console the oppressed and gives confidence and divine support to their struggle. The interreligious experience of the Sikh Gurus is very relevant to the present world situation. We need the courage and competence to look critically at in-dwelling oppressive structures in various religions and work for their reformation. The Sikh Gurus undertook such an exercise and they are correctly celebrated for it.[31]

Although Sikhs around the world retain many of the attributes of their distinctive cultural community (with over 50 gurdwaras in the UK alone) and although many cling to at least some of the five Ks of the Khalsa, most of the Sikhs who wear the distinctive trimmings of the Khalsa identity do so in order to remind themselves of their duty to uphold the universal values of Guru Nanak and the Guru Granth Sahib. These values, however we dress and whatever language we speak, complement those of the earlier teachers and prophets in providing guidance for the achievement of a harmonious and sustainable world civilization, within which the Sikhs themselves would surely continue to exist as a small, but colorful and beneficial community.

9
MIRZA HUSAIN ALI
NURI & GOD'S UNITY
RECLAIMED 3

Mirza Husain Ali Nuri was born in 1817 into a noble family in Tehran. The once stable Shia Islamic Empire of the Safavid Dynasty (see Chapter 7) had collapsed into chaos in 1722, but modern Iran was beginning to take shape under Shah Fath Ali (1797-1835), who had succeeded his uncle, Aga Muhammad, a chief of the Kajar tribe. Aga Muhammad had reunited the country in the mid-1790s and ruthlessly put down local revolts against the new Kajar power before being assassinated in 1797.

Mirza Husain's father was a landowner and worked as provincial governor for Shah Fath Ali and then for his successor, Shah Muhammad (1835-48), so the boy had a relatively secure and comfortable childhood, albeit within a country still racked by division and insecurity. The Shahs were generally recognized as rulers throughout Iran, but central power was patchy and unstable, with some local leaders remaining largely autonomous. The country was also uncomfortably divided between a small minority of wealthy landowners on the one hand and growing masses of peasants on the other. It was also wary of the powers around its borders: the relatively strong, prosperous and stable Ottoman Empire to its west and the emerging technological and military imperial powers of Christian Europe beyond, not least because of the expansionist threats posed by Russia from the north and the British Empire from the east.

Although Shia Islam remained the dominant religion in Iran and a force for national unity, significant communities of Sunni Muslims, Christians, Jews and Zoroastrians still survived, along with a variety of heterodox branches of

Shia Islam (see Chapter 7). Most of these minorities were seen as a threat to national stability, and regularly suffered from persecution. But new Shia sects continued to emerge, possibly because of the messianic nature of the Shia legacy and the generally unsatisfactory situation of most Iranians.

One of the new sects was founded by Shaykh Ahmad Al-Ahsai (1753-1826). This sect, the Shaykhis, claimed to be the unveilers of hidden knowledge and the heralds of the resurrection. When Shaykh Ahmad died he was succeeded by Sayyid[1] Kazam Rashti who led the Shaykhis until his death in 1844. Some of the Shaykhis were then drawn to a new leader, Sayyid Ali Muhammad, a man from outside the original group who had been born into a merchant family in the southern city of Shiraz in 1819.

Sayyid Ali Muhammad left his family business to make a pilgrimage around Iran's holy shrines in 1841. He returned to Shiraz in 1842, married and had one child. The child died in infancy. Ali then left Shiraz again to adopt the life of a wandering ascetic holy man. He made contact with the Shaykhis during the course of his wandering.

The Shaykhis were already expecting the resurrection of the Mahdi or Messiah and, when Kazam Rashti died, Ali Muhammad told of a vision he had had of the severed head of the Third Imam, Husain, who was killed in 680 at the Battle of Karbala (see Chapter 7). He told of how the spirit of God had permeated his soul as a result of his vision. He then claimed to be the Mahdi, the Twelfth Imam, returning from hiding (Chapter 7 again) and "One who God has made manifest."[2]

These were much greater personal claims than those made by the earlier Shaykhi leaders, but many Shaykhis still continued to follow him. Sayyid Ali also described himself as the *Bab* (Gate), preparing the way for yet another manifestation of God, whose appearance would mark the true resurrection. Those Shaykhis who accepted Sayyid Ali as the Bab became known as the Babis, and his missionaries took his message throughout Iran.

In 1845 the Bab also took his message to Mecca and planned to go from there to Karbala in Ottoman Iraq to await the resurrection, but this plan was aborted when his writings were denounced as blasphemous and one of his missionaries was arrested in Iraq, tried for heresy and sentenced to a life of hard labor in the docks of Istanbul. The Bab returned to Iran and went home to Shiraz. Soon after his arrival, he was subjected to house arrest and his followers were expelled from the city, but he used his detention to write prolifically, continuing to predict the imminent resurrection of "He whom God shall make manifest" in succession to Adam, Abraham, Jesus, Muhammad and himself, saying of the prophets:

▷ "Each is the rising and setting of the same sun, but each gives a more comprehensive and developed expression of the divine message."

The Bab condemned the injustices of Iranian society, the intolerance and misogyny of the Islamic leadership and the dogmatism and exclusivity that closed the minds of the other religious groups. He specifically rejected Koranic texts allowing instant divorce and insisted that divorce without at least a year's notice was unholy. He declared that his own writings superseded the Koran and predicted that his opponents would go to Hell. The numbers of Babis continued to grow, mostly among existing Shaykhi communities, but also among other communities throughout Iran, including that of Mirza Husain Ali Nuri and his first wife in Tehran.

In 1846 Shiraz was hit by a cholera epidemic. The Bab escaped the city and was able to take refuge in Isfahan as a protected guest of the local governor. This protection lasted only a year, however. The governor died in 1847 and the Bab was taken under armed escort to Tehran, and thence to imprisonment in remote fortresses in Maku, then Chihriq. In 1848, still refusing to give up his claim to be the Mahdi, the Bab was tried and beaten in Tabriz. He was then sent back to Chihriq.

In the meantime, Fatimah Baraghani, a feminist Babi was accused of heresy in Karbala and expelled from Iraq. She returned to Iran where she emerged from a Babi conference in Badasht as the leader of a radicalized movement. Now known as Tahirih (the pure one) she led a demonstration in her hometown of Qasvin. It ended in violence and was followed by further violent encounters between the Babis and the authorities. At one point, an armed group of around 700 Babis marched on Barfurush near the Caspian coast, only to be forced back to the shrine of Shayk Tabarsi where they held out until 1849 before being overcome and massacred. In 1850 there were further conflicts in the cities of Yazd, Tehran, Zanjan (home to 3,000 Babis in a population of 20,000) and Nayriz (1,500 Babis in a population of 3,000).

Seven Babis were also arrested and executed in Tehran and the Bab was taken back from Chihriq to Tabriz to face a firing squad. He actually faced two firing squads, because the first, composed of Christian Armenian soldiers, all missed him. This squad was then replaced by Muslim soldiers, who didn't. Leadership of the Babis then fell to the Bab's teenage nominee, Mirza Yahya Nuri (1832-1912), younger half-brother of Mirza Husain Ali Nuri. The community moved to Ottoman Baghdad, where Babis were now tolerated.

In 1852 a failed Babi attempt to assassinate Shah Nasir Ud-Din (1848-1896) led to a renewed persecution of the Babis still in Iran. Those in Tehran, including Mirza Husain Ali Nuri, were rounded up and imprisoned. While in prison, Mirza Husain Ali Nuri experienced visions that would soon lead to the birth of another new religion. He was released in 1853 after four months' incarceration and exiled, along with his wife and nine-year-old son, Abbas, to Baghdad. After a short time with the Babi refugee community, which was still led by his younger half-brother, Mirza Yahya Nuri, Mirza Husain withdrew to the mountains of Kurdistan for two years (1854-6), then returned to challenge his half-brother for the leadership of the community. Those Babis who remained loyal to Mirza Yahya Nuri – now renamed Subhi Azal (the Morn of Eternity) – were soon to become known as the Azalis, a sect that subsequently faded. Those who accepted Mirza Husain Ali Nuri – soon to be renamed Baha'ullah (the Glory of God) and revered by his followers as the Manifestation of God for the current age – were the progenitors of the Bahai Faith.

During seven years in Baghdad, Mirza Husain wrote extensively. His writings included letters to the Ottoman Sultan and other imperial and national leaders, and a series of books, including *The Hidden Words* (1858) and the *Book of Certitude* (1862). Selected highlights from his writings follow on the next page. Verses whose numbers are preceded with an H have been taken from the *Hidden Words*. Those with numbers preceded with a G are taken from the official Bahai compilation of *Gleanings from the Writings of Baha-ullah*.[3] Extended highlights appear in Chapter 10.

THE VISION – SELECTED HIGHLIGHTS

On The Nature of God

G19 God, the unknowable essence, the divine Being is immensely exalted beyond every human attribute. Far be it from God's glory that human tongue should adequately recount God's praise, or that human heart should comprehend God's fathomless mystery. Tabernacles of holiness, these primal mirrors that reflect the light of unfading glory, are but expressions of God, the Invisible of the invisibles. By the revelation of divine virtue, the attributes of God, such as knowledge and power, sovereignty and dominion, mercy and wisdom, glory, bounty and grace, are made manifest [but] have never been vouchsafed to certain prophets and withheld from others. G22 God is the innermost Spirit of spirits and eternal Essence of essences. H6 Your paradise is the love of God; your heavenly home, reunion with God. H11 You are God's light and God's light is in you.

On God's Purpose and Human Responsibility

G24 A drop of the billowing ocean of God's endless mercy has adorned all creation with the ornament of existence and a breath wafted from God's peerless paradise has invested all beings with the robe of God's sanctity and glory. A sprinkling from the unfathomed deep of God's sovereign and all pervasive will has, out of utter nothingness, called into being a creation which is infinite in its range and deathless in its duration. The process of God's creation had no beginning and can have no end. G4 It is incumbent upon all the peoples of the world to reconcile their differences and, with perfect unity and peace, abide beneath the shadow of the tree of God's care and loving kindness. G52 Depend not on the sight of anyone except yourself, for God has never burdened any soul beyond its power. G66 Beware that you do not swell with pride before God and reject His loved ones. Lay not on any soul a load which you would not wish to be laid upon you, and do not wish on anyone the things you would not wish for yourself. G72 Cast away that which you possess and, on the wings of detachment, soar beyond all created things. Beware lest the desires of the flesh and of a corrupt inclination provoke divisions among you. Be as the fingers of one hand, the members of one body. G76 Meditate diligently upon the purpose of the Lord. Strive to know God directly and not through others. G110 The fundamental purpose animating faith in God is to safeguard the interests and promote the unity of the human race, to foster the spirit of love and fellowship among men and not to allow religion to become a source of dissension and discord, of hate and enmity. G112 Don't regard each other as strangers. You are the fruits of one tree; the leaves of one branch. G120 Elected representatives of the people in every land, take counsel together and let your concern be only for that which profits mankind. G146 Beware lest you prefer yourselves above your neighbors.

On Worship

G52 Pray to be forgiven, O people, for having failed in your duty towards God and for having trespassed against God's cause, and be not of the foolish. G93 Wonder not that God is closer to you than your own self. Wonder only that, despite such nearness, you can still be so far from God.

Prayer

G18 Praise be to God, the Lord of all worlds.

Prophecy

G133 Whoever keeps the commandments of God shall attain everlasting felicity. G163 This civilization, so often vaunted by the learned exponents of arts and science, will bring great evil upon men. If carried to excess, civilization will prove as prolific a source of evil as it had been of goodness when it kept within the bounds of moderation. Its flame will devour the cities.

See Chapter 10 for further highlights from the Vision of Mirza Husain Ali Nuri.

THE LEGACY

In May 1863 Mirza Husain Ali Nuri left Baghdad for Istanbul with a number of his closest followers. He met and impressed many influential people: Ottoman officials, Muslim clerics and Iranian exiles. The Iranian government sought his repatriation, but the Ottomans refused to expel him and accepted him as an

Ottoman citizen. He was allowed to preach freely in the Ottoman capital, but by December, Istanbuls's welcome for the growing Babi group cooled and they were removed to Edirne in the far west of the Ottoman Empire (now in European Turkey). Edirne became the center of Babi activity for the next five years. It was during this period that the claim of Mirza Husain Ali Nuri to be Baha'ullah, the Glory of God and the Manifestation of God for the current age, was publicized. The claim acrimoniously and irreversibly split the Babis into the Azali and Bahai factions. Both factions fought among each other in Edirne and sent competing messengers to the Babis in Iran. The Azalis rejected Mirza Husain's new claim and advocated continuing political agitation. The Bahais worshipped Baha'ullah, advocated the separation of religion from politics, and accused the Azalis of attempting to murder Baha'ullah.

In 1868, the Ottomans removed the Azali group from Edirne to Famagusta in Cyprus and the Bahais to Acre in Palestine where Mirza Husain was initially imprisoned in a fortress then held under house arrest. He was able to strengthen Bahai Faith from his places of captivity:

> ▷ G 126 To whatever place I may be banished, however great the tribulation I may suffer, you who are the people of God must, with fixed resolve and perfect confidence, keep your eyes directed to the Day Spring of Glory, and be busy in whatever may be conducive to the betterment of the world and the education of its peoples. All that has befallen Me in the past has advanced the interests of My Revelation; and all that may befall Me in the future will have a like result. Cling with your inmost hearts to the Cause of God, a Cause that has been sent down by Him who is the Ordainer, the All Wise. I have, with the utmost kindliness, summoned and directed all peoples and nations to that which shall truly profit them. People of God have no ambition except to revive the world, to ennoble its life and to regenerate its peoples.

Sporadic outbreaks of violence between Azalis and Bahais continued for several more years, both around Acre and in Iran, and the authorities continued to regard both groups as a threat. At the height of the violence, in 1869, a Bahai envoy attempting to deliver a message of peace to the Shah of Iran was tortured and killed, but by 1873, the Bahais' situation had become considerably safer. Mirza Husain's *Holy Book of Law* was published and his son, Abbas, married an Iranian Bahai from Isfahan. Abbas, now renamed Abdul Baha (Servant of Glory), took over organizational control of the Bahai community and, in 1877, Mirza Husain's confinement was relaxed. He was allowed to move to a mansion in nearby Bahji, Haifa, where he lived peacefully with his wife and family until his death in 1892. His will stated that his "sons would be his successors."[4]

By this time, Abdul Baha had already become an active missionary of the Bahai Faith and supplemented his father's writings with many of his own, including *The Secret of Divine Civilization* (1875) and *A Traveler's Narrative* (1886). During the 1880s the number of Bahais in Iran grew to around 100,000, attracting converts from Shia, Zoroastrian and Jewish communities. The faith also spread east to India and north to Russian Turkestan. Acre and Bahji became places of pilgrimage, attracting visitors from Europe as well as Asia.

Following Mirza Husain's death, his younger son, Mirza Muhammad Ali, challenged Abdul Baha's supremacy, accusing him of over-reaching his mandate. Abdul Baha's response was to have his half-brother excommunicated. This response contributed to the ongoing divisions within the Babi/Azali/Bahai communities back in Iran, raising their profiles again and re-igniting their persecution there. Pogroms against the communities in Iran continued well into the 1900s.

Back in Palestine, Abdul Baha was able to consolidate his authority over the Bahai community in the Acre/Haifa area. He also undertook his missionary trips to Europe and North America, where he gained converts among emigrant Iranian communities and others.

His missionary activity was curtailed for seven years from 1901, when the Ottoman authorities confined him to Acre, but he was released following the Young Turks' revolution of 1908. He then moved the Bahai headquarters to Haifa, arranged to have the remains of the Bab taken there and initiated plans for a shrine on Mount Carmel. He traveled to Egypt in 1910, visited London, Bristol and Paris in 1911, and undertook an extensive mission to the West in 1912-13, visiting the USA, Canada, the UK, France, Germany and Austria-Hungary.

The expansion of the faith under Abdul Baha included the development of Bahai communities in all these countries and an increase in the number of Bahais in the Russian Empire to around 4,000, mostly Iranian refugees. The first Bahai House of Worship was built Ashkhabad in Turkestan in 1907. Abdul Baha also oversaw the establishment of a Bahai Women's Assembly in Tehran (1910), a National Teaching Council in India (1911) and the foundation of

Bahai communities in Hawaii (1901), Japan (1914), Australia (1920) and Brazil (1921). During World War I and its immediate aftermath, he organized relief work in Palestine, an activity that brought him a knighthood from the British in 1920. He died in 1921 and was buried with the Bab. Their shrine on Mount Carmel was eventually completed in 1953.

In his will, Abdul Baha appointed his eldest grandson, Shoghi Effendi (1897-1957), as his successor, or "Guardian of the Faith." He also made provision for the recognition of four "Hands of the Cause of God" to advise in guiding the faithful, and for the eventual establishment of an elected governing body, to be known as "The Universal House of Justice."

Shoghi Effendi was educated at a Western college in Syria and at the universities of Beirut and Oxford before taking charge of the Bahai World Center in Haifa at the age of 24. He introduced a cycle of 19-day fasts, issued membership cards, and instituted elected nine-member "Local Spiritual Assemblies" and "National Spiritual Assemblies" with elected secretaries to administer the Bahai communities around the world. He undertook missionary tours in Africa from 1929, married an American in 1937, published his own work, *As God Passes By* in 1944 and excommunicated many Bahais, including members of his own extended family, who challenged his approach. In 1947 he addressed the UN Palestine Committee on "The Faith of Baha'ullah" and, in 1948, the Bahai Faith was affiliated to the UN. He established an International Bahai Council in 1950, an Auxiliary Board for Expansion in 1953, and an Auxiliary Board for Protection in 1957. He died during a missionary visit to London in November 1957 and was buried there.

The faith also suffered some reverses under Shoghi Effendi. These included banning in Nazi Germany (1933-45) and Indonesia (from 1953), and mass arrests and deportations in the USSR, along with the expropriation and demolition of the Ashkhabad House of Worship in 1938. Despite these setbacks, the faith expanded steadily around the world. By 1935 there were 139 Local Spiritual Assemblies and 10 National Spiritual Assemblies and, by 1957, these figures had risen to 670 and 12. A seven-year plan to settle Bahai pioneers in every state of the USA and every province of Canada (1937-44) succeeded and, in 1953, a House of Worship in Wilmette, Illinois, was completed as a focal point for the faith in the Americas.

The expansion continued gathering momentum after Shoghi Effendi's death. By 1963, there were over 4,000 Local Spiritual Assemblies and 56 National

Spiritual Assemblies. There are now over 20,000 and 180 respectively, serving over six million Bahais around the world, including around two million in India, one million in South America and 200,000 in the USA.

Houses of Worship have been completed in Kampala, Uganda (1961), Sydney, Australia (1961), Frankfurt (1964), Panama (1972), Western Samoa (1984) and New Delhi (1986). World Congresses were held in London (1963) and New York (1992), the latter attracting 27,000 delegates from 180 countries. The Universal House of Justice, established in 1963, has been augmented by Continental Boards of Councilors since 1968 and supports a number of other Bahai bodies: the Office for Social and Economic Development (established in 1983), the Bahai University of Bolivia (founded in 1985), the Office for the Environment (1989) and the Office for the Advancement of Women (1992).

The Bahai World Center in Haifa now employs over 700 staff. Bahai literature has been published in 800 languages. The Bahai community is involved in development projects in every continent. It is also active in preserving local cultures (insofar as they don't clash with Bahai values) and features indigenous music programs on its radio stations.

Converts to the faith in the USA have included the jazz trumpeter, Dizzy Gillespie, a founding father of both be-bop in the 40s and latin jazz in the 50s, and a stalwart of UN musical goodwill tours until his death in 1993; and both members of the 70s pop duo, Seals & Crofts.

The expansion of the worldwide Bahai community in the last half-century has been dramatic, but it has been accompanied by further reverses. There were more excommunications and splits during the period between Shoghi Effendi's death and the establishment of the Universal House of Justice, notably in the USA, where Charles Mason Remy, one of the four "Hands of the Cause of God" opposed the emerging details of Bahai organizational plans and proclaimed himself Shoghi Effendi's successor as the "Guardian of the Faith," effectively founding an American Bahai sect in opposition to Haifa. Elsewhere, the mainstream Bahai Faith was banned in several more countries (Egypt from 1960; Iraq from 1970; Vietnam from 1976, and Iran again from 1979). A Bahai missionary was sentenced to death in Morocco in 1962, but the sentence was commuted. Another was executed in Guinea-Bissau in 1966. And many thousands of Bahais were tortured, imprisoned or executed in Iran following the Islamic revolution of 1979.

Bahai values and the Bahai messages of unity and peace make it hard to understand the mentality of those who would persecute members of such an apparently tolerant and inoffensive faith, but despite Bahai claims to recognize "all God's prophets," and despite the continuing dramatic international expansion of its membership, the faith has effectively ruled itself out as the progressive world religion it claims to be. It has done this in several ways, three of which are listed below:

1. The level of deification of its founder, implied in the separation of Mirza Husain Ali Nuri from his real name and referring to him only as Baha'ullah, the Glory of God, imbues the faith with the same level of arrogance it rejects in Christianity's claim that Jesus is the [one and only] Son of God and Islam's claim that Muhammad was the last of all prophets.

2. Mirza Husain Ali Nuri's statement that "whoever lays claim to a revelation direct from God, ere the expiration of a full thousand years is assuredly a lying impostor"[5] contradicts the openness of other parts of his writing, such as, "knowledge of God is not vouchsafed specially unto certain prophets and withheld from others"[6] and "I have never aspired after worldly leadership. My sole purpose has been to hand down to men that which I was bidden to deliver by God, the Gracious, the Incomparable, that it may detach them from all that pertains to this world."[7]

3. The Bahai Faith claims to keep politics and religion separate and requires its members to refrain from participating in party politics, but this very requirement, combined with Bahai organizational development, has effectively turned the Bahai Faith into a parallel political organization – a theocratic world government-in-waiting.

Perhaps the only reason that, unlike at least six of the eight older religions considered here, the legacy of the Bahai Faith remains unstained by war and mass murder, is that it is the only one whose faithful have always been a minority without the power to inflict such persecution on those who would disagree with the details of their religion. As this is likely to remain the case, there is little to fear and much to be admired in the Bahai Faith, as can be seen from the further highlights of the Vision of Mirza Husain Ali Nuri, collected, along with those of his eight predecessors, in the following chapter.

10
COLLECTED
VISIONS*

On The Nature of God

Chapter 1 – Zarathustra

Who in the beginning, at creation, was the Father of order?
Who established the course of the sun and stars?
Through whom does the moon wax then wane?
Who has upheld the Earth from below and the heavens from falling?
Who sustains the waters and plants?
Who harnesses swift steeds to winds and clouds?
Who, O God, is the Creator of good purpose?
What Craftsman created darkness and light?
What Craftsman created sleep and activity?
Through Whom exist dawn, noon and eve,
which remind us of our duty?
Who fashioned power and devotion?
Who made the child respect the parent?
By these questions, O Lord
I help to identify You as Creator of all things through the Holy Spirit.[10]

With power, God came to this world, by good purpose and by truth,[11]
Then, through order, God made plants grow.[12]
Then, by long-lasting devotion, gave body and breath.[13]

---

* Superscripts throughout these Collected Visions refer to notes on Chapters 1-9 as indicated.

God fashioned for us in the beginning creatures and inner selves and intentions
And acts and words, through which one who has free will expresses choices.[14]

I recognized You as holy, God, when I saw You as First at the birth of life,
Then when You appointed rewards for acts and words,

Bad for the bad, good for the good
By Your innate virtue at the final turning point of creation,
At which turning point, You come to the world, O God, with Your Holy Spirit,
With power through good purpose, by Your acts, the people of good purpose
prosper.[15]

God is all-seeing and not to be deceived.[16]

Chapter 2 – Moses

God is the Lord. There is no other.
God is the Rock. All God's works are perfect. All God's ways are just.
God is without iniquity.[3]

In the beginning, God created the heavens and the earth. The earth was
without form and void and the Spirit of God moved ...[4]

Chapter 3 – Atharva

1.1

2. There are two kinds of knowledge, as those who know God declare, the
   higher as well as the lower.

3. Of these, the lower includes the Rig Veda, the Yajur Veda, the Sama Veda,
   the Atharva Veda, phonetics, ritual, grammar, etymology, metrics and
   astronomy, and the higher is that by which the Undecaying is
   understood.

4. That which is ungraspable, beyond family, beyond caste, beyond sight or
   hearing, without hands or feet, eternal, all-pervading, omnipresent,
   exceedingly subtle, that is the Undecaying that the wise perceive as the
   source of beings.

5. As a spider sends forth and draws in its thread, as plants grow on the
   earth, so from the Imperishable arises the universe.

2.1

1. This is the truth. As from a blazing fire, sparks issue forth by the thousand, so beings issue forth from God, and to God they return.

2. God is without and within, beyond breath, beyond mind, pure and higher than the highest immutable.

3. From God are born life, mind, senses, space, air, light, water and earth.

9. From God, all the seas and the mountains; from God flow rivers of every kind; from God come all plants and their juices, through which, together with the elements, the inner soul is upheld.

3.1

7. Vast, divine, of unthinkable form, subtler than the subtle, God's spirit shines forth, farther than the far, yet here, near at hand, set down in the secret place of the soul, and even here it is seen by the intelligent.

6. God is not grasped by the eye, nor by other senses, but when one's intellectual nature is purified by the light of knowledge, then one, by meditation, sees God, who is without parts.

Chapter 4 – Lao-tzu

1.2 The God that can be described is not the enduring and unchanging One – the originator of Heaven and Earth, the Mother of all things – the Mystery.

1.3 Where the Mystery is the deepest is the gate of all that is subtle and wonderful.

25 Before the world existed and the sky was filled with stars, there was Something complete and beyond definition; silent, beyond all substance and sensing, standing alone and undergoing no change, reaching everywhere and in no danger. It has always been here and always will be. Everything comes from It. It is the Mother of Everything. Its Way is great. It is greater than the heavens, greater than earth, greater than kings. Humanity is schooled by the earth. The earth's nature is derived from Heaven. Heaven's nature follows the Way.

5.1 The Way is greater than human ways. The heavens and earth do not act as humans. They don't expect to be thanked for making life.

7.1 The universe is eternal because it does not exist for itself.

14 Because the eye gazes and can catch no glimpse of the Way, it is called elusive.

Because the ear listens but cannot hear it, it is called inaudible.

Because the hand feels for it but cannot find it, it is called subtle.

These three cannot be further described, but blend into One.

39 From the beginning, the universe came from God.

The heavens are at one with God, and bright and clear.

Earth is at one with God, and firm and sure.

God is at one with all living things.

If this were not so, the heavens would soon rend;

The earth would break and bend;

God would not bless, and faith would fail;

Rivers would run dry and parch each vale.

Without this, life would pass away.

However grand and high, all would decay.

32 Heaven and Earth unite to send down sweet rain, which flows of its own accord without the directions of men, and gathers together like music. The relation of the Way to all the world is like that of the great rivers and seas to the streams of the valleys.

51 All things are produced by the Way and nourished by its outflowing operation. They receive their form according to their nature and are completed according to their circumstances; therefore all things honor the Way and exalt its outflowing operation. This honoring of the Way and exalting of its operation is not the result of any ordination, but always a spontaneous tribute.

62 The Way has, of all things, the most honored place. No treasures give good men so rich a grace. The Way of Heaven is always on the side of the good man.

Chapter 5 – Siddhartha Gautama

No section on the nature of God is included. The Buddha had no words to add to those already available on this matter. For a follower of the Buddhist Way, an understanding of the nature of God can only come with enlightenment, the path to which starts with the Four Noble Truths (see below).

Chapter 6 – Jesus

In the beginning was the Word, and the Word was with God, and the Word was God.[2]

God causes the sun to rise on the evil and the good, and sends rain on the righteous and the unrighteous.

Your heavenly Father is perfect.

Your Father is unseen.

Your Father sees what is done in secret.

No one can see the Kingdom of God, unless he is born again.[3]

No one can enter the Kingdom of God, unless he is born of water and the Spirit. Flesh gives birth to flesh, but the Spirit gives birth to spirit. You must be born again. The wind blows wherever it pleases; you hear its sound, but you cannot tell where it comes from, or where it is going; so it is with everyone born of the Spirit.[4]

The Kingdom of God does not come with your careful observation. You can't say, "Here it is," or, "There it is," because the Kingdom of God is within you.[5]

The Kingdom of God belongs to such as these (little children).[6]

Chapter 7 – Muhammad

2.115 God is omnipresent and all-knowing.

2.120 The guidance of God is the only guidance.

2.255 God knows what is before and behind us. We can grasp only the part of God's knowledge that God wills. God's throne is as vast as the heavens and the Earth, and the preservation of both does not weary God, the Exalted, the Immense One.

2.256 God is the patron of the righteous and leads them from darkness into light.

2.268 Wisdom is given according to God's will. Those that receive it are rich indeed.

3.18 God is the executor of justice, the only God, the Mighty, the wise One.

3.159 God loves those that trust in God.

8.24 God stands between man and his desires.

8.40 God is the noblest helper and protector.

8.46 God is with those who are patient.

10.5 God makes his revelation plain to those of understanding.

10.65 God owns all who dwell on Earth and in Heaven.

11.113 God is watching over all your actions.

12.6 Your Lord is all-knowing and wise.

13.9 God knows the visible and the unseen. God is the supreme One, the Most High.

13.16 God is the Creator of all things – the One, the Almighty.

13.31 All things are subject to God's will.

16.9 God alone can show the right path.

16.11 God brings up corn and olives, dates and grapes and other fruit. Surely in this there is a sign for thinking men.

16.20 Your God is one God.

16.91 God has knowledge of all your actions.

16.128 God is with those who keep from evil and do good works.

31.34 God guides to the light at will.

27.65 No-one in the heavens or on the Earth has knowledge of what is hidden, except God.

29.7 God has no need of his creatures' help.

35.38 God knows the mysteries of Heaven and Earth, the hidden thoughts of men.

38.61 God is the Lord of the heavens and the Earth and all that lies between them, the illustrious, the benign One.

42.9 God alone is the Guardian. God brings back the dead to life and has power over all things. God's are the keys of the heavens and the Earth. God gives abundantly to some and sparingly to others. God alone has knowledge of all things.

42.26 God hears the prayers of those who have faith and do good works.

42.50 God gives sons and daughters to some and none to others. God alone is mighty and all-knowing.

43.85 God is God in Heaven and God on Earth.

46.9 God is our all-sufficient witness.

47.19 Know that there is no god but God.

47.30 & 63.11 God has knowledge of all your actions.

50.10 God sends down precious water from the sky, giving new life to dead land, bringing forth gardens and harvest grain, tall palm trees laden with clusters of dates – a sustenance for all.

51.59 God alone is the munificent giver, the mighty one, the invincible.

55.1 God created man and gave him articulate speech. God raised the heavens on high and set the balance of all things that you might not transgress it. God laid the Earth for His creatures, with all its fruits and blossom-bearing palm, chaff-covered grain and scented herbs.

57.2 God is the mighty, the wise One. His is the kingdom of the heavens and the Earth. God ordains life and death and has power over all things. God is the First and the Last, the visible and the unseen. God has knowledge of all things. God created the heavens and the Earth. God knows all that goes in to the earth and all that emerges from it, all that comes down from Heaven and all that ascends to it. God is with you wherever you are. God is cognizant of all your actions.

59.22 God is God, besides whom there is no other god. God knows the visible and the unseen. God is the Compassionate, the Merciful, the Sovereign Lord, the Holy One, the Giver of Peace, the Keeper of Faith, the Mighty One, the All-powerful, the Most High, the Creator, the Originator, the Modeler, the Wise One.

64.4 God knows what the heavens and the Earth contain. God knows all that you hide and all that you reveal. God knows your innermost thoughts.

64.18 God has knowledge of the visible and the unseen. God is the mighty and wise One.

67.2 God has power over all things.

73.5 God is the Lord of East and West. There is no god but God.

73.30 God is forgiving and merciful.

74.56 No-one takes heed except by the Will of God, the spring of goodness and forgiveness.

God is wise and all knowing.

85.11 Forgiving and benign, God is the Lord of the glorious throne, the executor of His will.

87.7 God has knowledge of all that is manifest and all that is hidden.

96.1 God is the Most Bountiful One, who teaches us what we do not know.

112.1 God is One, the eternal God, who begat no man, nor was begotten. No-one is equal to God.

Chapter 8 – Nanak Dev

There is but one God.
God is all that is.
God is the Creator of all things and is all-pervasive.
God is without fear and without enmity.
God is timeless, unborn and self-existent.
God is the enlightener and can be realized by grace alone.
God was in the beginning and in all ages.
The true One is, was, and forever shall be.[1]

God's seat is everywhere.
God's treasure houses are in all places.[2]
The one Lord made us all.[3]

The Lord is true, plainly known, His loving kindness infinite.
To those who crave and seek, God gives with full abandon.[4]

God's state is beyond description. One who undertakes description will regret it afterwards. No use of pen or paper is availing. One knows God in his heart on due reflection.[5]

Chapter 9 – Mirza Husain Ali Nuri

G19 God, the unknowable essence, the divine Being is immensely exalted beyond every human attribute, such as corporeal existence, ascent and descent, egress and regress. Far be it from God's glory that human tongue should adequately recount God's praise, or that human heart should comprehend God's fathomless mystery. Tabernacles of holiness, these primal mirrors, which reflect the light of unfading glory, are but expressions of God, who is the Invisible of the invisibles. By the revelation of divine virtue, the attributes of God, such as knowledge and power, sovereignty and dominion, mercy and wisdom, glory, bounty and grace, are made manifest [but] have never been vouchsafed to certain prophets and withheld from others.

G22 God is the innermost Spirit of spirits and eternal Essence of essences.

G51 From God all the suns have been generated and to God they will all return.

G66 The greatness of God's mercy surpasses the fury of His wrath and His grace encompasses all who have been called into being and clothed with the robe of life.

G72 God can well dispense with all creatures. Your evil doings can never harm God, neither can your good works profit God.

G78 In the beginning was God; there was no creature to know God. The Lord was alone. God will always remain.

G79 God's creation embraces worlds besides this world and creatures apart from these creatures. In each of these worlds, God has ordained things which none can know except God, the All-knowing, the All-wise.

G82 Every fixed star has its own planets and every planet its own creatures, whose number no man can compute.

G84 The Divine Being transcends the limitations of numbers.

G93 There is no other god but God, the One, the Incomparable, the Almighty, the most exalted, the Most Great.

G94 God has, throughout eternity, been one in essence, attributes and works. God alone occupies the seat of transcendent majesty, of supreme and inaccessible glory. The birds of men's hearts, however high they soar, can never hope to attain the heights of God's unknowable essence. It is God who has called into being the whole of creation; Who has caused every created thing to spring forth. Far be it from God's glory that human pen or tongue should hint at God's mystery, or that human heart conceive God's essence.

G124 How wondrous is the living, the ever-abiding God – a unity that is exalted above all limitations – that transcends the comprehension of all living things! How lofty is God's incorruptible essence, how completely independent of the knowledge of all created things, and how immensely exalted will it remain above the praise of all the inhabitants of the heavens and the Earth! From the exalted source and out of God's favor and bounty, every created thing is entrusted with a sign of the knowledge of God, so that none of God's creatures may be deprived of its share in expressing this knowledge. This sign is the mirror of God's beauty in the world of creation and, as a result of the exertion of our own spiritual faculties, this mirror can be so cleansed from the dross of earthly defilements and purged from satanic fancies as to be able to draw nigh unto the meadows of eternal holiness and attain the courts of everlasting fellowship.

G129 God ordains as He pleases by virtue of His sovereignty and does whatever He wills at His own behest. He shall not be asked of the things it pleases Him to ordain. God is the Unrestrained, the All-powerful, the All-wise.

G134 The spirit that animates the human heart is the knowledge of God, and its truest adorning is the recognition that God does whatever he wills and ordains whatever He pleases.

G148 All that is in Heaven and Earth has come to exist at God's bidding and, by God's will, all has stepped out of utter nothingness into the realm of being. How can the creature that God's word has fashioned comprehend the nature of God?

G160 A true believer in the unity of God regards Him as One immeasurably exalted above all the comparisons and likenesses with which men have compared Him. Can it ever be maintained that the work of a craftsman is the same as the craftsman himself? God's creation can be regarded in no other light than as evidence of God's existence.

H6 Your paradise is the love of God. Your heavenly home is reunion with God. Enter therein and tarry not.

H11 You are God's light and God's light is in you.

On God's Purpose and Human Responsibility

Chapter 1 – Zarathustra

I am Zarathustra.
Were I able, I would be a true foe to the deceiver, but a strong support to the Just One.
To Your question: "Who do you wish to serve?",
I declare: "Your fire; at the offering made in reverence,
I shall think upon truth for as long as I am able."
Meditation teaches the best things to be uttered.
One should not seek to satisfy the wicked, for they declare the just to be

enemies.

Zarathustra chooses The Spirit of God.[17]

For seekers, I shall speak of those things to be pondered.
Hear with your ears the truth I preach.
Reflect with clear understanding on the two choices for decision,
being alert indeed to declare yourselves for God before the great requital.[18]
The most holy spirits, who are clad in the hardest stone, choose rightly,
and so do those who shall satisfy God continually with rightful acts.
The daevas[19] did not choose rightly.
They chose worst purpose.
They then rushed to fury, with which they have afflicted the world and mankind.[20]

Learn the commands which God has given.[21] Seek to satisfy those who are poorly protected.[22]

Chapter 2 – Moses

God is the Lord. Have no other gods before God.
Do not make, bow down to, or serve any graven image or likeness of anything that is in the heavens above or in the earth beneath.
Do not take the name of God in vain.[5]

Honor your father and your mother, so that your days may be long in the land that the Lord your God gives you.
Do not kill.
Do not commit adultery.
Do not steal.
Do not bear false witness against your neighbor.
Do not covet your neighbor's house, wife, servants, ox, ass, or anything else that is your neighbor's.[6]
Do not make yourselves gods of silver or gold.[7]
Do not have sexual relations with close relatives – your mother, your father's wife, your sister, your father's daughter or your mother's daughter, your son's daughter or your daughter's daughter, the daughter of your father's wife, your father's sister, your mother's sister, your father's brother's wife, your daughter-in-law or your brother's wife.
Do not have sexual relations with both a woman and her daughter or

granddaughter.

Do not have sexual relations with a neighbor's wife.

Do not have sexual relations with an animal and defile yourself with it.

Do not lie.

Do not deceive one another.

Do not oppress your neighbor or rob him.

Do not oppress the poor and needy hired servant.

Do not withhold the wages of hired servants.

Do not curse the deaf or put a stumbling block before the blind.

Do no injustice in judgment.

Do not be partial to the poor or defer to the great.

Judge your neighbor fairly.

Love your neighbors as yourself.

And when strangers sojourn in your land, do not do them wrong. Love them as yourself. Have the same law for the sojourner and the native.

When you reap the harvest, you shall not reap your field to its very border, nor shall you gather the gleanings after your harvest; leave them for the poor and the stranger.

If your brother becomes poor and cannot maintain himself, you shall maintain him.

Do not make him a slave. He shall be as a hired servant and a sojourner.

Do not accept a ransom for a person committed to destruction; he must be put to death.

Do not accept a ransom for a murderer who deserves to die; he must be put to death.

Do not pollute the land.

Do not follow the practices of the soothsayer, charmer, medium, wizard or necromancer.

Love and serve the Lord your God with all your heart and with all your soul and with all your might.

These words shall be upon your heart. Teach them diligently to your children and talk of them when you sit in your house, when you walk by the way, when you lie down and when you rise.

Respect the Lord and walk in God's ways.[8]

Proverbs[9] from Chapter 2

Respect for the Lord is the start of wisdom, but fools despise wisdom and discipline.

Happy are those who find wisdom, for its value is greater than gold.

Go to the ant, O sluggard, consider its ways and be wise. It has no ruler, yet it stores its provisions in summer and gathers its food at harvest.

Lazy hands bring poverty, but diligent hands bring wealth.

Ill-gotten gains have no value, but righteousness delivers peace.

Those who walk in integrity walk securely, but those who take crooked paths will stumble.

Those who wink maliciously cause grief and a chattering fool comes to ruin.

The mouth of the righteous is a fountain of life, but the mouth of the wicked brings strife.

Hatred stirs up strife, but love overcomes all wrongs.

Fools find pleasure in evil conduct, but the wise delight in wisdom.

The prospect of the righteous is joy, but the hopes of the wicked come to nothing.

When a wicked man dies, his hope perishes; all his desires comes to nothing.

The Way of the Lord is a refuge for the righteous.

A man who lacks judgment derides his neighbor, but a man of understanding holds his tongue.

The lips of the righteous know what is fitting, but the mouth of the wicked knows only what is perverse.

A gentle answer turns away wrath, but a harsh word stirs up anger.

Reckless words pierce like a sword, but the tongue of the wise brings healing.

The lips of the righteous nourish many, but fools die for lack of judgment.

A fool shows his annoyance at once, but the prudent man overlooks an insult.

Truthful words endure forever but lies last only a moment.

The ways of fools seem right to them, but the wise listen to advice.

Plans fail for lack of counsel, but with many advisors they succeed.

One who hates correction is stupid.

Pride only breeds quarrels, but wisdom is found in those who take advice.

Pride comes before a fall, but wisdom comes with humility.

The kind-hearted gain respect, but the ruthless gain only wealth.

The truly righteous attain life, but those who pursue evil go to their death.

The wicked will not go unpunished, but the righteous will go free.

Whoever trusts in riches will fall, but the righteous will thrive like green leaves.

The fruit of the righteous is a tree of life, and one who wins souls is wise.

The wicked desire the plunder of the evil, but the root of the righteous flourishes.

In the way of righteousness, there is life. Along that path is immortality.

The teaching of the wise is the fountain of life, turning us from the snares of death.

One who walks with the wise grows wise, but companions of fools suffer harm.

Right understanding wins favor, but the way of the foolish is hard.

The prudent act out of knowledge, but fools expose their folly.

The eyes of the Lord are everywhere, keeping watch on the wicked and the good.

Those who walk upright respect the Lord, but those who are devious despise God.

Those who despise a neighbor sin, but blessed are those who are kind to the needy.

One who is kind to the poor lends to the Lord and will be rewarded.

A heart at peace gives life to the body, but envy rots the bones.

Better a little with respect for the Lord than great wealth with turmoil.

Better a little with righteousness than much gain with injustice.

Better a meal of vegetables with love than a fattened calf with hatred.

Wine is a mocker and beer a brawler. Whoever they lead astray is not wise.

Our spirit is the Lord's lamp. It searches our innermost being.

Haughty eyes and a proud heart – the lamp of the wicked is sin.

Through love and faith, sin is atoned for; through respect for the Lord, evil is avoided. Do not say, "I'll pay you back for this wrong." Wait for the Lord and He will deliver us.

Whoever gloats over disaster will not go unpunished.

A man with many companions may come to ruin, but there is a friend that sticks closer than any other.

Respect for the Lord leads to life, then one rests content, untouched by trouble.

Better a patient man than a warrior: one who controls his temper rather than taking a city.

Charm is deceptive and beauty is fleeting, but a woman who respects the Lord is to be praised. Give her the reward she has earned. Let her works bring her praise at the city gate.

The first to present a case seems right, until questioned by another.

It is not good to have zeal without knowledge, or to be hasty and miss the way.

Teach your children the way they should go. When they grow up they will not turn from it.

Discipline your children and they will bring you peace. They will bring delight to your soul.

Chapter 3 – Atharva

1.2

9. The immature, living in ignorance, think, "We have accomplished our aim." Those who perform rituals do not understand the truth because of attachment and sink down wretched when their worlds are exhausted.

10. These deluded men, regarding sacrifices and works for gain as most important, do not know any other good.

11. Those who practice austerity and faith in the forest, the tranquil knowers, depart freed from sin, through the door of the sun to where dwells the Immortal Imperishable One.

12. Having scrutinized the worlds won by works, let us arrive at non-attachment.

13. Let the knowing teacher teach in its very truth that knowledge of God by which one knows the truth.

2.2

5. God in whom the sky, the earth and space are woven with the mind and all living breath, know Him alone as the One. Dismiss other utterances. This is the bridge to immortality.

Chapter 4 – Lao-tzu

1.1 The way that can be trodden is not the enduring and unchanging Way.

1.3 Without desire we must be found, if the Way's deep mystery we would sound.

But if desire within us be, its outer fringe is all we'll see.

2.1 People can only recognize beauty and mercy because they know the opposite, which is ugly and mean.

3 Not to prize things that are difficult to procure is the way for people not to become thieves. If a leader governs according to the Way, then his people will not go wrong, so, in his wisdom, he will restrain himself by not being greedy, by not dominating the state, and by keeping himself healthy and fit. If there is nothing to fight for, good order is universal.

4 We should blunt our sharp points and unravel the complications of things. We should temper our brightness and bring ourselves into agreement with the obscurity of others. How pure and still the Way is, as if it should continue so forever.

5 If Heaven and Earth are worked, they will produce more. Work should be valued above words. Much speech will lead to swift exhaustion. Guard your inner being and keep it free.

7 The wise leader guides his people by putting himself last. Desiring nothing for himself, he knows how to channel desires. He can achieve everything because he wants nothing. The way of the wise is the way of water. There must be water for life to exist and its flow is true to the Way. Those following the Way, like water, accept where they find themselves and that may often be where the water goes – the lowest place. Like a lake, the heart must be calm and quiet, having great depth. The wise leader rules with compassion and his word needs to be trusted. He needs to know, like water, how to flow around obstacles, how to find a way through without violence. He should wait for the moment to ripen and be right.

9 One may amass gold and jade in plenty, but the more one has, the less safety. When wealth and honors lead to arrogance, they attract evil. Let go when your work is done. That is the Way of Heaven. Can you nurture your soul by holding it in unity with the Way? Can you rid your mind of all its dross? Can you do it without self-interest so as to become as flawless as a diamond? Can you love the people around you? Can you embrace the world without losing your humility? The Way nurtures without owning. It gives without reward.

It knows without flouting knowledge. It is serene beyond desire.

11 Clay is fashioned into vessels, but it is on their empty hollowness that their use depends. Walls, doors and windows form a room, but it is on the space

within that its use depends. That which has substance serves for adaptation. That which has not may serve for actual usefulness.

12 Too much color blinds the eyes. Too much music deafens the ears. Too much taste deadens the mouth. Too much riding drives you crazy. The wise seek to satisfy the craving of the belly, but not the desires of the eyes.

13.3 If you can put yourself aside, you can do things for the whole world, and if you love the world like this, then you are ready to serve it.

15.3 Who can make muddy water clear? Let it be still and it will become clear. It may be hard to wait for mud to settle, but if you can, then you can act. If you follow the Way without pretension, you will never burn yourself out.

22 One whose desires are few overcomes suffering. One whose desires are many goes astray. Learn to yield and be soft to survive. Learn to empty yourself and be filled by the Way. Learn to be satisfied with nothing and you will have everything. The wise always act like this and are the children of the Way. Never trying to impress, their being shines forth. Never boasting, they leave the space they can be valued in. Be true to yourself and all will be well with you.

23 It is natural to talk sparingly. Violent wind and lashing rain never last long. If nature cannot sustain such actions, how much less can man? If you go the way of virtue, its purity will sustain you.

24 Those who stand on tip-toe cannot walk easily; those who stride ahead are bound to tire; those who always insist on their own way of seeing things can never learn from anyone; those who always want to be seen will never be a help to others. They are not worthy of respect; they are as leftover food at a feast, as tumors on the body.

27 Skilful travelers leave no traces of their wheels or footsteps. Skilful speakers say nothing that can be faulted. The wise never calculate the profit they can make from their actions. Skilful negotiators need no bolts or bars. They keep out thieves with wisdom. They need no strings or knots. Their rules are clear and binding. The skilful ruler is aware of everyone, leaving no one uncounted, caring like a parent, wasting nothing. This is the essence of harmony.

28 The wise understand the strength of the yang yet maintain the gentleness of the yin. They are as streams that flow to the sea. They are born again, innocent, humble. They are channels for excellence. They weave energies in a true and practical way, so they can link up with the Way and become one again.

29 If a ruler acts as if he owns the land, he will do no good at all. The land is sacred. It cannot be owned. If he tries to possess it, he will destroy it. If he tries to hold on to it, he will lose it. In the course of nature, those in front can fall behind, those with warmth can cool, strength can fail and stores can spoil, so the wise abandon greed, extravagance and pride.

30 If a ruler's advisors follow the Way, they will not recommend mastery by force of arms. Strategies of warfare will always invite revenge. When troops trample the land, only weeds will grow in the broken ground. There will be no harvest. Everyone will be left starving. When action is needed, the wise leader strikes only as necessary. He does not abuse his power. When successful, he guards against arrogance. Those who do otherwise eventually lose. They do not act in accordance with the Way, and what is not in accordance with the Way will always come to an end.

31 Arms, however beautiful, are instruments of evil omen, hateful to all creatures. Those who follow the Way avoid them. The wise want peace and quiet. No military victory is free of grief. To celebrate one is to glory in the death of innocent people. No one who revels in death can follow the Way or be fit to rule. One who has killed should weep for his victims with the bitterest grief.

33 Those who know others are discerning. Those who know themselves are wise. Those who overcome others are strong. Those who overcome themselves are mighty. Those who are satisfied with what they have are rich. Those who are not satisfied with what they have will never have enough.

38 Those who follow the Way have innate virtue yet do not seek to flaunt it. Lesser men act from their egos and seek gratification. Those who rule through the Way act with compassion and subtlety. Those who rule through strict legality may act judiciously, but still seek to serve their own ends. The rigid ruler uses laws and, if people do not respond, bears arms to threaten them. If the Way is lost, mere morality remains; if this is lost, mere conscience; if this is lost, mere justice; if this is lost, confusion reigns; forecasts and prophesies abound, and they are merely a gloss on the Way; they are the root of twisted guidance. The wise abide by what is solid and eschew the superficial. They blow away the dust and drink the water. They live with the roots and the fruit, not just the flowers. Blow away the dust now. Come to the living water.

41 When wise students hear about the Way, they follow it without ceasing. When average students hear about it, they follow it some of the time. When

failing students hear about it, they laugh like idiots. If this were not so, it wouldn't be the Way.

43 Those who live violently die violently.

46 Greed is the seed of the apocalypse.

47 Without leaving your soul, you can know the whole world.

49 The wise are never opinionated. They listen to other people. They are kind to those who are kind to them. They are kind to those who are not kind to them; thus all will be improved. Virtue is its own reward. The wise are sincere to those who are sincere to them. They are sincere to those who are not; thus all will become sincere.

52 To bend like a reed in the wind – that is real strength. Use your mind, but stay close to the light and it will lengthen its glow right through your life.

53 The Way is easy, but people are forever choosing sidetracks. They care for their palaces, but leave their fields uncultivated and their granaries empty. They wear fine clothes, but carry arms. They gorge themselves and accumulate property at the expense of the poor. They are robbers and bloaters. This is not the Way.

57 A state may be ruled by law and defended with cunning, but the more prohibitions there are, the more unhappy the people are; the more weapons there are, the more bad things happen; the more laws there are, the more they will be broken.

59 Governing a great state is like cooking a small fish. The wise ruler uses simplicity in everything.

61 What makes a great state is its following of the stream. It becomes the center to attract the small states. By condescending to the small states, the great state wins them over. The great state gains adherents; the small states procure favor. The great state seeks to unite men together and nourish them. Each gets what it desires, but the great state must learn to abase itself.

63 The wise do not seek to own precious things. They help others to be true to themselves without standing in their way. They achieve without trying. They take on the greatest challenges while they are still small; start the hardest things while they are still easy. The person that thinks things easy finds them harder than anticipated. The wise see the difficulty in what seems easy, so never get out of their depth.

64 When everything is peaceful, don't forget the dangers. When things seem safe, don't lose your edge. A brittle thing can break easily. Act before it happens. Secure order before disorder has begun. Great trees start from small seeds. Tall towers begin on the ground. A journey of a thousand miles starts with a single step.

66 A wise leader seeks to serve the people. If he has no desire to control them, they will not feel oppressed. They will trust him and not tire of him.

78 There is nothing in the earth more soft and weak than water, yet for attacking things that seem firm and strong, there is nothing that can take precedence over it.

79 When reconciliation is effected between two parties after a great animosity, there is sure to be a grudge remaining, so the wise and good will not insist on speedy fulfillment. One who has the attributes of the Way regards all the conditions. One without these attributes regards only those conditions favorable to himself.

67 I have three priceless treasures: the first is love, the second thrift, and the third is that I never want to be ahead of you. With love, I can be bold. With thrift, I can be generous. With humility, I can be trusted. These days, people scorn compassion and try to be tough; they spend all they have, yet want to be generous; they despise humility and want to be the best. This is the way of death. In the long run, love will be victorious. Heaven will be its protection.

71 To know without thinking we know is the highest attainment. Not to know while thinking we do know is a disease. It is by being pained at the thought of this disease that we are preserved from it.

Chapter 5 – Siddhartha Gautama
The Four Noble Truths

1. It is noble to realize that suffering is an integral part of life, involved in birth, in ageing and sickness, in death and loss, in parting from loved ones, and in longing for that which we do not have. It is therefore noble to be aware of the world's afflictions and to be compassionate.

2. It is noble to acknowledge that the key causes of suffering and sorrows are our passions: desire, lust, craving, selfishness, greed and attachment to material things.

3. It is possible to rise above suffering and achieve enlightenment by overcoming such passions. This is the way that will allow us to deal with the world's afflictions and to strive towards attaining better state of mind (Nirvana) and hence a better world.

4. Nirvana can be attained by keeping to The Middle Way, between the extremes of the pursuit of wealth and living as an ascetic, and by following the Noble Eightfold Path of

(i) right views and understanding
(ii) right thoughts and intentions
(iii) right speech
(iv) right action
(v) right livelihood
(vi) right effort
(vii) right awareness, mindfulness and watchfulness
(viii) right concentration, contemplation and meditation.

The Dhammapada

146 How can there be laughter, how can there be pleasure, when the whole world is burning? When you are in deep darkness, will you not ask for a lamp?

151 The glorious chariots of kings wear out; and the body wears out and grows old, but the virtue of the good never grows old and can therefore teach the truth.

273-5 The best of all truths are the Four Noble Truths. The best of states is freedom from passion. The best of all people are those who see. The best of all ways is the Noble Eightfold Path. There is no other that leads to enlightenment. Whoever goes this Way travels to the end of sorrow.

(i) Right Views and Understanding

1 What we are today comes from our thoughts of yesterday. Our present thoughts build our life of tomorrow. If we speak or act with impure minds, suffering follows, just as the wheel of the cart follows the beast that draws the cart.

2 Speak or act with a pure mind, and joy follows you as surely as your shadow.

6 Many do not know that we are here in this world to live in harmony. Those

who know this do not fight against each other.

45 The wise student can overcome the worlds of pain and death, and find the Way, even as one who seeks flowers can find the most beautiful flower.

46 One who knows that his body is as the foam of a wave, the shadow of a mirage, breaks the sharp arrows of evil concealed in the flowers of sensual passion.

(ii) Right Thoughts and Intentions

33 The mind is wavering and restless, difficult to guard and restrain. Let the wise straighten their minds as arrowsmiths straighten their arrows.

34 Like a fish on dry land, the mind strives and struggles to get free from the power of evil.

35-6 The mind is invisible and subtle, fickle and flighty. It flies after fancies wherever it likes. Let the wise guard their minds, for a mind well guarded is a source of great joy.

37-9 Those who set their minds in harmony become free from the bonds of death. Those whose minds are unsteady, who don't know the Way, whose faith and peace are ever wavering, shall never reach the fullness of wisdom, but those whose minds, in calm self-control, are free from passion, are awake and have conquered fear.

40-1 The body is frail, like a jar, and will soon lie lifeless on the earth, cast aside like a useless log, so the mind must be strong to fight the great fight against evil temptations. After victory, guard your conquests well and stay forever watchful.

42 One who hates can harm others, but one's own mind, if wrongly directed, can do far greater harm.

5 Hate is not conquered by hate. Hate is conquered by love. This is an eternal law.

3 In those who harbor such thoughts as, "He abused me. He struck me. He overcame me. He robbed me," hatred never ceases. It comes to an end through non-violence. We overcome anger by loving kindness, evil by good, miserliness with generosity, lies with truth.

233 Watch for anger of the mind. Let your mind be self-controlled. Hurt not with your mind, but use your mind well.

50 Don't think of the faults of others, of what they have done or not done. Think rather of your own sins, of the things you have done or not done.

253 If one sees the sins of others and forever thinks of their faults, one's own sins increase forever and far off is he from the end of his faults.

63 If a fool can see his own folly, then, in this at least, he is wise, but the fool who thinks he is wise is indeed the real fool.

70 A fool may fast month after month, yet be worth only a fraction of a wise man whose thoughts feed on the truth.

74 "Let people think it was I who did that work and let them ask me what they should do or not do." These are the thoughts of a fool, puffed up with pride and desire.

285 (i) Pluck out your vanity as you would pluck out a faded lotus in autumn.

81 Just as a great rock is unaffected by the wind, a wise man is unaffected by praise or blame.

283-4 Cut down the forest of desires, not just one tree, for danger lies in this forest. As long as desires are not controlled the mind is not free, but is bound like a calf tied to a cow.

340 The creeper of craving grows everywhere. If you see the creeper grow, cut off its roots by the power of wisdom.

347 Those who are slaves to their cravings run to the forest of desires just as a spider runs to its web. Those who cut the fetters and follow the Way will attain enlightenment.

(iii) Right Speech

83 (ii) The holy don't spend idle words on matters of desire.

100 A single word that gives peace is better than a thousand words that don't.

101 A single verse that gives peace is better than a thousand verses that don't.

102 A single poem that gives peace is better than a thousand poems that don't.

133 Never speak harsh words. Once spoken, they may return to you. Angry words are painful and there may be blows for blows.

176 If a man lies, transgresses the great law and scorns the higher world, there is no evil he may not do.

224 Speak the truth. Yield not to anger. Give what you can to those who ask.

232 Watch for anger of words. Let your words be self-controlled. Hurt not with words, but use your words well.

258 Those who talk and talk again are not wise. The wise are peaceful, loving and fearless.

(iv) Right Action

116-9 Make haste and do what is good. This will keep your mind away from evil. One who is slow to do good will find pleasure in evil, and the accumulation of wrongdoings will be painful. Find joy in good work, for the accumulation of good work is joyful, but when the fruit of evil ripens, it is evil indeed.

84 One who does not crave power or wealth, or put material success before righteousness, is virtuous and wise.

91 Those who have high thoughts are ever striving. They are not happy to remain in the same place. Like swans that leave their lake and rise into the air, they leave their home for a higher home.

7-8 Those who live only for pleasure and whose souls are not in harmony, who don't consider the food they eat, are idle and without virtue, are easily moved by selfish temptations, even as a weak tree is shaken by the wind; but those who don't live for pleasure alone, whose souls are in harmony, who eat or fast in moderation, and have faith and the power of virtue, are not moved by temptation, even as a great rock is not shaken by the wind.

27 Never surrender to carelessness. Never sink into weak pleasures and lust. Those who are watchful, in deep contemplation, reach, in the end, the joy supreme.

69-73 A wrong action seems sweet to the fool until the reaction comes and brings pain. The bitter fruits have then to be eaten by the fool. The action may not bring its reaction at once, even as fresh milk turns not sour at once, but, like a smoldering fire, concealed under its ashes, it consumes the wrongdoer – and, if he increases the cleverness of his deception, wishing for reputation, precedence, authority or veneration, the fool eventually destroys his mind and makes his fate even worse than it would have been.

76 Look to the one who tells you your faults as if telling of a hidden treasure, the wise one who tells you of the dangers of life. Follow and you

will see good, not evil.

103-5 If one man conquers thousands in battle and another conquers his desire, the latter has achieved the greater victory. Nothing can overturn the victory of such a man.

121-2 Do not underestimate the evil effect of a sin, thinking, "This is little to me." Just as falling drops of water will in time fill a jar, so the fool becomes full of evil.

129 (ii) Do not kill or cause to kill.

167 Do not live a low life. Do not follow wrong ideas. Do not sink into the world.

177 The noble find joy in generosity.

185 Do not hurt by words or deeds.

211-2 Do not become addicted to pleasure, for its loss will bring pain. There are no fetters for those who rise above pleasure and pain. They are free from fear and sorrow.

221 Forsake anger. Give up pride. Sorrow cannot touch those who are not in bondage to anything.

222 One who can control rising anger as a coachman controls his carriage at full speed is as a good driver; others merely hold the reins.

223 Overcome anger by peacefulness. Overcome evil by good. Overcome meanness by generosity and those who lie by truth.

231 (ii) Hurt not with your body, but use your body well.

239 Remove impurities from yourself as the silversmith removes impurities from silver – one after one, little by little, again and again.

246-8 One who destroys life, who utters lies, who takes what is not given, who goes to another's wife, who gets drunk, digs up the very roots of life. Lack of self-control means wrongdoing. Watch that greed and vice do not bring you long suffering.

251 There is no fire like that of lust. There are no chains like those of hatred. There is no net like that of illusion. There is no rushing torrent like that of desire.

256-7. Do not attempt to settle matters in violent haste. Calmly consider what is right and what is wrong. Face differing opinions with truth, non-violence and peace.

282 Spiritual yoga leads to light. Lack of yoga leads to darkness. Walk the path that leads to light.

314 It is better to do nothing than to do what is wrong, for wrongdoing brings burning sorrow. Do only what is right, for good deeds never bring pain.

328-30 If, on the journey of life, you can find a wise and intelligent friend who is good and self-controlled, go with that traveler, and in joy and recollection, overcome the dangers of the journey. Otherwise, travel alone, for this is better than to take a fool as a companion.

(v) Right Livelihood

49 As the bee takes the nectar from a flower and flies away without destroying its beauty and perfume, so let the wise wander in the world.

53 There is much good work to be done in a lifetime, just as there are many garlands and wreaths to be made from beautiful flowers.

51-2 The beautiful words of those who live by them are like flowers with beautiful color and perfume; but the words of those who speak them, but do not live by them are fruitless, just as the seed of a beautiful flower that has no pollen.

55 The sandalwood, rose, lotus and jasmine flowers have beautiful perfumes, but far above the perfume of flowers is the perfume of virtue. The perfume of virtue is supreme.

54-6 The perfumes of flowers do not travel far, but the perfume of virtue reaches all round the world; the perfume of virtue reaches Heaven.

64-5 Fools can live among the wise all their lives but never know the path of wisdom, just as a spoon never knows the taste of soup; but those who watch and see will soon know the path of wisdom, just as they know they taste of soup.

136 When fools do evil work, they forget that they are lighting fires wherein they must burn one day.

158-9 First find the truth then teach it to others. Make yourself as good as you tell others to be. Stay aware of the difficulty of self-control.

263 Uproot envy, greed and deceit. Practice love and compassion.

266 Accept the law of righteousness. Reject the law of the flesh.

270 It is not great to be a warrior and kill others; but only to avoid hurting others.

304-5 The good shine from far away like the Himalayan Mountains; but the wicked are in darkness, like arrows thrown in the night. One who can be alone and rest alone and who is never weary of great work can live in joy, beyond the forest of desires.

331-3 It is sweet to have friends in need, to share enjoyment, to do good before death, to surrender all pain. It is sweet in this world to be a mother, a father, a monk, or a saintly person. It is sweet to enjoy a virtuous life; a pure, firm faith. It is sweet to attain wisdom and to be free from sin.

(vi) Right Effort

112 A single day lived with courage and powerful striving is better than a hundred years lived in idleness and weakness.

276 It is you who must make the effort. The great of the past only show the way. Those who think and follow the path become free from bondage.

313 When you have something to do, do it with all your might and concentration. A thoughtless pilgrim only raises dust on the path – the dust of dangerous desires.

280 If the young and strong do not rise and strive when they should, and thus sink into laziness and lack of determination, they will not find the path to wisdom.

289 Those who are virtuous and wise will understand the truth then strive with all their might to follow the path to Nirvana.

325 Those who are lazy and gluttonous, who eat large meals, then roll in sleep, who are like pigs fed in the sty, these fools are reborn to a life of death.

(vii) Right Awareness, Mindfulness and Watchfulness

113 Considering for one day how all things arise and pass away is better than a hundred years without considering how all things arise and pass away.

21 Watchfulness is the way of immortality. Negligence is the path of death. Those who are watchful are alive. Those who are not are already as dead.

22 Those who with a clear mind have seen this truth. Those who are wise and ever watchful feel the joy of watchfulness, the joy of the way of the great.

25 By arising in faith and watchfulness, by self-control and self-harmony, the wise make an island for the soul that no waters can overflow.

26 Those who are foolish and ignorant are never watchful, but those who live in watchfulness consider it their greatest treasure.

29 Watchful among the unwatchful, awake among those who sleep, the wise, like swift horses, outrun those who are slow.

13 Passions break in to an ill-guarded mind, just as rain breaks in to a badly thatched house.

233 (i) Watch for anger of the mind. Let your mind be self-controlled.

232 (i) Watch for anger of words. Let your words be self-controlled.

231 (i) Watch for anger of the body. Let the body be self-controlled.

293 For those who are ever careful of their actions, who are watchful and wise, sinful desires come to an end.

297-300 The followers of the Buddha are awake and forever watch and, ever by night and day, they remember the teaching of the Buddha, the truth of the law, the holy brotherhood and the mystery of the body, and find joy in love for all beings.

327 Find joy in watchfulness. Guard your mind well. Uplift yourself from your lower self, even as an elephant lifts itself from a muddy swamp.

334 For those who watch not for Nirvana, cravings grow like creepers; and they jump from death to death, like monkeys in a forest jump from one tree without fruit to another.

(viii) Right Concentration, Contemplation and Meditation

111 A single day of life lived in wisdom and deep contemplation is better than a hundred years lived in ignorance and without contemplation.

249-50 If you can uproot and burn away all jealousies, then you can achieve supreme contemplation.

134 If you can achieve contemplation with the silence of a broken gong, you have reached the peace of Nirvana and your anger is in peace.

301 The followers of the Buddha are awake and forever watch, and ever by

night and day, they find joy in supreme contemplation.

Chapter 6 – Jesus

Love the Lord your God with all your heart and with all your soul and with all your mind. This is the first and greatest commandment. And the second is like it: Love your neighbor as yourself. All the Law and the prophets hang on these two commandments.[7]

You are the salt of the Earth. Salt is good, but if it loses its saltiness, how can you make it salty again? Have salt in yourselves and be at peace with each other. Watch yourselves. If your brother sins, rebuke him, and if he repents, forgive him. If he sins against you seven times in a day and seven times comes back to you and repents, forgive him[8].

You are the light of the world. Let your light shine before men, that they may see your good deeds and praise your Father in Heaven.

Be careful not to do acts of righteousness before men simply in order to be seen. When you give to the needy, do not announce it with trumpets, to be honored by men. When you give to the needy, do not let your left hand know what your right hand is doing, so that your giving may be in secret.

When you fast, do not look somber as the hypocrites do. Put oil on you head and wash your face, so that it will not be obvious that you are fasting, except to your Father, who is unseen.

Settle matters quickly with an adversary who would take you to court. Do it while you are still with him on the way.

If your right eye would cause you to sin, gouge it out and throw it away; or if your right hand would cause you to sin, cut it off and throw it away; it is better for you to lose a part of your body than for your whole body to be thrown into torment.

Do not swear by Heaven, for it is God's throne, or by Earth, for it is God's footstool. Simply let your yes be yes and your no be no.

Do not resist an evil person. If someone strikes you on the right cheek, turn to him the other also. If someone wants to sue you and take your tunic, let him take your cloak as well. If someone forces you to go one mile, go with him two miles. Give to the one who asks you, and do not turn away from the one who wants to borrow from you.

Love your enemies and pray for those who persecute you, that you may be sons of your Father in Heaven.

Do not store up for yourselves treasures on Earth, where moths and rust destroy, and where thieves break in and steal; but store up for yourselves treasures in Heaven, where moths and rust do not destroy, and where thieves do not break in and steal; for where your treasure is, there your heart will be also.

No one can serve two masters. Either he will hate the one and love the other, or he will be devoted to one and despise the other. You cannot serve both God and money.

Do not worry about your life – what you will eat, drink or wear. Isn't life more important than food, and the body more important than clothes? Look at the birds of the air. They do not sow or reap or store away in barns, and yet your heavenly Father feeds them. Are you not much more valuable than they? Who of you by worrying can add a single hour to his life? And why do you worry about clothes? See how the lilies of the field grow. They do not labor or spin; yet I tell you that not even Solomon in all his splendor was dressed like one of these, which is here today and thrown into the fire tomorrow. Will God not much more clothe you? So do not worry, saying, "What shall we eat? What shall we drink? What shall we wear?" for the pagans run after all these things, and your heavenly Father knows that you need them; but seek first His Kingdom and righteousness. Do not worry about tomorrow. Today has enough worries of its own.

Do not judge, or you too will be judged; for in the same way you judge others, you too will be judged. Why do you look at the speck of sawdust in your brother's eye and pay no attention to the plank in your own eye. How can you say to your brother, "Let me take the speck out of your eye," when all the time there is a plank in your own eye? First take the plank out of your own eye then you will see clearly to remove the speck from your brother's eye.

Do not give dogs what is sacred; do not throw your pearls to pigs; if you do, they may trample them underfoot, then turn and tear you to pieces.

Ask and it will be given; seek and you will find; knock and the door will be opened.

Do unto others what you would have them do to you.

Enter through the narrow gate, for wide is the gate that leads to destruction, and many enter through it; but small is the gate and narrow the road that leads to life, and only a few find it.

Watch out for false prophets. They come to you in sheep's clothing, but inwardly they are ferocious wolves. By their fruit you will recognize them. Do people pick grapes from thorn bushes?

Do not be afraid of those who kill the body, but cannot kill the soul, rather be afraid of the One that can destroy both soul and body in hell. Are not two sparrows sold for a penny? Yet not one of them will fall to the ground apart from the will of your Father, and even the hairs of your head are numbered, so don't be afraid at all; you are worth more than many sparrows.

What God has joined together (in marriage), let man not separate.

What good will it be for a man if he gains the whole world, but forfeits his soul?

Be perfect, as your heavenly Father is perfect.

If you want to be perfect, go, sell your possessions and give to the poor, and you will have treasure in Heaven.

Give to Caesar what is Caesar's and to God what is God's.[9]

Whoever wants to be great among you must be your servant, and whoever wants to be first must be your slave.

Watch out! Be on your guard against all kinds of greed; a man's life does not consist of the abundance of his possessions. Be careful, or your hearts will be weighed down with dissipation, drunkenness and the anxieties of life.[10]

Watch out for the teachers of the law. They like to walk around in flowing robes and be greeted in the market places, and have the most important seats in the synagogues and the places of honor in banquets. They devour widows' houses and for show make lengthy prayers.[11]

When you are brought before synagogues, rulers and authorities, do not worry about how you will defend yourselves or what you will say, for the Holy Spirit will teach you what to say at that time.[12]

He, who has ears to hear, let him hear.[13]

Repent, for the Kingdom of Heaven is near.[14]

Be dressed and keep your lamps burning.[15]

Any of you who does not give up everything he has, cannot be my disciple.[16]

Chapter 7 – Muhammad

4.1 Men, have fear of your Lord who created you from a single soul (Adam); from that soul, God created woman (Eve) and, through them, filled the Earth with men and women.

14.11 God's grace is bestowed on those God chooses.

47.38 You are called upon to give to the cause of God. Some of you are ungenerous, yet whoever is ungenerous to this cause is ungenerous to himself. Indeed, God does not need you. It is you who need God.

57.22 Every misfortune that befalls the Earth is pre-ordained, so you should not grieve for the good things you miss or be overjoyed by what you gain. God does not respect the haughty, the vainglorious or those who, being niggardly themselves, enjoin others to be niggardly also. God alone is self-sufficient and worthy of praise.

76.2 God created man from the union of the two sexes in order to test him. God endowed him with sight and hearing, and, be he thankful or oblivious of God's favors, God has shown him the right path.

90.1 God created man to test him with afflictions.

2.190 Fight for the sake of God those who fight against you, but do not attack them first. God does not love the aggressors.

2.24 Proclaim good tidings to those who have faith and do good works.[4]

2.195 Be charitable. God loves the charitable.

2.271 To be charitable in public is good, but to give alms to the poor in private is better.

2.213 Mankind was once one nation.

4.86 If a man greets you, return his greeting.

4.114 Enjoin charity, kindness and peace among men.

6.106 Do not revile their idols, lest they in their ignorance should spitefully revile God.

6.159 Have nothing to do with those who have split us into sects.

6.165 God has given us the Earth for our heritage and exalted some of us above others only to test us. Swift is the Lord in retribution, yet forgiving and merciful.

7.35 God has forbidden all indecent acts, whether overt or disguised: both sin and oppression.

8.25 Guard yourselves against temptation.

8.27 Your worldly goods are but a temptation.

8.46 Have patience. God is with those who are patient.

8.61 If your enemies incline to peace, make peace with them, and put your trust in God.

8.73 Give aid to one another. If you do not, there will be persecution in the land and great corruption.

10.24 God invites you to the Home of Peace.

10.49 Only by the will of God do we acquire benefits and avert evil.

11.2 & 17.39 Serve none but God.

16.50 You shall not serve two gods, for God is but one God. Revere none but God.

16.78 God brought you out of your mothers' wombs devoid of all knowledge, and gave you ears and eyes and hearts, so that you may give thanks.

16.90 God enjoins justice, kindness and charity to one's kindred and forbids indecency, wickedness and oppression.

16.91 Keep faith with God. Do not break your oaths.

16.124 Call men to the path of your Lord with wisdom and kindly exhortation. Reason with them in the most courteous manner.

17.23 Show kindness to your parents. If either or both of them attain old age within your dwelling, show them no sign of impatience and do not rebuke them. Speak kind words to them. Treat them with humility and tenderness. Say, "Lord, be merciful to them. They nursed me when I was an infant."

4.1 Honor the mothers who bore you.

17.25 Give your near of kin their due. Give also to the destitute and to wayfarers, but do not squander your substance wastefully. If you lack the means to assist them, at least speak to them kindly. Be neither miserly nor prodigal.

4.2 Give orphans the property that belongs to them. Do not exchange their valuables for worthless things or cheat them. Do not deprive them of their property by squandering it before they come of age.

4.4 Give women their dowry as a free gift.[5]

4.5 Do not give the feeble-minded the property with which you have been entrusted for their support, but maintain and clothe them with its proceeds and give them good advice.

4.7 Men and women shall share in what their parents and kinsfolk leave.

17.31 Do not kill your children for fear of want.

17.32 Do not commit adultery, for it is foul and indecent.

17.33 Do not kill any man, except for a just cause.[6]

17.34 Do not interfere with the property of orphans, except with the best of motives.

17.35 Give full measure and weigh with even scales.

17.36 Do not follow what you do not know.

17.37 Do not walk proudly on the Earth. You cannot cleave the Earth nor rival the mountains in stature.

17.53 Be courteous in your speech.

18.23 Do not say of anything, "I will do it tomorrow," without adding, "God willing."

24.24 Let the rich and powerful among you swear[7] not to withhold their gifts from their kindred, the poor, and those who have left their homes for the cause of God.

24.27-29 Do not enter the dwellings of others until you have asked their permission and wished them peace. If you find no one there, do not enter until you are given leave. If this is refused, it is right that you should go away. It shall be no offence for you to seek shelter in empty dwellings. God knows what you hide and what you reveal.

24.30 Enjoin believing men to turn their eyes away from temptation and to restrain their carnal desires. This will make their lives purer.

24.31 Enjoin believing women to turn their eyes away from temptation and to preserve their chastity; to cover their adornments, except such as are normally displayed.[8]

24.53 Your obedience rather than your oaths will count. God has cognizance of all your actions.

28.77 Be good to others as God has been good to you.

30.30 Stand firm in your devotion to the true faith, the upright nature with which God has endowed us.

30.33 Do not split up religion into sects, each exulting in its own beliefs.

31.17 Endure with fortitude all that befalls you. This is a duty incumbent on all. Do not treat men with scorn, nor walk proudly on the earth. Let your gait be modest and your voice low. The harshest of voices is the braying of the ass.

39.56 Follow the best of what is revealed to you without arrogance.

39.72 The dwelling place of the arrogant is evil.

42.15 Call men to the true faith, and follow the straight path as you are bidden. Do not be led by their desires. Say, "God will bring us all together."

50.55 Do not use force against them [people who disagree with you].

49.11 Do not mock one another, defame one another, or call one another nicknames.

49.12 Avoid immoderate suspicion. Do not spy on one another or backbite one another, but get to know one another.

51.51 Set up no other god but God.

55.5 Give just weight and full measure.

57.8 Put your trust in God, so that God may lead you out of darkness into the light.

61.2 It is most odious in God's sight that you should say one thing and do another.

68.6 Give no heed to the disbelievers, nor yield to the wretch of many oaths, the mischief-making slanderer, the opponent of good, the wicked transgressor, the bully.

73.3 Remember the name of the Lord and dedicate yourself to God utterly. Accept God as your Protector and leave to God those who deny the truth.

74.1 Magnify your Lord. Cleanse your garments and keep away from all pollution. Bestow no favors where you expect in return more than you have given.

76.20 Your high endeavors are gratifying to God. Do not yield to the wicked and unbelieving.

76.29 Let those that will take the right path to the Lord.

84.25 Proclaim to all a woeful doom, save those who embrace the true faith and do good works.

93.11 Do not wrong the orphan, nor chide the beggar, but proclaim the goodness of the Lord.

94.8 When your task is ended, resume your toil and seek your Lord with all fervor.

2.219 There is great harm in drinking and gambling. Their harm is far greater than their benefit.

2.241 Reasonable provision should be made for divorced women. This is incumbent on righteous men.[9]

2.275 God permits trading, but forbids usury.

42.43 To endure with fortitude and to forgive are duties incumbent on all.

45.19 God has set you on the right path. Follow it and do not yield to the lust of ignorant men, for they can in no way protect you from the wrath of God. Wrongdoers are patrons to each other but the righteous have God for their patron.

Chapter 8 – Nanak Dev

Air is the vital force. Water is the progenitor. Earth is the mother of all. Day and night are nurses, fondling all creation. Air gives us mobility and liberty. Water gives us purity and cleanliness. Earth instills patience and love. The sky teaches us of equality and broad-mindedness.[6]

If we remember God, we live. If we forget God, we die.[7]

Let no man be proud because of his caste. The man who has God in his heart, he, no other, is the true Brahmin, so, O fool, do not be vainglorious about your caste, for vainglory leads to most of the mind's evils. Though they say there are four castes, one God created us all; all of us are molded of the same clay. The Great Potter has merely varied our shapes. All of us are made of the same elements. No one can reduce an element in one or increase it in another.[8]

Out of the cotton of compassion, spin the thread of contentment; tie the knot of continence and the twist of virtue. Make such a sacred thread, O Pundit, for your inner self.[9]

Let compassion be your mosque. Let faith be your prayer mat. Let honest living be your Koran. Let modesty be the rule of observance. Let piety be the fast you keep. In such wisdom try to become a muslim [i.e. one who is at peace with God, rather than traditional Muslim]. Let right conduct be your Kaba [after the

Muslim House of God in Mecca]. Let submission to God's will be your rosary. If you do these things, the Lord will be your protector.[10]

Pilgrimages, penances, compassion and alms-giving bring a little merit, the size of a sesame seed, but one who hears and believes and loves God shall bathe and be made clean in a place of pilgrimage within.[11]

Of woman we are born, of woman conceived, to woman engaged, to woman married. Woman we befriend. By woman is civilization continued. When woman dies, woman is sought. It is by woman that order is maintained. From woman is woman born. And without woman, no one would exist.[12]

If you believe in pollution at birth, there is pollution everywhere. There are creatures in cow-dung and wood. There is life in each grain of corn. Water is the source of life, the sap for all things. Then how can one escape pollution? Pollution pollutes only the ignorant. The pollution of the mind is greed. The pollution of the tongue is lying. The pollution of the eyes is to look with covetousness upon another's wealth, upon another's wife, and upon the beauty of another's woman. The pollution of the ears is to listen to slander. The pollution in which people commonly believe is all superstition. Birth and death are by divine will. Those who arrive at the truth are untouched by pollution.[13]

One may read for years and years and spend every month of the year in reading only, and thus read all one's life, right up to one's last breath. Of all things, a contemplative life is what really matters. All else is the fret and fever of egoistic minds.[14]

Chapter 9 – Mirza Husain Ali Nuri

H11 Get your radiance from God and seek none other than God, for God has created you rich and has bountifully shed favor upon you.

G24 A drop of the billowing ocean of God's endless mercy has adorned all creation with the ornament of existence and a breath wafted from God's peerless paradise has invested all beings with the robe of God's sanctity and glory. A sprinkling from the unfathomed deep of God's sovereign and all-pervasive will has, out of utter nothingness, called into being a creation which is infinite in its range and deathless in its duration. The wonders of God's bounty can never cease and the stream of God's merciful grace can never be arrested. The process of God's creation had no beginning and can have no end.

G27 God chose to confer upon mankind the unique distinction and capacity to know and to love God – a capacity that must be regarded as the generating impulse and the primary purpose underlying the whole of creation.

G38 The light of divine revelation has been vouchsafed to men in direct proportion to their spiritual capacity. Consider the sun: how feeble its rays the moment it appears above the horizon; how gradually its warmth and potency increase as it approaches its zenith, enabling all created things to adapt themselves to the growing intensity of its light. Were it to manifest its energies suddenly, it would cause injury to all created things. In like manner, if the sun of truth were suddenly to reveal the full measure of its potency, human understanding would be consumed, for men's hearts would neither be able to sustain the intensity of its revelation nor to mirror forth the radiance of its light.

G3 O you lovers of the one true God! Strive that you may truly recognize and know God and observe befittingly God's precepts.

G4 It is incumbent upon all the peoples of the world to reconcile their differences and, with perfect unity and peace, abide beneath the shadow of the tree of God's care and loving kindness.

G5 Now is the time to cheer and refresh the downcast through the invigorating breeze of love and fellowship and the living waters of friendliness and charity. Show forbearance and benevolence and love to one another. Should any one among you be incapable of grasping a certain truth, or be striving to comprehend it, show forth when conversing with him, a spirit of extreme kindliness and goodwill. Help him to see and recognize the truth, without esteeming yourself to be in the least superior to him, or to be possessed of greater endowments. Every eye should seek what will best promote the cause of God. Nothing whatever can inflict a greater harm than dissension and strife, contention, estrangement and apathy, among the loved ones of God. Strive to knit together the hearts of men, in God's name, the Unifier, the All-knowing, the All-wise.

G43 Arise, O people, and, by the power of God, resolve to gain victory over your selfish desires, that haply the whole Earth may be sanctified and freed from its servitude to the gods of its idle fancies – gods that have inflicted such loss upon, and are responsible for the misery of, their wretched worshippers. These idols are the obstacles that impede us in our efforts to advance upon the path of perfection. O people of God, do not busy yourselves in your own concerns; let your thoughts be fixed upon that which will rehabilitate the fortunes of mankind and sanctify the hearts and souls of men. This can best be achieved through pure and holy deeds, through a virtuous life and goodly behavior. Valiant acts will ensure the triumph of the cause and a saintly character will reinforce its power. It is incumbent upon every man to hold fast unto whatsoever will promote the interests and exalt the station of all nations and just governments. O people of justice, be as brilliant as the light and as splendid as the fire that blazed in the burning bush. The brightness of the fire of your love will no doubt fuse and unify the contending peoples of the Earth, whilst the flame of enmity and hatred cannot but result in strife and ruin.

G52 Depend not on the sight of anyone except yourself, for God has never burdened any soul beyond its power.

G66 Beware that you do not swell with pride before God and reject His loved ones. Lay not on any soul a load which you would not wish to be laid upon you, and do not wish on anyone the things you would not wish for yourself. Return to God and repent, that He through His grace, may have mercy upon you, may wash away your sins and forgive your trespasses.

G72 Cast away that which you possess and, on the wings of detachment, soar beyond all created things. Beware lest the desires of the flesh and of a corrupt inclination provoke divisions among you. Be as the fingers of one hand, the members of one body.

G76 Meditate diligently upon the purpose of the Lord. Strive to know God directly and not through others.

G77 We have all been created in the nature made by God; each of us prescribed a pre-ordained measure. All that we potentially possess can, however, be manifested only as a result of our own volition.

G96 Don't be careless of the virtues with which you have been endowed, neither be neglectful of your high destiny. Don't suffer your labors to be wasted through the vain imaginations that certain hearts have devised. You are the stars of the heaven of understanding, the breeze that stirs at the break of day, the soft flowing waters on which other lives depend, the letters inscribed upon God's sacred scroll. With the utmost unity and in a spirit of perfect fellowship, exert yourselves that you may be able to achieve that which becomes this day of God. Strife and dissension are entirely unworthy. Center your energies in the propagation of faith in God. Whoever is worthy of so high a calling, arise and promote it. Whoever are unable have a duty to appoint those who will.

G100 It is incumbent upon you to summon all to whatsoever shall sanctify them from all attachment to the things of the Earth and purge them of all its defilements, so that the sweet smell of the raiment of the All-glorious may be smelled from all them that love. You who have riches must have the utmost regard for the poor, for great is the honor destined by God for those poor who are steadfast in patience. There is no honor apart from that which God bestows. Great is the blessedness awaiting the poor that endure patiently and endure their sufferings, and well is it with the rich who bestow their riches on the needy and prefer them before themselves. Please God, may the poor exert themselves and strive to earn the means of livelihood. Equity is the most fundamental among human values. The evaluation of all things depends on it. Observe equity in your judgment.

G106 Every age has its own problems and every soul its particular aspirations. Be anxiously concerned with the needs of the age you live in and center your deliberations on its exigencies and requirements. Arise and lift up your voices that they who are asleep may be awakened. Say, "You who are as dead, the Hand of divine bounty proffers to you the water of life. Hasten and drink your fill. Whoever is reborn shall never die. Whoever remains dead shall never live."

G107 How great the felicity that awaits the man that forsakes all he has in a desire to strive for God.

G109 To act like the beasts of the field is unworthy of man. Those virtues that befit his dignity are forbearance, mercy, compassion and loving kindness towards all the peoples and kindred of the Earth.

G110 The fundamental purpose animating faith in God is to safeguard the interests and promote the unity of the human race, to foster the spirit of love and fellowship among men and not to allow religion to become a source of dissension and discord, of hate and enmity. This is the straight path, the fixed and immovable foundation. The world can never impair its strength, nor the revolutions of countless centuries undermine its structure. Our hope is that the world's rulers and religious leaders will arise in unison for the reformation of this age and the rehabilitation of its fortunes. Let them, after meditating on its needs, take counsel together and, through full and earnest deliberation, administer to a diseased and sorely afflicted world the remedy it requires. It is incumbent on those in authority to exercise moderation in all things.

G111 O contending peoples and kindred of the Earth! Set your faces towards unity and let the radiance of its light shine upon you. Gather together and, for the sake of God, resolve to root out whatever is the source of contention amongst you. Then will the effulgence of the world's great Luminary envelop the whole Earth and its inhabitants become the citizens of one city. There can be no doubt whatever that the peoples of the world, of whatever race or religion, derive their inspiration from one heavenly source and are the subjects of one God. The difference between the ordinances under which they should abide should be attributed to the varying requirements and exigencies of the age in which they were revealed. All of them, except a few that were the outcome of human perversity, were ordained of God and are a reflection of God's will and purpose. Arise and, armed with the power of faith, shatter to pieces the gods of your vain imaginings, the sowers of dissension amongst you. Cling to what draws you together and unites you. This is the most exalted word. To this bears witness the Tongue of grandeur from His habitation of glory.

G112 Don't regard each other as strangers. You are the fruits of one tree; the leaves of one branch.

G113 Don't follow, under any condition, the promptings of your evil desires. Keep the law of God, your Lord, the Beneficent, the Ancient of days.

G118 Be vigilant, that you may not do injustice to anyone. Tread the path of justice, for this is the straight path. Resolve your differences and reduce your armaments, that the burden of your expenditures may be lightened, and that your minds and hearts may be tranquil. Heal the dissensions that divide you, and you will no longer need any armaments, except what the protection of your cities and territories demand. Beware not to deal unjustly with anyone who appeals to you and enters beneath your shadow. Know that the poor are the trust of God in your midst. Watch that you don't betray God's trust and that you don't walk the ways of the treacherous.

G119 Rulers of the Earth, don't lay excessive burdens on your peoples. Do not rob them to rear palaces for yourselves; nay, rather choose for them that which you choose for yourselves. Be reconciled among yourselves, that you may need no more armaments. Be united, for thereby will the tempest of discord be stilled, and your peoples find rest. Should any one among you take up arms against another, rise you all up against him, for this is naught other than manifest justice.

G120 Elected representatives of the people in every land, take counsel together and let your concern be only for that which profits mankind. Regard the world as the human body that, though at its creation whole and perfect, has been afflicted with grave disorders and maladies. The Lord has ordained that the sovereign remedy and the mightiest instrument for the healing of the world is the union of all its peoples in one universal cause, one common faith.

G122 Regard man as a mine rich in gems of inestimable value. Education can cause it to reveal its treasures and enable man to benefit therefrom.

G125 When a true seeker determines to take the step of search on the path leading to knowledge of God, he must, before all else, cleanse his heart, which is the seat of the revelation of the inner mysteries of God, from the obscuring dust of all acquired knowledge and the illusions of the embodiments of satanic fancy. He must purge his breast, which is the sanctuary of the abiding love of God, of every defilement. He must sanctify his soul from all that pertains to water and clay – from all shadowy and ephemeral attachments. He must so cleanse his heart that no remnant of either desire or hate may linger therein, lest that desire blindly incline him to error, or that hate repel him from the truth. Witness that most people, because of such desire and hate, bereft of the immortal Face, have strayed far and, shepherdless, are roaming through the wilderness of oblivion and error. The seeker must at all times put his trust in God, must detach himself from the world of dust and cling to God. He must never seek to exalt himself above anyone. He must wash away from the tablet of his heart every trace of pride and vainglory. He must cling to patience and resignation. He must observe silence and refrain from idle talk, for the tongue is a smoldering fire, and excess of speech a deadly poison. Material fire consumes the body, but the fire of the tongue devours both heart and soul. The seeker should regard backbiting as serious error; it quenches the light of the heart and extinguishes the life of the soul. The seeker should be content with little and be freed from all inordinate desire. At the dawn of every day, he should commune with God and, with all his soul, he should persevere in the quest of his Beloved. He should consume every wayward thought with the flame of God's loving mention. He should succor the dispossessed and never withhold his favor from the destitute. He should show kindness to animals and to his fellow men. He should not wish for others that which he does not wish for himself, nor promise that which he does not fulfill. He should forgive the sinful. He should regard all but God as transient and count all things but God as utter nothingness. These are among the attributes that constitute the hallmark of the spiritually minded.

G126 Be busied in whatever may be conducive to the betterment of the world and the education of its peoples. Cling to the cause of God. Revive the world, ennoble its life and regenerate its peoples. Outward conduct is but a reflection of inward life and inward life a mirror of outward conduct. No veil hides or obscures the truth on which faith is established. One's acts attest the truth of these words.

G128 Eat of the good things that God has allowed you and don't deprive yourselves of God's wondrous bounties. Proclaim unto men the message of your Lord, that it may deter them from following the promptings of their evil and corrupt desires, and bring them to the remembrance of God. Whoever arises among you to teach the cause of the Lord, let him teach himself first, so that his words may attract those that hear him. Without this, his words will not attract the seeker. Take heed, O people, lest you be of those that give good counsel to others, but fail to follow it yourselves. Be fair to yourselves and to others, so that the evidence of justice may be revealed through your deeds. Beware, lest you contend with anyone, nay, strive to make him aware of the truth with kindly manner and most convincing exhortation. Dispute not with anyone concerning the things of this world and its affairs, for God has abandoned them to those that have set their affection upon them.

G132 The purpose of God in revealing Himself to men is to lay bare those gems that lie hidden within the mine of their true and inmost selves. That the diverse communities of the Earth and the manifold systems of religious belief should never be allowed to foster feelings of animosity among men is the essence of faith in God. Religious principles have proceeded from one source and are the rays of one light. The utterance of God is a lamp whose light is these words: You are the fruits of one tree, the leaves of one branch. Deal with each other with the utmost love and harmony, with friendliness and fellowship. So powerful is the light of unity that it can illuminate the whole Earth. Exert yourselves that you may attain this transcendent and most sublime station, the station that can ensure the protection and security of all mankind. This goal excels every other goal.

G136 Deliver your souls, O people, from the bondage of self and purify yourselves from all attachment to anything besides God. Remembrance of God cleanses all things from defilement. Sow not the seeds of dissension amongst men and contend not with your neighbor. Be patient under all conditions and place your whole trust and confidence in God. Unlock your hearts with the keys of remembrance of God. Beautify your tongues with truthfulness and adorn your souls with honesty.

G138 Cleanse yourselves thoroughly from the defilement of the world and all that pertains to it. These things of the Earth ill become you. Cast them away unto those that may desire them and fasten your eyes upon the most holy and effulgent vision. That which becomes you is the love of God. Let truthfulness and courtesy be your adorning. Beware lest you walk in the ways of those whose words differ from their deeds. Strive that you may be enabled to manifest to the peoples of the Earth the signs of God and to mirror forth his commandments. Let your acts be a guide unto all mankind, for the words of most men differ from their conduct. Through your deeds the brightness of your light can be shed upon the whole Earth.

G141 Walk not after the imaginings that the sowers of mischief have devised, they that commit wickedness and impute it to God.

G143 Walk steadfastly in the love of God and keep straight on in faith. If tribulation touches you for God's sake call to mind my (Mirza Husain Ali Nuri's) ills and troubles and remember my banishment and imprisonment.

G134 No act, however meritorious, can ever compare to steadfastness.

G144 Were you to consider this world and realize how fleeting are the things that pertain to it, you would choose to tread no path except the path of service to the cause of the Lord. O, you rich ones of the Earth! Flee not from the face of the poor that lie in the dust, nay rather befriend them and allow them to recount the tale of the woes with which God's inscrutable decree has forced him to be afflicted. Blessed are the learned that pride not themselves on their attainments and well is it with the righteous that mock not the sinful.

G146 Beware lest you prefer yourselves above your neighbors.

G151 Release yourselves, O nightingales of God, from the thorns and brambles of wretchedness and misery, and wing your flight to the garden of unfading splendor. O my friends that dwell upon the dust, hasten forth unto your celestial habitation.

G152 Be as resigned and submissive as the earth, so that from the soil of your being there may blossom the fragrant, holy and multicolored hyacinths of the knowledge of God. Be ablaze as the fire, that you may burn away the veils of heedlessness and set aglow, through the quickening energies of the love of God, the chilled and wayward heart. Be light and untrammeled as the breeze, that you may obtain admittance into the precincts of God's court, God's inviolable sanctuary.

G153 Quench the thirst of heedlessness with the sanctified waters of God's grace and chase away the gloom of remoteness through the morning light of God's divine presence. Don't be destroyed by the tyranny of covetous desires and the dust of self and passion. Clothe yourself with the essence of righteousness and let your heart be afraid of no one but God. Don't obstruct the luminous spring of your soul with the thorns and brambles of vain and inordinate affections or impede the flow of the living waters from the fountain of your heart. Set your hope in God and cling tenaciously to God's unfailing mercy. Let the flame of search burn within your heart so as to enable you to attain your supreme and most exalted goal – to be united with God.

G156 Address yourselves to the well-being and tranquility of the children of men. Bend your minds and wills to the education of the peoples and kindred of the Earth, that the dissensions that divide it may be blotted out from its face and all mankind become the upholders of one order and the inhabitants of one city. Illuminate and hallow your hearts; let them not be profaned by the thorns of hate or the thistles of malice. You dwell in one world and have been created through the operation of one Will. Blessed is he who mingles with all men in a spirit of utmost kindliness and love.

G159 That which becomes man is submission to the restraints that will protect him from his own ignorance and guard him against the harm of the mischief-maker. False liberty causes man to overstep the bounds of propriety and to infringe upon his dignity. It debases him; true liberty consists in man's submission to God.

C161 Wholly for the sake of God, proclaim God's message and, with the same spirit, listen to whatever response your words may evoke in your hearer.

G163 Whoever clings to justice can, under no circumstances, transgress the limits of moderation; he discerns the truth in all things through the guidance of God, the All-seeing.

G6, 102 & 163 Happy are those that harken and observe God's counsel and woe betide the heedless.

On Worship

Chapter 1 – Zarathustra

I am eager to behold and take counsel with God,
Devotion, world-furthering Truth, Good Purpose, Power.[23]

Truly, praising, I shall worship you, O God of truth, good purpose and power.
Zarathustra, maker of mantras, friend of truth,
lifts up his voice with reverence, O God.
Truly I shall harness for You the swiftest steeds, which, You, O God, shall drive,
should You be ready for my help.[24]

We worship with reverence for God, Who offers us support.
Holy are those of piety, through their understanding, their words, their acts
and their inner selves. Bounteous is God's truth and power with good
purpose.
God created all. It is God that I shall entreat for the good reward.
God knows the best for me.[25]

Chapter 2 – Moses

Sing to the Lord, for God is highly exalted.[10]

Chapter 3 – Atharva

3.2

2 The wise, who, free from desires, worship God, pass beyond the seed.

3 Those who entertain desires, thinking of them, are born here and there
   on account of their desires, but, for those who are perfected souls, desires
   vanish, even here.

4 This cannot be attained by instruction alone, nor by intellectual power
   alone, nor even through much hearing.

5 It cannot be attained by one without strength, nor through heedlessness,
   nor through austerity without purpose, but one who strives by these
   means may enter God's abode.

8 Just as the flowing rivers disappear into the ocean, casting off name
   and shape, even so, the knower, freed of name and shape, joins the

Divine, higher than the high.

9 One who knows God joins God; crossing over sorrows, crossing over sins, liberated from the knots of the soul, becoming immortal.

Chapter 4 – Lao-tzu

51.2 Every living thing should bow to the Way and its virtue.

Chapter 5 – Siddhartha Gautama

107-9 A moment's reverence to the teachings of a holy man is worth more than a hundred years of worship; whatever may be offered in worship or in gifts to earn merit is not worth a fraction of the merit earned by one's reverence to these teachings; and whosoever honors in reverence those who are old in virtue and holiness, indeed conquers four treasures: long life, health, power and joy.

141 Neither nakedness, nor sleeping on the ground, nor fasting, nor covering the body with ashes, nor squatting in a meditative pose, can purify those who harbor doubts and desires.

9-10 If a man puts on a pure yellow robe with a soul which is impure, without self-harmony and truth, he is not worthy of the holy robe, but one who is pure from sin and whose soul is strong in virtue, who has self-harmony and truth, is worthy of the yellow robe.

190 One who follows the Buddha, his teachings and his disciples, goes indeed to a great refuge.

195-6 Who could measure the excellence of one who reveres those worthy of reverence, a Buddha or his disciples, who have left evil behind and crossed the river of sorrow, who, free from all fear, are in the glory of Nirvana.

Chapter 6 – Jesus

Get up and pray, so that you do not fall into temptation.[17]

If you are offering a gift at the altar and remember that your brother has something against you, leave your gift. First go and be reconciled with your brother, then come and offer your gift.

When you pray, do not be like the hypocrites, for they love to pray standing in the synagogues and on street corners to be seen by men. When you pray, go into you room, close the door and pray to your Father, who is unseen.

Do not keep on babbling like pagans. Your Father knows what you need before you ask him.

It is lawful to do good on the Sabbath.

Have faith. Never give up.[18]

Chapter 7 – Muhammad

2.46 Fortify yourselves with patience and prayer. This may indeed be an exacting discipline, but not to the devout who know that they will meet their Lord.

2.172 Eat the wholesome things that God has provided and give thanks to God.

2.177 Righteousness does not consist in whether you face towards the east or the west. The righteous are those who, for the love of God, give their wealth to their kinfolk, to the orphans, to the needy, to the wayfarers and to the beggars; who attend to their prayers and pay their taxes; who are true to their promises and steadfast in trial and adversity and in times of war.

2.183 Fasting is decreed for you as it was decreed for those before you; perchance you will guard yourselves against evil. Fast a certain number of days, but if you are ill or on a journey, fast a similar number of days later on.

4.43 Do not approach your prayers when you are drunk, but wait until you can grasp the meaning of your words; nor when you are polluted, except when traveling, until you have washed.[10]

10.58 Rejoice in God's grace and mercy, for these are better than worldly riches.

10.66 Those that worship false gods follow nothing but idle fancies and preach nothing but falsehoods.

10.106 Do not pray to idols which can neither help nor harm you.

17.111 Pray neither too loudly nor in silence, but seek between these extremes a middle way. Say, "Praise be to God, who has never begotten a son, who has no partner and needs no defense." Proclaim God's greatness.

14.39 All prayers are heard by God.

17.78 Recite your prayers at sunset, at nightfall and at dawn. Pray during the night as well, an additional duty for the fulfillment of which your Lord may exalt you to an honorable station.

19.65 Worship God and be loyal in God's service; for is there any other god like God?

24.56 Attend to your prayers. Pay your taxes.

30.17 Give glory to God morning and evening. Praise God in the heavens and the Earth, at twilight and at noon.

36.34 God gave the Earth life, and from it produced grain for your sustenance. God planted it with palms and vines, and watered it with gushing springs, so that we may feed on its fruit. It was not our hands that made all this. Should we not give thanks?

39.66 Serve God and give thanks to God.

52.49 Give glory to your Lord when you waken. In the night time, praise God, and at the setting of the stars.

56.58-77 Behold the semen you discharge. Did you create it or did God? It was God that ordained death among you. Nothing can hinder God from replacing you with others like you, or with beings you know nothing of. Consider the seeds you grow. Is it you that gives them growth or God? God could turn your harvest into chaff. Consider the water you drink. Was it you that poured it from the clouds or God? God could turn it bitter. Why then do you not give thanks? Observe the fire you light. Is it you that created the wood or God? God made it a reminder for man, and, for the traveler, a comfort. Praise then the name of your Lord, the Supreme One.

61.2 Believers, why do you profess what you never do? It is most odious in God's sight that you should say one thing and do another.

62.9 When you are summoned to Friday prayers, hasten to the remembrance of God and cease your trading.

76.27 Remember the name of your Lord morning and evening. In the night time, worship God. Praise God all night long.

87.1 Praise the name of your Lord, the Most High, who has created all things and well-proportioned them, who has ordained their destinies and guided them, who brings forth the green pasture, then turns it to withered grass.

96.19 Prostrate yourself and come nearer.

Chapter 8 – Nanak Dev

We cannot comprehend God through thinking, although there be thoughts by
the thousand.

We cannot discover God through silence, although it be continuous silence.

We are persistently hungry, although we eat of tasty abundance.

Not one of a hundred thousand devices avails God!

How may the truth be attained, the bonds of falsehood broken?

By obeying the will of God as surely recorded.[15]

Devotion leads to happiness.

Sins and sorrows are destroyed by harkening.

Death itself is overcome by harkening.

Yoga skill and mystery come by harkening.

Truth, knowledge and contentment come by harkening.

Honor and the art of reading come by harkening.

And by it the last stage of meditation.

By harkening one knows the avatars, the role of saints, prelates and rulers.

The blind find their own paths by harkening.

By harkening, impassable streams are forded.

One knows God in one's heart on due reflection.

Wisdom and understanding come by reflection.

Slights and slaps are brought to nothing by reflection.

Death's ties are cut asunder by reflection.

One's path is rid of hindrance by reflection.

Through reflection one appears at last with honor.

By reflection one may journey quite unshaken.

And find companionship at last with dharma.[16]

Let good deeds be your prayers.[17]

Put on the garb of deeds and salvation's way is open.[18]

Chapter 9 – Mirza Husain Ali Nuri

G5 They who are beloved of God, in whatever place they gather and
whomsoever they may meet, must evince, in their attitude toward God, and
in the manner of their celebration of God's praise and glory, such humility
and submissiveness that every atom of the dust beneath their feet may

attest the depth of their devotion.

G52 Pray to be forgiven, O people, for having failed in your duty towards God and for having trespassed against God's cause, and be not of the foolish.

G93 Wonder not that God is closer to you than your own self. Wonder only that, despite such nearness, you can still be so far from God.

G94 The tie of servitude between worshippers and the adored One, between creatures and the Creator, should be regarded as a token of God's gracious favor, and not as an indication of any merit they may possess.

G95 The favors vouchsafed by God unto mankind are limitless in their range. First and foremost is the gift of understanding. God's purpose in conferring such a gift is to enable us to know and recognize God. This gift gives us the power to discern the truth in all things, leads us to that which is right and helps us to discover the secrets of creation. Next in rank is the power of vision, the chief instrument whereby our understanding can function. The sense of hearing, the heart and the like are similarly to be reckoned with among the gifts with which the human body is endowed. Render thanks unto the Lord for having vouchsafed unto you so great a bounty. Lift up your voice and say, "All praise to God, the Desire of every understanding heart."

G100 Adorn yourselves with the ornament of God's remembrance and illuminate your hearts with the light of God's love. This is the key that unlocks the hearts, the burnish that shall cleanse the souls of all beings. Beseech God to enable us to adorn ourselves with the ornament of pure and holy deeds.

G105 Worship none but God and, with radiant hearts, lift up your faces unto the Lord. Wash your hearts from all earthly defilements and hasten to enter the Kingdom of your Lord, the Creator of Heaven and Earth.

G135 Render thanks to the Almighty and magnify His name, inasmuch as He has aided you to recognize a cause through which the hidden secrets of men's breasts have been searched out and tested.

G136 Intone the verses of God that you have received, as intoned by them that have drawn nigh to Him, that the sweetness of your melody may kindle your soul, and attract the hearts of all men.

G160 Beseech God to enable you to remain steadfast in His path. This is the essence of faith and certitude. They that are worshippers of the idols that their imaginations have carved and who have called it inner reality are accounted among the heathen.

H18 Don't ask of God that which God does not desire for you. Be content with what God has ordained for you, for this is what profits you, if you content yourself with it.

Prayers

Chapter 1 – Zarathustra

God, who, by Your Most Holy Spirit, has fashioned the cow, the waters and plants, Grant me immortality and wholeness, endurance and strength.[26]

As Healer of the world, promise us a judge, then let hearkening come to those of us with good intentions, O God, to whomsoever You wish.[27]

I shall serve You with good purpose.
Grant me the gifts of both worlds – of matter and mind –
through Your truth.
I shall praise you in song as never before.
Come, at invocation, to my support.
I fix my mind solely on lifting up my soul by good intentions
And, with knowledge of God's justice, as long as I shall have life and strength,
So long shall I look in quest of Your truth.
God, Who guards truth and good purpose eternally,
Teach me through the eloquence of Your spirit
Those things through which the foremost existence shall here come to be.[28]
Be present to me with Your support and truth,
So that my thoughts may be concentrated where understanding falters.[29]

God, who sees afar, reveal to me for support, the incomparable things of Your realm,
Which are the recompense for good purpose,
For, as a gift, Zarathustra gives the breath even of his body.[30]

Let salvation be granted to the beneficent
We wish Your fire, Lord, strong through truth, very swift, mighty
To be of manifest help to Your supporters,
But of visible harm, O God, to your enemy.[31]

Grant to me this through devotion: recompenses of riches, a life of good purpose

And grant success to those who would teach us the straight paths of
salvation,
Paths of the material world and the mind, leading to the true heights where
dwells the Lord.
By the Hand that holds the recompenses that You give through the strong fire
of Your truth, God help me.[32]
Who, O God, have You appointed protector for one like me,
if the wicked shall dare to harm me?
Who, but Your fire and good purpose, by whose acts, Lord, truth is
nourished?
Proclaim this teaching to my inner self.[33]
Grant to my followers strength through truth
And that power of good purpose that gives dwellings and peace.[34]
Let those of good power rule with acts of good understanding.
Let the best purification be made for the cow on Earth,
To nurture her for our food.[35]
May the Creator of life accomplish through good purpose
the true fulfillment of what is most wonderful.[36]

Chapter 2 – Moses

I will sing to the Lord for God is highly exalted.
The Lord is my strength and my song.
This is my God, I will praise and exalt Him.
Who is like You, O Lord, among the gods?
Majestic in Holiness, doing wonders.[10]

Let the Lord go with us.
Forgive our iniquity and sin and take us for Your inheritance.[11]

May the Lord Bless you and keep you.
May the Lord's face shine upon you, be gracious to you and give you peace.[12]

Psalms[9] from Chapter 2

1. Blessed is the man
who walks not in the counsel of the wicked
nor lives in the way of sinners
nor sits in the seat of scoffers

but who delights in the law of the Lord
and meditates on the law day and night.
He is like a tree planted by streams of water,
which yields its fruit in season
and whose leaf does not wither.
In all that he does, he prospers.
Not so the wicked. They are like chaff that the wind blows away.
Therefore the wicked will not stand in the judgment,
nor sinners in the assembly of the righteous.
For the Lord watches over the righteous, but the way of the wicked will perish.

9. I will praise you, O Lord, with all my heart.
I will tell of all Your wonders.
I will be glad and rejoice in You.
I will sing praise to Your name most high.

The Lord reigns forever.
He has established his throne for judgment.
He will judge the world in righteousness.
He will govern the people with justice.
The Lord is a refuge for the oppressed, a stronghold in times of trouble.
Those who know You shall trust in You,
for You, Lord, have never forsaken those who seek You.

18. I love You, O Lord, my Strength.
The Lord is my Rock, my Fortress and my Deliverer.
God is my Rock, in whom I take refuge.
The Lord is my Shield and the Horn of my salvation.
I call to the Lord, who is worthy of praise, and I am saved.

19. The heavens declare the Glory of God.
The skies proclaim his work.
Day after day, they pour forth speech.
Night after night they display knowledge.
There is no speech nor language where their voice is not heard.
Their voice goes out to all the earth; their words to the end of the world.
Let the words of my mouth and the meditation of my heart
be acceptable in your sight, O Lord, my Rock and my Redeemer.

23. The Lord is my Shepherd, I shall not want.

He makes me lie down in green pastures.

He leads me beside quiet waters.

He restores my soul.

He guides me in paths of righteousness.

Even though I walk through the valley of the shadow of death,
I will fear no evil.

For You are with me. Your rod and staff comfort me.

You prepare a table for me.

You anoint my head with oil. My cup overflows.

Surely goodness and mercy shall follow me all the days of my life
and I shall dwell in the House of the Lord forever.

27. The Lord is my Light and my Salvation. Who shall I Fear?

The Lord is the stronghold of my life.

Teach me Your way, O Lord, and lead me on a level path.

I believe that I shall see the goodness of the Lord in the land of the living.

Wait for the Lord. Be strong and take heart. Yeah! Wait for the Lord.

32. Blessed are we whose transgressions are forgiven.

Let us all pray to You, while You may be found.

Surely, when the mighty waters rise, they will not reach us.

You are our hiding place.

You will protect us and surround us with songs of deliverance.

33. Rejoice in the Lord and be glad, you righteous.

Sing, all you who are upright in heart.

Praise the Lord with the harp.

Make music for God on the ten-stringed lyre.

Sing God a new song. Play skillfully and shout for joy,

for the Word of the Lord is right and true.

The earth is full of the steadfast Love of the Lord.

Let Your steadfast Love be upon us, even as we put our hope in You.

37. Don't fret because of the wicked or envy those who do wrong.

Like the grass, they will wither; like green plants, they will die away.

Trust in the Lord and do good.

Take delight in the Lord.

Commit your way to the Lord,

and your righteousness will shine like the dawn.

The justice of your cause will shine like the sun.

Refrain from anger and turn from wrath.

Do not fret. It leads only to evil.

And the evil will be cut off, but those who trust in the Lord will prevail.

The meek will inherit the land and enjoy great peace.

Turn from evil and do good.

Wait for the Lord and keep his way.

The Lord helps the righteous and delivers them,

because they take refuge in God.

38. Blessed are those who consider the poor and weak.

The Lord will deliver them in times of trouble.

The Lord will protect them and preserve their lives.

42. As a deer longs for flowing streams,

my heart longs for you, O Lord.

My soul thirsts for God; for the living God.

When can I go and meet with God?

Why are you downcast, O my soul?

Put you hope in God, for I will praise him.

By day the Lord directs his love.

At night his song is with me.

92. It is good to give thanks to God,

and sing praises to the Lord most high;

to proclaim your love in the morning,

and your faithfulness at night,

to the music of the ten-stringed lyre

and the melody of the harp.

95. O come let us sing to the Lord,

to the rock of our salvation.

Let us come to the Lord with thanksgiving,

And extol God with music and song.

96. Sing to the Lord a new song.

Sing to the Lord all the earth.

Sing to the Lord. Praise God.

Proclaim God's salvation daily.

Declare God's glory among all nations.

The Lord will judge the world in righteousness

and the peoples in God's truth.

103. Praise the Lord, O my soul.

All my inmost being praise God's holy name.

Praise the Lord, O my soul, and forget not all his benefits.

Who forgives all your sins and heals all your diseases?

Who redeems your life from the pit and crowns you with love and compassion?

Who satisfies you with good as long as you live, so your youth is renewed like the eagle's?

104. Praise the Lord O my soul.

O Lord my God, You are very Great.

You are clothed with honor and majesty.

You cover Yourself with light as a garment.

You have stretched out the heavens like a tent.

You make the clouds Your chariot.

You ride on the wings of the wind ...

Praise the Lord O my soul. Praise the Lord!

108. My heart is steadfast, O Lord.

I will sing and make music with all my soul.

Awake, harp and lyre! I will awaken the dawn.

I will praise You, O Lord, among the nations.

I will sing of Your love among all the peoples,

for great is your love, higher than the heavens.

117. Praise the Lord all nations.

Extol God all you peoples.

For great is God's love toward us,

And the faith of the Lord endures forever.

119. Blessed are those whose ways are blameless,

who walk with the law of the Lord.

Blessed are they who keep God's statutes,

And seek the Lord with all their heart.

I seek You with all my heart.

Do not let me stray from your commands.

Praise be to you O Lord.

Teach me Your decrees.

I rejoice in following Your statutes, as one rejoices in great riches.

I meditate on Your precepts and consider Your ways.

I delight in Your decrees. I will not neglect Your word.

136. Give thanks to the Lord for God is good. God's love endures forever.

150. Praise the Lord.
Praise God in the sanctuary.
Praise God in the mighty heavens.
Praise God with the sounding of the trumpet.
Praise God with the harp and lyre.
Praise God with the tambourine and dancing.
Praise God with the strings and flute.
Praise God with the clash of cymbals.
Praise God with resounding cymbals.
Let everything that has breath praise the Lord

Chapter 3 – Atharva

2.2

5 God in whom the sky, the Earth and space are woven in the mind and all living breath, know Him alone as the One. Dismiss all other utterances. This is the bridge to immortality.

Chapter 4 – Lao-tzu

Lao-tzu's Tao Te Ching offers advice, but no prayers.

Chapter 5 – Siddhartha Gautama

197-200 O let us live in joy; in love among those who hate; in health among those who are ill; in peace among those who fight.

201 O let us live in joy, although having nothing. In joy, let us live like spirits of light.

Chapter 6 – Jesus

This is how you should pray:

Our Father in Heaven, hallowed be Your name.
Your kingdom come; Your will be done, on Earth as it is in Heaven.
Give us this day our daily bread.

Forgive us our trespasses, as we forgive them that trespass against us.
Lead us not into temptation, but deliver us from evil,
For yours is the kingdom, the power and the glory for ever. Amen.

Chapter 7 – Muhammad

1.1 (The Exordium) Say: In the name of God, Lord of Creation, the Compassionate, the Merciful, King of Judgment Day. You alone we worship, and to you alone, we pray for help. Guide us to the straight path, the path of those whom You have favored, not of those who have incurred your wrath, nor of those who have gone astray.

2.287 Lord, do not be angry with us, if we forget or lapse into error. Lord, do not lay on us the burden You laid on those before us. Lord, do not charge us with more than we can bear. Pardon us. Forgive us our sins and have mercy upon us. You alone are our Protector.

6.161 Say: My Lord has guided me to a straight path, to an upright religion, to the faith of saintly Abraham, who was no idolater.

6.162 Say: My prayers and my devotions, my life and my death are for God, the Lord of Creation. God has no peer.

7.55 Pray to your Lord with humility and in secret.

17.80 Say: Lord grant me a goodly entrance and a goodly exit, and sustain me with Your power.

27.93 Say: Praise be to God.

God will show you His signs and you will recognize them. Your Lord is watching over all your actions.

28.50 Say: Bring down from God a scripture that is a better guide than the Torah and the Koran, and we will follow it.

66.8 Say: Lord, perfect our light for us and forgive us. You have power over all things.

67.29 Say: God is the Lord of mercy. In God we believe and in God we put our trust.

Chapter 8 – Nanak Dev

Unity, Active One, True God, Fearless One, devoid of enmity, whom time and the ages do not encumber, Self-existent, Perceptible – Praise! Pre-eminent Truth, primordial Truth, Truth that is and will abide forever.[19]

Words are vain, but teach me the mystery, O Lord. Such wisdom may I cherish.[20]

Impressive are the varied forms of beauty. Who knows the generous bounty of the whole? What mighty power for man to fix his thought on! No self-denial comprehends it all.

To please God is a man's best aspiration. O God, You are eternal, dwelling in repose.[21]

Chapter 9 – Mirza Husain Ali Nuri

G1 Lauded and glorified are You, O Lord, my God! How can I make mention of You, assured as I am that no tongue, however deep its wisdom, can befittingly magnify Your name, nor can the bird of the human heart, however great its longing, ever hope to ascend into the heaven of Your majesty and knowledge. Exalted, immeasurably exalted, are You above the strivings of mortal man to unravel Your mystery, to describe Your glory, or even to hint at the nature of Your essence. For whatever such strivings may accomplish, they never can hope to transcend the limitations imposed upon Your creatures, inasmuch as these efforts are actuated by Your decree, and are begotten of Your invention. High above the praise of men will You remain forever. There is no other God but You, the Inaccessible, the Omnipotent, the Holy of Holies.

G11 May my life be a sacrifice to You, inasmuch as You have fixed Your gaze upon me, have bestowed Your bounty upon me. All praise be to You for having enabled me to harken to Your call.

G18 Praise be to God, the Lord of all worlds.

G24 Praise be to God, the All-possessing, the King of incomparable glory, a praise which is immeasurably above the understanding of all created beings, and is exalted beyond the grasp of the minds of men. From each and every revelation emanating from the source of God's glory, holy and never-ending evidence of unimaginable splendor have appeared, and out of every manifestation of God's invincible power, oceans of eternal light have outpoured.

G27 All praise to the unity of God, and all honor to God, the sovereign Lord, the incomparable and all-glorious Ruler of the universe, Who, out of nothingness, has created the reality of all things, Who, from naught, has brought into being the most refined and subtle elements of creation and, Who, rescuing His creatures from the abasement of remoteness and the perils of ultimate extinction, has received them into his kingdom of incorruptible glory; Who chose to confer upon mankind the unique distinction and capacity to know and to love God – a capacity that must be regarded as the generating impulse and the primary purpose underlying the whole of creation.

G43 The world is in great turmoil and the minds of its people are in a state of utter confusion. We entreat the Almighty to graciously illuminate us with the glory of God's justice and enable us to discover that which will be enlightening to us at all times and under all conditions.

G93 God grant that, with a penetrating vision, we may perceive in all things the revelation of the Lord and recognize how exalted and sanctified from the whole creation is that most holy and sacred Being. This, in truth, is the very root and essence of belief in the unity and singularity of God.

G96 Please God may we all be strengthened to carry out Your will and may we be graciously assisted to appreciate the rank conferred upon such of Your loved ones as have arisen to serve You and magnify Your name.

G100 Please God, may the poor exert themselves and strive to earn the means of livelihood. This is a duty that has been prescribed unto everyone and is accounted in the sight of God as a goodly deed. Whoever observes this duty, the help of the invisible One shall certainly aid. Praise be to God, concealer of the sins of the weak and helpless. Magnified be Your name, O God that forgives the heedless ones that trespass against You! We beseech You to vouchsafe grace to us all, to enable us all to attain knowledge of God and ourselves. Whoever knows the Lord shall soar in the immensity of God's love and shall be detached from the world and all that is therein. Nothing on Earth shall deflect him from his course. Amity and rectitude of conduct, rather than dissension and mischief, are the marks of true faith.

G110 How long will humanity persist in its waywardness? How long will injustice continue? How long will chaos and confusion reign amongst men? How long will discord agitate the face of society? The winds of despair are blowing from every direction. The signs of impending convulsions and chaos can now be discerned inasmuch as the prevailing order appears to be lamentably defective. I beseech God, exalted be His glory, that He may graciously awaken the peoples of the Earth, may grant that the end of their conduct may be profitable unto them and aid them to accomplish that which becomes them.

G127 Guide Your servants, O Lord, to the court of Your favor and bounty, and suffer them not to be deprived of the wonders of Your grace and manifold blessings. Outwardly, we are weak and helpless. Inwardly we are but orphans. We ask Your forgiveness for the things we have committed against You. Verily, You are the Forgiving, the All-merciful.

G138 Shield us from the assaults of our evil passions and desires, and help us to obtain the things that shall profit us in this world and the next. You see, O Lord, our hands lifted up toward the heaven of Your favor and bounty. Grant that they may be filled with the treasures of Your munificence. Forgive us and our fathers and mothers and fulfill whatsoever we have desired from the ocean of Your grace and divine generosity. Accept, O Beloved, our hearts and all our works in Your path.

Prophecy

Chapter 1 – Zarathustra

When, O God, shall devotion bring order,
bringing good dwellings, bringing pasturage through Your power?
Who will stop cruelty by bloodthirsty wicked men?
To whom will come the teaching of good purpose?
They truly shall be saoshyants of the lands that follow Your teaching.
They indeed have been appointed opponents of fury.[37]

Falsehood brings on age-long punishment, and truth leads on to fuller, higher life.[38]

Within the span of this one life on Earth, perfection can be reached by fervent souls,
Ardent in their zeal, sincere in their toil.[39]

What will the punishment be for whoever promotes power for the wicked men of evil actions – for whoever finds no other means of livelihood than harming the cattle and men of the honest pastor – when, by God's bright-blazing fire, the distribution in good shall take place for all parties and Heavenly glory shall be the future possession of whoever comes to the help of the just? A long life of darkness, foul food, the crying of woe – to that existence, O wicked ones, your inner selves shall lead you.[40]

The seeds of bad purpose, lies and arrogance have defrauded mankind of good life and immortality, much as you have defrauded yourselves, you daevas and bad spirits. Those wicked ones, who appear in grandeur as chieftains and their ladies, have ruined life, stealing property from its inheritor. Those who have deflected the just from best purpose, who, with their life of pleasure have ruined the life of the cow. They shall not be brought to the House of Good Purpose.[41]

Evil-doers yoke mankind to destroy life, but their souls and inner selves will torment them when they reach the Chinvat Bridge. They will be guests forever in the house of the lie. And those who I shall bring to Your worship, with all these shall I cross over the Chinvat Bridge.[42]

God has promised by truth and good purpose that there shall be wholeness and immortality within God's realm, strength and perpetuity within God's house.[43]

You have promised the just all the best things. The wicked man shall have his share remote from Your affection, since he abides by acts inspired by bad purpose. By Your Holy Spirit, God, You will distribute justice to both parties by fire.[44]

God's bright blazing fire and molten metal is a sign to be given among all living things to destroy the wicked and save the just. The inner selves of the wicked destroy for themselves the reality of the straight way. God shall surely vex them at the Chinvat Bridge, for they have strayed from the path of truth by their acts and words. Their pleasure is from hurt to the cow, by their acts and teachings, which shall at the end set them in the house of the lie.[45]

The best wish of Zarathustra Spitama has been heard. If God will grant boons in accord with truth, a good life forever to those who have accepted and taught the words and the acts of the good religion, making straight the paths for the religion of the saoshyant, which God has ordained, then indeed there shall be reward for us all. If you abandon this teaching, then there shall be woe for you at the end. Such is the power by which God gives what is better to the honest poor.[46]

Chapter 2 – Moses

God will reign for ever and ever.[11]

If you walk in God's statutes and observe God's commandments, God will give rains in their season, the land will yield its increase and the trees will yield their fruit. You will eat to the full and dwell in your land securely. God will give peace and no one shall make you afraid.[12]

God will raise up prophets and if we do not heed words spoken in God's name, God will call us to account, but if what a prophet proclaims in the name of the Lord does not take place or come true, then the prophet has spoken it presumptuously and we need have no fear of false Prophecy.[13]

Chapter 3 – Atharva

3.2

8 Just as the flowing rivers disappear into the ocean, casting off name and shape, even so, the knower, freed of name and shape, joins the Divine, higher than the high.

9 One who knows God joins God; crossing over sorrows, crossing over sins, liberated from the knots of the soul, becoming immortal.

Chapter 4 – Lao-tzu

46 When the Way prevails in the world, the war-horses may be sent to draw carts.

When the Way is disregarded in the world, war-horses will breed in the borderlands.

61 A great state is like a low-lying estuary. It is a place where all the lesser states mingle and merge. If a great state takes a low place, it wins over the trust of smaller states.

79.3 In the Way of Heaven there is no partiality of love; it is always on the side of the good.

32 A ruler who follows the Way is like a river reaching the sea, gathering the waters of the streams as he goes.

30.4 & 55.4 That which is not in accordance with the Way soon comes to an end. Those who follow the Way will last forever.

Chapter 5 – Siddhartha Gautama

15 Those who do evil will suffer, and mourn when they see the wrong they have done. Those who do good will be happy. They will feel great gladness when they see the good they have done.

20 If we speak but a few holy words, yet live the life of those words, free from passion and hate and illusion, with right vision and a free mind, craving for nothing, either now or hereafter, our lives will be holy.

23 Those who in high thought and in deep contemplation, advance on the path with ever-living power will eventually reach Nirvana.

24 Those who arise in faith, who ever remember the high purpose, whose work is pure and carefully considered, who, in self-possession, live the life of perfection, shall rise in glory.

27 (ii) Those who are watchful, in deep contemplation, reach in the end the joy supreme.

47-8 Death carries away those who gather the flowers of sensuous passions, even as a torrent of rushing water overflows a sleeping village and goes on is way. Death, the end of all, makes an end of those ever thirsty with desire.

57-9 The Way of those who are rich in virtue, who are ever watchful, whose true light makes them free, cannot be crossed by death. Even as a lotus may grow and blossom on a heap of rubbish, so the pure light of the wisdom of the student who follows the Buddha may shine among the blind multitudes.

79 One who drinks the waters of truth rests in joy with mind serene. The wise find their delight in the Way, in the truth revealed by the Great.

85-6 Few cross the river of time and are able to reach Nirvana. Most run up and down only on this side of the river; but those who, when they know the law, follow the path of the law, shall reach the other shore and go beyond the realm of death.

89 Those whose minds are well trained in the ways that lead to light, who surrender the bondage of attachments and find joy in freedom from attachments, who, free from the darkness of passions, shine pure in a radiance of light, enjoy the immortal Nirvana even in their mortal lives.

90 The traveler who has reached the end of the journey is free from all sorrows in the freedom of the infinite; fetters thrown away, the burning fever of life is no more.

94-6 The man who wisely controls his senses as a good driver controls his horses and is free from lower passions and pride is calm like the earth that endures. He is steady like a column that is firm. He is free from *samsara*, the ever returning life-in-death. In the light of his vision, he has found his freedom. His thoughts are peace. His words are peace. His work is peace.

97 He who has seen the eternal Nirvana, who has thrown off the bondage of the lower life and, far beyond temptations, has surrendered all his desires, is indeed great among men.

98 Wherever holy men dwell is indeed a place of joy, be it in a village, in the forest, in a valley or on the hills.

119 One may find pleasure in doing evil as long as the evil has not borne fruit, but when the fruit of evil comes, one finds evil indeed.

125 (ii)/127-8 Evil returns like dust thrown against the wind. Neither in the sky nor deep in the ocean, nor in a mountain cave, nor anywhere, can a man be free from the evil he has done, or from the power of death.

120 One may find pain in doing good as long as the good has not borne fruit, but when the fruit of good comes, one finds good indeed.

126 Those who do evil may go to Hell and the righteous to Heaven, but those who are pure find Nirvana.

131-2 Those who for the sake of happiness hurt others who also want happiness shall not hereafter find happiness, but those who do not hurt others shall find happiness.

144 By faith, by virtue and energy, by deep contemplation and vision, by wisdom and by right action, you shall overcome the sorrows of life.

148-51 The body is a house of bones covered with flesh and blood. Pride and hypocrisy dwell in this house, and also old age and death. All life ends in death. The body wears out and grows old. The chariots of kings wear out, but the virtue of the good never grows old.

201 Victory over others brings hate, because the defeated are unhappy. Those who rise above such victory and defeat find joy.

155-6 Those who in their youth did not live in self-harmony and did not gain the true treasures of life are later like long-legged old herons standing sadly by a lake without fish, like broken bows, ever deploring things past and gone.

164 The fool who scorns the teaching of the holy gathers fruits for his destruction.

172-3 One who was unwise, but later finds wisdom – one who overcomes the evil he has done with good – sheds a light over the world, like the moon when freed from clouds.

175 Swans follow the path of the sun by the miracle of flying through the air. Men who are strong conquer evil and its armies and rise far above the world.

178 Better than power over all the earth, better than going to Heaven, is the joy of entering the river of life that leads to Nirvana.

187 (ii) When desires go, joy comes. The followers of Buddha find this truth.

194 Happy is the birth of a buddha. Happy is the teaching of the Way. Happy is the harmony of his followers. Happy are the lives of those who live in harmony.

291 Those who seek happiness for themselves by making others unhappy are bound in the chains of hate.

350-1 Those who enjoy peaceful thoughts, who consider the sorrows of pleasure, and who ever remember the light of their lives, will see the end of their cravings and will break the chains of death. They have reached the end of their journey. They do not tremble. They are free from sin. They have burned the thorns of life. This is their last mortal body.

Chapter 6 – Jesus

Woe to the world because of the things that cause people to sin. Such things must come, but woe to the man through whom they come.[19]

Blessed are the poor in spirit, for theirs is the Kingdom of Heaven.
Blessed are those who mourn, for they will be comforted.
Blessed are the meek, for they will inherit the Earth.
Blessed are those who hunger and thirst for righteousness, for they will be filled.
Blessed are the merciful, for they will be shown mercy.
Blessed are the pure in heart, for they shall see God.
Blessed are the peacemakers, for they shall be called the sons of God.
Blessed are those who are persecuted because of righteousness, for theirs is the Kingdom of Heaven.

Blessed are you when people insult you, persecute you and falsely say all kinds of evil against you because of me; rejoice and be glad, for great is your reward in Heaven.

Blessed are those who hear the word of God and obey it.[20]

Blessed are those who will eat at the feast in the Kingdom of God.[21]

Anyone who breaks one of the least of God's commandments and teaches others to do the same will be called least in the Kingdom of Heaven, but whoever practices and teaches these commands will be called great in the Kingdom of Heaven, for I tell you that unless your righteousness surpasses that of the Pharisees and the teachers of the law, you will certainly not enter the Kingdom of Heaven. Only one who does the will of God will enter the Kingdom of Heaven. Unless you change and become like little children, you will never enter the Kingdom of Heaven.

Everyone who hears these words and puts them into practice is like a wise man who builds his house on a rock. The rains come down, the streams rise and the winds blow and beat against the house, yet it does not fall, because it has its foundation on a rock; but everyone who hears these words and does not put them into practice is like a foolish man who builds his house on sand. The rains come down, the streams rise, the winds blow and beat against the house, and it falls with a great crash.

There is nothing concealed that will not be disclosed. Anyone who receives a prophet because he is a prophet will receive a prophet's reward. Anyone who receives a righteous man because he is a righteous man will receive a righteous man's reward.

All who draw the sword will die by the sword. Every kingdom divided against itself will be ruined, and every city or household divided against itself will not stand.

Many who are first will be last, and many who are last will be first. How hard it is for the rich to enter the Kingdom of God! Indeed, it is easier for a camel to go through the eye of a needle than for a rich man to enter the Kingdom of God. Everyone who exalts himself will be humbled, and he who humbles himself will be exalted.[22]

Anyone who will not receive the Kingdom of God like a little child will never enter it.[23]

Whoever has (knowledge of the Kingdom of Heaven) will be given more, and he will have an abundance. Whoever does not have, even what he has will be taken from him.[24]

From everyone who has been given much, much will be demanded; and from the one who has been entrusted with much, much more will be asked.[25]

Everyone who does evil hates the light, and will not come into the light for fear that his deeds will be exposed, but whoever lives by the truth comes into the light, so that it may be seen plainly that what he has done has been done through God.[26]

The truth will set you free.[27]

There will be more rejoicing in Heaven over one sinner who repents than over ninety-nine righteous persons who do not need to repent.[28]

When you hear of wars and revolutions, do not be frightened. These things must happen first. The end will not come right away. Nation will rise against nation and kingdom against kingdom. There will be great earthquakes, famines and pestilences in various places, and great signs from Heaven.[29]

Chapter 7 – Muhammad

2.261 One who gives for the cause of God is like a grain of corn which brings forth seven ears, each bearing a hundred grains. Abundance is given according to God's will.

2.264-5 Those who mar their almsgiving with taunts and mischief-making, and those who spend their wealth for the sake of ostentation are like rocks covered with earth; showers will fall and leave them hard and bare. They shall gain nothing from their works, but those that give away their wealth from a desire to please God are like a garden on a hillside: if a shower falls upon it, it yields up twice its normal crop, and if no rain falls upon it, it is watered by the dew.

4.128 Man is prone to avarice, but if you do what is right and guard yourselves against evil, know then that God is cognizant of all your actions.

6.131 Your Lord would not destroy a nation without just cause and due warning.

6.133 God could destroy and replace you at will.

10.26 Those that do good works shall be rewarded with abundant blessings. Neither darkness nor misery shall cover their faces. They are the heirs of

Paradise: in it they shall abide forever. Whoever plants a tree and diligently looks after it until it matures and bears fruit is rewarded.

10.108 Those that follow the right path follow it to their advantage; those that go astray do so at their own peril.

11.7 After death you shall be raised to life.

13.11 God does not change a people's lot unless they change what is in their hearts. If God seeks to afflict them with misfortune, none can ward it off. Besides God, they have no protector.

13.29 Blessed are those who have faith and do good works; blissful is their end.

13.39 Every age has its scripture. God confirms or abrogates at will. God alone is the eternal book.

16.127 It shall be best for you to endure your wrongs with patience.

18.27 You shall find no refuge besides God.

18.46 Wealth and children are the ornament of this life, but deeds of lasting merit are better rewarded by God and hold for you a better hope of salvation.

18.107 & 14.22 Those that have faith and do good works shall dwell forever in the gardens of Paradise, desiring no change to befall them.

15.47 The righteous shall dwell in peace and safety. God will remove all hatred from their hearts.[11]

17.58 There is no nation that shall not be destroyed or sternly punished before the Day of Resurrection.

28.80 None shall attain God's reward except those that have endured with fortitude.

19.96 God will cherish those who have faith and are charitable.

23.1 Blessed are the believers who are humble in their prayers; who avoid profane talk and give alms to the destitute, who restrain their carnal desires[12] and do not transgress through lusting after other women; who are true to their trusts and promises and never neglect their prayers. These are the heirs of Paradise. They shall abide in it forever.

39.9 None will take heed, but those of understanding.

39.22 One whose heart God has opened, shall receive light from the Lord, but woe to those whose hearts are hardened against the remembrance of God.

Truly they are in the grossest error.

41.7 Woe to those who serve other gods.

42.15 God will bring us all together. To God we shall return.

42.53 All things shall in the end return to God.

43.40 You cannot make the deaf hear or the blind see, nor can you guide those who are in gross error.

45.15 God will reward us according to our deeds. Those that do what is right do so to their advantage. Those that commit evil do so at their peril.

45.28 You shall see all the nations on their knees.

47.1 God will bring to nothing the deeds of disbelievers who would bar others from God's path.

47.38 If you give no heed, God will replace you by others different from you.

53.32 To those who avoid the grossest sins and indecencies and commit only small offences, God will show abundant mercy.

55.26 All who live on Earth are doomed to die, but the face of your Lord will abide forever, in all its majesty and glory.

57.28 God will bestow on you a light to walk in and will forgive you.

61.8 God's light will be perfect.

62.12 That which God has in store is far better than any merchandise or merriment.

63.9 Those that forget God shall have much to lose.

64.7 By the Lord, you may assuredly be raised to life!

64.16 Those that preserve themselves from greed shall surely prosper.

73.30 Whatever good you do, you shall surely find it with God, ennobling and richly rewarding.

76.8 God will deliver the poor, the orphans and the captives and make their faces shine with joy. God will reward them for their steadfastness.[13]

76.30 God is merciful to whom God wills, but for the wrongdoers, God has prepared a grievous punishment.

85.11 Those that have faith and do good works shall be rewarded. Theirs is the supreme triumph.[14]

87.15 Happy are those that purify themselves; who remember God and pray.

90.17 Would that you knew what the height of happiness is. It is the freeing of a bondsman, the feeding of a hungry orphan or a needy man in distress; it is having faith and enjoining fortitude and mercy.

91.7 Blessed are those that keep the soul pure and ruined are those that corrupt it.

92.18 Those who purify themselves by almsgiving and do good works for the sake of the Most High only, not in recompense for a favor, shall be content.

98.7 Of all creatures, those that embrace faith and do good works are the noblest. God will reward them. God is well pleased with them and they with God. Thus are they rewarded.[15]

104.1 Woe to all back-biting slanderers who amass riches and sedulously hoard them, thinking their treasures will render them immortal. By no means! They shall be flung into the destroying flame – God's own kindled fire, which will rise up to their hearts.

107.6 Woe to those who pray, but are heedless in their prayers, who make a show of piety, but give no alms to the destitute.

Chapter 8 – Nanak Dev

There is no Hindu. There is no Muslim.[22]

Whoever sings and listens, heart-felt praise retaining, his sorrows fade and he will dwell in blessing.[23]

Chapter 9 – Mirza Husain Ali Nuri

G6 Happy are those that harken and strive, and woe betide the heedless.

G10 It is incumbent upon everyone to place trust in the manifold bounties of God and arise to disseminate, with the utmost wisdom, the verities of God's cause. Then, and only then, will the whole Earth be enveloped with the morning light of God's revelation.

G56 Ere long will the state of affairs within [Tehran] be changed and the reins of power fall into the hands of the people.

G71 Neither the pomp of the mighty, nor the wealth of the rich, nor the ascendancy of the ungodly will endure. All will perish at a word from God. What advantage is there in earthly things which men possess? That which would enlighten them, they utterly neglect. Ere long they will escape from their slumber and find themselves unable to obtain that which has escaped them in the days of their Lord. Did they but know it, they would renounce their all, that their names may be mentioned before God's throne. They, verily, are accounted among the dead.

G72 Did you but know it, you would renounce the world and hasten with your whole hearts to the presence of God. Your spirits would be so transported as to throw the greater world into commotion – how much more this small and petty one!

G80 The soul is exalted above, and is independent of, all infirmities of body or mind. That a sick person shows signs of weakness is due to the hindrances that impose themselves between the soul and the body, for the soul remains unaffected by bodily ailments. Consider the light of a lamp. Though an external object may interfere with its radiance, the light continues to shine. In like manner, every malady afflicting the body is an impediment that prevents the soul from manifesting its inherent light and power. When it leaves the body, however, it will evince such ascendancy and reveal such influence as no force on Earth can equal. Every pure, refined and sanctified soul will be endowed with tremendous power and rejoice with exceeding gladness.

G81 The world beyond is as different from this world as this world is different from that of the child in the womb of its mother. When the soul attains the presence of God, it will assume the form that best befits its immortality and is worthy of its celestial habitation.

G82 The soul is a sign of God, a heavenly gem whose reality the most learned of men have failed to grasp, and whose mystery no mind of man, however acute, can hope to unravel. Within it lies concealed that which the world is now utterly incapable of apprehending.

G86 Each shall receive their share from the Lord. Blessed are those that turn their faces towards God and walk steadfastly in God's love until their souls wing in flight to God, the sovereign Lord of all, the Most Powerful, the Ever-forgiving, the All-merciful.

G91 Those who act unjustly shall soon know what lot awaits them.

G93 Every created thing is a sign of the revelation of God. Each, according to its capacity, is a token of the Almighty. So pervasive and general is this revelation that nothing whatsoever in the whole universe can be discovered that does not reflect God's splendor.

G103 God shall cleanse the Earth from the defilement of corruption and give it for a heritage to those who are close to Him.

G104 People of the world! An unforeseen calamity is following you and grievous retribution awaits you. Don't think the deeds you have committed are blotted from God's sight.

G108 God has fixed a time for you, O peoples. If you fail to turn toward God, He will lay violent hold on you and cause grievous afflictions to assail you from every direction.

G112 There is no force on Earth that can equal in its conquering power the force of justice and wisdom. Blessed is the leader who marches with the ensign of wisdom unfurled before him and the battalions of justice massed in his rear. He is the ornament that adorns the brow of peace and the countenance of security. There can be no doubt whatever that if the day star of justice, which the clouds of tyranny have obscured, were to shed its light upon men, the face of the Earth would be completely transformed.

G125 Only when the lamp of search, of earnest striving of passionate devotion, of fervid love, of rapture, of ecstasy is kindled within the seeker's heart, and the breeze of loving kindness is wafted upon his soul, will the darkness of error be dispelled, the mists of doubts and misgivings be dissipated and the lights of knowledge and certitude envelop his being. At that hour will the mystic herald, bearing joyful tidings of the spirit, shine forth from the city of God. Then will the manifold favors and outpouring grace of the holy and everlasting spirit confer such new life upon the seeker that he will find himself endowed with a new eye, a new ear, a new heart and a new mind. He will contemplate the manifest signs of the universe and will penetrate the hidden mysteries of the soul. When the channel of the human soul is cleansed of all worldly and impeding attachments, it will unfailingly perceive the breath of God across immeasurable distances and attain and enter the city of certitude. The attainment of this city quenches thirst without water and kindles the love of God without fire. Within every blade of grass are enshrined the mysteries of an inscrutable wisdom and upon every rose bush a myriad nightingales pour out their melody in blissful rapture. The city is none other than the word of God.

G131 Through the power of the word, the whole human race can be illuminated with the light of unity. The remembrance of God is able to set the hearts of us all on fire and burn away the veils that intervene between us and God's glory.

G133 Whoever keeps the commandments of God shall attain everlasting felicity.

G137 Whoever has tasted the sweetness of God's word will never consent to transgress the bounds, which God as fixed. Such a man will, with his inner eye, readily recognize how altogether vain and fleeting are the things of this world and will set his affections on things above.

G138 Ere long, the world and all that is therein shall be as a thing forgotten and all honor shall belong to the loved ones of the Lord, the All-glorious, the most bountiful.

G160 The condition of self-surrender transcends, and will ever remain exalted above, every other condition. So complete must be your consecration, that every trace of worldly desire will be washed from your heart. This is the meaning of true unity.

G161 Those who shall accept and believe shall receive their reward. Those who shall turn away shall receive none other than their own punishment. Well it is with those whom the changes and chances of this world have failed to deter from recognizing the unity of God. They shall be numbered with the inmates of Paradise in the book of God, the Lord of all worlds.

G163 This civilization, so often vaunted by the learned exponents of arts and science, will, if allowed to overstep the bounds of moderation, bring great evil upon men. If carried to excess, civilization will prove as prolific a source of evil as it had been of goodness when it kept within the bounds of moderation. The day is approaching when its flame will devour the cities.

11

UNITY RECLAIMED 4
– THE QUEST
CONTINUES

———•••———

Over a century has passed since the death of Mirza Husain Ali Nuri, aka Baha'ullah, the last of the nine "Sons/Prophets/Manifestations" of God in whose names the great religions considered in this book were founded.

There have been no new additions to their ranks. The last hundred years have produced many new cults and many new sects within old religions, but no Prophets in the same league as the nine whose visions I have presented and whose legacies I have discussed. Science and reason are now seen as more significant than subjective and/or unprovable visions. Many still swear by one or more of the old visionaries and are willingly bound within one of their legacies, but modern science and the traditional religions have – in their separate ways – effectively blocked the space that prophets once filled. Unless our global community disintegrates completely and collapses into a new dark age, the days of new prophets are surely all behind us, and the days of scientific understanding and/or wonder and a spiritually enlightened civilization are just beginning.

But some old-mold characters who may be classed as prophets of new religions did emerge in the 20th century and, before looking toward the spiritual quest of the new millennium, I will briefly review the backgrounds, visions and legacies of just two of them: Marcus Garvey (1887-1940), the prophet of Rastafarianism, and Lafayette Ronald Hubbard (1911-86), inventor of *dianetics,* an approach to mental health that he promoted through another personal creation, his Church of Scientology.

Marcus Garvey was a Jamaican who emigrated to the USA in 1911. A devout Christian, repelled by America's endemic racial discrimination – against blacks in particular – he reacted by founding the "Universal Negro Improvement Association" (UNIA) in 1914, followed by a newspaper, *Negro World*, a "Back to Africa" movement and the Black Star Shipping Line. His links with Africa led him to discover Ras Tafari, progressive heir to the throne of Queen Zauditi, Empress of Ethiopia, the only African state to survive the onslaught of European colonial domination. Empress Zauditi reigned from 1916 to 1930 and Ras Tafari served her as Governor of Harrar, then as regent, taking Ethiopia into the League of Nations in 1923 and abolishing slavery in Ethiopia in 1924. Marcus Garvey promoted Ras Tafari as a role model for his followers. But even before this – from as early as 1916 – Garvey was making the prophecy that would spawn Rastafarianism:

▷ Look to Africa for the crowning of a black king.
He shall be the Redeemer.[1]

Both UNIA and the Black Star Shipping Line collapsed in the early 20s. Garvey was convicted of fraud and jailed in 1925, then pardoned by President Coolidge, but deported to Jamaica in 1927, where he continued, albeit at a more modest level, to work for social reform. Back in Ethiopia, Empress Zauditi died in 1930 and Ras Tafari succeeded her, taking the title Haile Selassie I at his coronation. Some of Garvey's followers then began to revere Ras Tafari, now an earthly emperor, as the Redeemer and an incarnation of God. His deification survived his flight into exile in London during the Italian occupation of Ethiopia (1936-42) and his overthrow by a military coup in 1974. It was spectacularly boosted by his 1966 state visit to Jamaica, following independence in 1962, and also by his grants of land for Rastafarian settlement in Ethiopia, by his role in founding the Organization of African Unity in 1963, and by his death in 1975.

Rastafarianism remains a minority religion in Jamaica and among Jamaican communities elsewhere, but it has also become a global cultural phenomenon, associated with dreadlocks, marijuana-smoking and the reggae music popularized internationally since the 70s by Bob Marley (1945-81) and his successors. It is an ongoing religious response to the racism and oppression endemic in our current global organization. Although there are now many Rastafarian sects with widely differing beliefs – including the meaning of the central idea of the eventual return to Ethiopia – the various sects remain linked in a loose alliance that is much bigger than the sum of its parts.

The vision of Scientology is very different. It is a personal response to alienation, rather than a communal response to oppression. Its founder, L Ron Hubbard, made his way as a science fiction writer in the USA until the late 40s, then, at the age of 39, he decided that it may be more lucrative to create his own religion, or "applied religious philosophy." His next two books, *Dianetics: The Modern Science of Mental Health* (1950) and *Science and Survival* (1951) prepared the ground for this mission. He advocated confrontation with painful experiences from the past as the means of achieving true mental health and becoming "clear."

In 1954 he set up the Church of Scientology in California to promote his ideas. His followers progress through levels of mental wellbeing rising from "pre-clear" through "clear" to the highest level, that of an "Operating Thetan" (OT). Hubbard served as executive director of the Church from 1955 to 1966. He subsequently returned to writing science fiction and died in 1986.

The Church of Scientology has continued to grow since Hubbard's death, particularly in California, but also across the USA and Europe. It claims over a million members worldwide, including many Hollywood stars, such as Tom Cruise, Nicole Kidman and John Travolta. Its description as a cult or as a new religion, rather than simply as an approach to mental health, is based partly on its financial organization as a church – very tax-effective in the USA – and partly on Hubbard's references to gods as a plurality and his rejection of earlier religious leaders in general and of Christian views on sin, repentance and Hell in particular. Some brief quotations from Hubbard's vision illustrate these views:

> ▷ There are gods above all other gods, and gods beyond the gods of the universes.[2]

> ▷ Neither Lord Buddha nor Jesus Christ were OTs. They were just a shade above clear.[3]

> ▷ It is despicable and utterly beneath contempt to tell a man he must repent, that he is evil.[4]

> ▷ Hell is a total myth, an invention just to make people very unhappy and is a vicious lie.[5]

Rastafarianism was developed as a reaction to racism and injustice. Scientology arose from an imagination steeped in science fiction in a society being dramatically transformed by real science. Both have been adopted as religions by only tiny minorities of the world's population. But, like the nine great religions of the preceding chapters, they seek to satisfy the spiritual needs of their devotees and have thus become new parts of the ever-expanding mosaic of human response to both the problems and the mysteries of our existence and environment.

It is inevitable that the human imagination will continue to respond to these ongoing problems and mysteries, but there is nothing inevitable about this response leading us to adopt new religions or constraining us within any one of the old religions. If it is to have any real meaning, our developing spiritual understanding must surely take into account all the old visions and all the new knowledge discovered by genuine experimental and inductive science: new discoveries about time and space, about matter and energy – their applications and their implications.

The God of the Bible and the Koran created the Earth in six days, some six millennia ago. Deep water was already there, but in darkness. Then God created light – but not the sun, moon or stars – to start the first day, then Heaven on the second day – but there is no mention of day and night having anything to do with the Earth revolving in space. Land and plants were created on the third day; the sun, moon and stars (finally!) on the fourth day; animals on the fifth, and man on the sixth.

We now know that the universe was created not in six days, but in less than a second; that this happened not six millennia, but 15 **million** millennia ago, and that the universe has been expanding ever since, generating all the galaxies of stars, other heavenly bodies and black holes that we have so far detected and countless others that we haven't – not to mention the "dark matter" that is needed to explain our detailed observations of the expansion of the universe.

We know that for two-thirds of the time since the universe's initiating Big Bang, our sun did not exist; that, in terms of size, it is a very average star in a very average galaxy, and that it was formed, along with the rest of the solar system, from interstellar gases and the debris of long-dead earlier stars, some five million millennia ago.

We know that all material life on Earth is guided by a chemical language of nucleic acids, giant molecules of DNA and RNA, all built from a handful of just five smaller molecules we call nucleic acid bases. We know that these bases combine to form genes. We know that the language of the genes carries information determining the nature of all living things; and we know that changes can happen in the patterns of the combinations of bases, altering the genes and thereby altering the nature of the living thing they are part of.

We know that the simplest life forms appeared on Earth some four million millennia ago. We know that life has been evolving ever since; and we know that the earliest man-like creatures appeared (in Ethiopia) only a few thousand millennia ago. In other words, we know that humanity has only been a part of life on Earth for the last thousandth part of its existence, but even this makes us a thousand times older than the age of the Earth and universe as estimated by biblical scholars.

So, if the universe is a million times older than man, what was God doing in the fifteen billion years between creating the universe and creating us? There is much more in God's universe than meets the eye. Indeed, the universe itself may only be a small part of creation.

Our Big Bang of fifteen billion years ago may just be a black hole in another universe. The matter and energy disappearing into our black holes may be giving birth to universes elsewhere. Whatever the details, the Earth is clearly just a miniscule part of creation, and our time on it so far is just a miniscule part of time.

Our knowledge of these facts should surely affect the way we see ourselves in the scheme of things, and should surely temper the arrogance of those presenting pre-scientific religious ideas. There is clearly no proper place on Earth for those who would force their religious ideas on others, or who would seek to establish theocratic states, let alone a theocratic world order, or for those who would use arguments based on religion to justify either the establishment or expansion of a state by force.

None of the nine faiths considered in this book, nor any of their variants, can lay total claim to God's Truth. None can justify the imposition of their will on others, or the use of force or terror against others. All should, instead, seek out and develop the ideas on which they can agree: that a complete idea of God is beyond our grasp; that the idea must be far greater than our universe, but that the spirit of the idea pervades the universe, from its first joule of energy to the farthest galaxies, from the dark matter of space to the depths of our souls. God may speak to us as his children, but we must agree to differ in the way we listen. The spiritual idea is one that transcends the state, the Earth and even the universe.

But there is extensive common ground between the great religions and between spirituality and science, particularly with respect to human responsibility. There is common ground between the words of all the nine founders of religions considered here – not only those presented in the Selected Highlights (See Chapters 1-9.), but also those in the Collected Visions (Chapter 10). Participation in any particular organized religion should only ever be a voluntary individual choice, guided only by the way we listen. And the decision as to whether we listen at all should also be a matter of choice.

And, if we choose to listen, should the way we listen ever be fixed for all time, or should it change with our scientific development? There is no doubt that our scientific understanding dramatically affects our perceptions of the world around us, and that these perceptions are currently undergoing revolutionary changes, particularly in the ways we perceive matter and energy.

We have discovered that what we see and feel as tangible matter, whether solid liquid or gas, is all built up from tiny moving particles. We have discovered that solids are made up of crystals built from atoms (and/or ions), and that liquids and gases are made of freely moving molecules, also built from atoms. We have also discovered that atoms are not the indestructible particles they were thought to be until the last century, and that both atoms and ions are, in fact, mostly space in which tiny nuclei are surrounded by even tinier fast-moving electrons. We have discovered that the nuclei themselves can be broken down into protons and neutrons, and, in the last 20 years, that these nuclear particles are, in turn, made up of a variety of even tinier entities we call quarks.

During the last hundred years, as we have begun to understand these sub-atomic particles, we have split the nucleus to release energy and begun to use the electron in particular to change our world. We have developed chemical, biochemical, electrical, electronic and telecommunications industries to produce modern weapons, wonder drugs, TVs, PCs, CDs, DVDs, mobile phones and the internet etc.

But we have had a vague awareness of the electron for much longer. We inherited our word for electricity, and hence for the electron itself, from the ancient Greeks, and their observation that the rubbing of amber jewelry (*electra*) on garments, produced flashes of light (arising from the conversion of static electricity into light energy). The ancient Greeks were a long way from picking up the electron and running with it, and would have found it difficult to believe that it could be understood and used as it is today. The vague awareness of the link between static electricity and light was there for over two thousand years before mankind began to understand it. But when understanding finally came, it was quickly followed by the development of the industries mentioned above.

During the same period, we have also discovered that energy is transmitted as waves, either mechanical (eg sound, earth tremors) or electromagnetic (eg light) and that light is only a small part of a much wider electromagnetic spectrum, which ranges from the longest radio waves to the shortest cosmic waves. We have learned how to tap in to these waves and use them as means of communication and as investigative tools. We broadcast radio signals on the long, medium and short waves and on even shorter VHF waves. We broadcast TV signals VHF and the still shorter UHF waves. We use even shorter waves to carry radar signals. We use the still shorter microwaves and infrared radiation not only for heating, but also for transmitting signals from hand-held remote control devices to TV sets, hi-fis and model trains etc. We use light waves themselves (shorter than all the above) to carry digital information around the world and beyond. We use the still shorter ultra-violet waves to investigate atomic structure. We use the still shorter waves we call X-rays, generated when fast electrons approach the nuclei of hot metals, to look inside materials opaque to light. And we use the even shorter γ-rays, emitted by radioactive nuclei, to destroy cancerous cells within our bodies. Little did Isaac Newton (1642-1727) know, when he first split a beam of white light with a prism and unlocked the mystery of the rainbow, how much we would soon be doing with the *spectrum* (Latin for ghost) he introduced us to!

Isaac Newton is also remembered for his mechanics and his work on the understanding of gravity. But, although still useful on earth, Newtonian mechanics proved incapable of explaining astronomical observations, such as the gravitational effects of stars on light. When some of the deficiencies of Newtonian mechanics were addressed by Albert Einstein (1879-1955) with his theories of Relativity, his calculations led him to predict that matter – the stuff of particles – could be converted into energy – the stuff of waves. The truth of this prediction was terrifyingly confirmed in the summer of 1945 with the explosion of atom bombs at Los Alamos, then over Hiroshima and Nagasaki, and we now know that our "particles" are not simply particles, but also have the characteristics of waves and that our "waves" are not simply waves, but also have the characteristics of particles: the smaller the particle, the longer its associated wave. In our everyday lives, we can think of balls as particles without worrying about their wave characteristics and we can think of radio broadcasts as being carried by waves not particles, but there are situations where the effects of light can be explained better by considering it as particles (photons) rather than waves, and where the effects of streams of electrons can be explained better by considering them as waves. In short, we now know that matter and energy are interchangeable – that all materials, despite the deceptive illusions of our senses, are just sets of energetic interactions; that particle size and wavelength meet at the level of electrons; and that the electrons surrounding the nuclei of every atom on Earth are as much energy (standing waves) as they are matter (moving particles).

Our new way of explaining matter and energy – as a wave-particle duality – is closer to the truth than the old ways of relying on the illusions of our senses alone. But it is not the whole picture. It is merely a useful model. The development of the above-mentioned industries provides evidence of the usefulness of the model, but a limited, incomplete model is all that it is.

There can no doubt that our understanding of matter and energy is better developed than that of the ancient Greeks or that of any of our nine Prophets; that modern science's explanation of light and the rest of the electromagnetic spectrum has come a long way since Newton; and that both nuclear technology and astronomy have come a long way since Einstein's contributions. But our understanding of God or Universal Spirit is as inchoate as was the ancient Greek understanding of matter and energy. The awareness is there, but we must rely on faith and intuitions – either our own or those of the prophets or scientists – in attempting to understand it. While we have an objective understanding that all matter is generated from energy, we can only speculate on whether matter, energy and consciousness are ultimately generated from Spirit; or on whether the ultimate reservoir of all Spirit is God, and on whether one day our own spirits will return to this spiritual reservoir, as raindrops return to the sea.

Our scientific understanding of consciousness and spirituality is still as shallow as the ancients' understanding of matter and energy was. We are as far from useful theories about consciousness and spiritual phenomena as they were from wave-particle duality explanations of material phenomena. The skeptics' rejections of the possibilities of so-called supernatural phenomena are as reasonable as an ancients' rejection of the possibility of many of the phenomena we take for granted today would have been. Imagine trying to convince Zarathustra's contemporaries of the possibility of electric light; or explaining radio, TV, the internet or mobile phones to Jesus, Mohammed, Guru Nanak or Baha'ullah. Electricity existed long before we did. We were in awe of it in the form of thunder and lightning long before we learned to understand it and use it. Today, we are still in awe of spiritual or extra-sensory phenomena: revelation, enlightenment, the power of prayer, near-death experiences, ghostly apparitions, faith healing, telepathy, séances, spiritual mediation and ESP all still challenge scientific explanation. All of them remain awesome to many. But all of them also attract the derision of skeptics; not least because of the way charlatans so often exploit our lack of understanding.

We are, however, beginning to make real progress in neurology – the scientific study of the brain and consciousness – and some neurologists are even beginning to investigate the bridge between spiritual experience and scientifically measurable phenomena. These are the neurotheologists. One particular line of neurotheological investigation is following epileptics' reports of seeing visions of Heaven, Hell or angels when suffering from seizures. The observation that such seizures are accompanied by increased brain activity in the temporal lobes has prompted the study of temporal lobe activity in volunteers from the wider population. At the University of California in San Diego, for example, Professor Vilyanur Ramachandran has established a link between temporal lobe activity and susceptibility to religious or spiritual stimulation. In doing so, he has also found that some people are much more susceptible than others. This has led to the postulation that we may all be hard-wired, to a greater or lesser degree, for spiritual experience, and that we all have a "God-spot" somewhere in one or both of our temporal lobes. It has been suggested that the seizures suffered by people such as St Paul and Ellen White (see Chapter 6) and even Muhammad (Chapter 7) – and the dramatic spiritual experiences they subsequently reported – may have been the products of increased temporal lobe activity, and that the seizures "enriched their mental lives enormously." [6]

Other neurotheologists have studied the brain activity of volunteers during quiet prayer and meditation. They have found that both are generally associated with reduced parietal lobe activity and sometimes with increased temporal lobe activity.[7] These observations beg the question of whether or not there may be measurable external stimuli related to such changes in brain activity, particularly in the temporal lobes. At Laurentian University in Canada, Michael Persinger has studied the effect of magnetic fields on temporal lobes and associated subjective experience: 80% of his subjects reported some form of induced alteration in consciousness, described by some as a "sensed presence". But for one specially selected skeptic, the noted scientific author and atheist, Professor Richard Dawkins from Oxford University, there was no such presence. Sitting in Persinger's magnetic helmet left him feeling only "pleasantly relaxed, dizzy and strange with some twitchiness in the legs" even though he would have liked to have experienced "a mystical oneness with the universe."[8]

On the basis of his research, Persinger has speculated that each of us may be born with our own level of temporal lobe sensitivity or "spiritual talent." He has also suggested that it may be possible to encourage and develop spiritual talent in the same way as we do musical talent. Even Dawkins suggests that "the kind of brain activity that manifests itself as religious belief" may have survival value.[9] Other studies have shown that people of religious faith may lead longer and happier, albeit more prejudiced, lives than people without.[10]

But the quest to understand spirituality is only just beginning. Today's neurotheologists searching for God can be compared with medieval alchemists searching for the "Elixir of Life" or the "Philosopher's Stone" that could transmute base metals to gold. They were a long way off the mark, but their endeavors were followed by real chemistry – and by the rest of modern science and technology – even including genetics with its life-expanding potential and nuclear chemistry with its ability to transmute one element into another, both much more fascinating than Elixir of Life and the Philosopher's Stone that the alchemists postulated.

Eventually, we may understand much more about theology too. The successors of today's neurotheologists may make significant discoveries about the bridge between matter and mind on the one hand, and God and Spirit on the other.

In the meantime, we have not only the visions of our nine Prophets and their interpreters, but also many other thoughts and visions from scientific, philosophical and religious thinkers from all over the world; thinkers whose spirits may also have been touched by God. Some of them are quoted in the following sections.

On the Nature of God

The physicist [thinking of the atom] sometimes as a wave and sometimes as a particle ... knows very well that both these terms are analogical – they are metaphors, "picture thinking," and, as pictures, they are incompatible and mutually contradictory. But he need not on that account refrain from using them for what they are worth. If he were to wait till he could have immediate experience of the atom, he would have to wait until he was set free from the framework of the universe. In the meantime, as long as he remembers that language and observation are human functions, partaking at every point of the limitations of humanity, he can get along quite well with them and carry out fruitful researches. To complain that man measures God by his own experience is a waste of time; man measures everything by his own experience. He has no other yardstick.

Dorothy L Sayers[11]

The God of the heart, the God who is felt, the God of living men, is the Universe itself, conceived as a personality: God is the consciousness of the universe."

Miguel de Unamuno[12]

Nature and spirit are not without communication; one has an intimate relationship with the other [and] there must be an even greater unifying force at the foundation of these two. This unity is God. Our consciousness is a part of the consciousness of God and its unity comes from the unity of God. Reason and conscience are [God's] voice.

Nishida Kitaro[13]

All language about God must necessarily be analogical.

Saint Thomas Aquinas[14]

The proofs that religious doctrines have bequeathed to us are deposited in writings that themselves bear every trace of being untrustworthy. They are full of contradictions, revisions and interpolations; where they speak of actual authentic proofs they are themselves of doubtful authenticity. It does not help much if divine revelation is asserted to be the origin of their text or only of their content. Just as they cannot be proved, neither can they be refuted. We still know too little to approach them critically. The riddles of the universe will only reveal themselves slowly to our enquiry. To many questions, science can as yet give no answer; but scientific work is our only way to the knowledge of external reality.

Sigmund Freud[15]

I cannot persuade myself that a beneficent and omnipotent God would have designedly created the ichneumonidae with the express intention of their feeding within the bodies of living caterpillars.

Asa Gray[16]

I do not believe in a personal God. If something is in me that can be called religious then it is the unbounded admiration for the structure of the world so far as it can be revealed by science. Scientists require evidence, plus testability, precision, quantifiability, consistency, intersubjectivity, repeatability, universality and independence of cultural milieu before ideas can be accepted. Religious authorities dispense with all of these conditions when requiring that their revelations from God be accepted. It is as though the faithful gain prestige by believing even more ridiculous things than their rivals succeed in believing. Is it possible that some religious doctrines are favored not in spite of being ridiculous, but because they are ridiculous? Any wimp in religion could believe that bread symbolically represents the body of Christ, but it takes a real red-blooded Catholic to believe something as daft as the transubstantiation. The Virgin Birth, the Resurrection, the raising of Lazarus, and the manifestations of Mary and the saints around the Catholic world, even the Old Testament miracles, are all freely used for religious propaganda, and very effective they are with an audience of unsophisticates and children. Every one of these miracles amounts to a scientific claim, a violation of the normal running of the natural world. Theologians wanting to remain honest should make a choice. You can claim your own magisterium, separate from science's but still deserving respect. But in that case you have to renounce miracles. Or you can keep your Lourdes and your miracles, and enjoy their huge recruiting potential among the uneducated. But then you must kiss goodbye to separate magisteria and your high-minded aspiration to converge on science. The desire to have it both ways is not surprising in a good propagandist. What is surprising is the readiness of liberal agnostics to go along with it. To an honest judge, the alleged convergence between [traditional religions] and science is a shallow, empty, hollow, spin-doctored sham [but] if you allow cosmic awe as true religion, then religion and science have indeed converged.

Richard Dawkins[17]

Religious stories should only be accepted insofar as they help us to find a meaning in our lives which will improve our behavior toward ourselves, our world and all we share it with. They should never be claimed as exclusively true, especially in the absence of rational evidence, or used to promote the interests of one group at the expense of others. The petty prejudices displayed by religious people about beliefs, morals and actions are a far stronger obstacle to reviving a widespread belief in a living God than are the more metaphysical, logical and philosophical arguments claiming to demonstrate the impossibility of the existence of God. Everything we "know" is provisional, held together and given direction by faith, the faith that trusts, and hope in the love of God and the resources of the Holy Spirit. The claim that the stamp of revelation authorizes one to ignore either history or science only guarantees that any form of belief in God will appear to the wider world to be an outmoded superstition. The sacred formulations of the past are rich resources to be read in the light of our present reality [but] what religious people claim to believe about God seems too often to make them smaller and more shallow human beings, rather than enlarging and deepening their humanity. Internecine quarrels about God encourage atheism. Faith knows that God is decisively (but not exclusively) as he is in Jesus – the hope of the future of all. God is love and love requires freedom in order that it may be received, developed and shared. So faith in God is basically a personal matter of encounter, response and pilgrimage – not a product or a set of beliefs sustained by authorities ecclesiastical or textual. It is a personal pilgrimage in company – the companions of the way of faith being those kept and maintained by God in the Spirit. Faith is received, sustained and lived within an expanding experience of living reality. It is not a taught religion or a series of detached beliefs received on authority. I fail to understand why so many people have taken our discoveries, from the vastness of the universe to the biochemical structure of our very bodies, as compelling evidence to reduce ourselves to selfish genes or beings whose lives are determined by the necessities of price exchanges in the market. Why this miserable, myopic, self-centered shrinking of vision? Churches contribute to this secular myopia by a determination to trap the dynamics of God within the self-centered constructions of religion.

David Jenkins, former Bishop of Durham[18]

On God's Purpose and Human Responsibility

The most beautiful thing we can experience is the mysterious. It is the source of all true art and science. He to whom this emotion is a stranger, who can no longer pause to wonder and stand rapt in awe is as good as dead: his eyes are closed. I cannot imagine a God who rewards and punishes the objects of His creation, whose purposes are modeled after our own – a God, in short, who is but a reflection of human frailty. It is enough for me to contemplate the mystery of conscious life perpetuating itself through all eternity, to reflect upon the marvelous structure of the universe which we can dimly perceive, and to try humbly to comprehend even an infinitesimal part of the intelligence manifested in nature. The ideals that have always shone before me and filled me with the joy of living are goodness, beauty and truth. To make a goal of comfort or happiness has never appealed to me; a system of ethics built on this basis would be sufficient only for a herd of cattle. Without the sense of collaborating with like-minded beings in the pursuit of the ever unattainable in art and scientific research, my life would have been empty. Possessions, outward success, publicity, luxury – to me these have always been contemptible. I believe that a simple and unassuming manner of life is best for everyone, best both for the body and the mind. I am independent of the customs, opinions and prejudices of others, and am not tempted to rest my peace of mind on such shifting foundations. I am convinced that degeneracy follows every autocratic system of violence. The man who enjoys marching in line to the strains of music falls beneath my contempt; he received his great brain by mistake – the spinal cord would have been sufficient.

Albert Einstein[19]

We all have a soul that is nourished by the good we do on this planet.

Michael Douglas[20]

Every soul has a tendency toward God.

Dorothy Day[21]

Ideas flow in upon me, directly from God.

Johannes Brahms[22]

The music was dictated to me by God; I was merely instrumental in putting it on paper and communicating it to the public.

Giacomo Puccini[23]

God continues to reveal himself in genius. The voice of God can speak to mankind even by lips that deny his existence.

Nathan Soderblom[24]

The ethical progress of society depends not on imitating or running away from the cosmic process, but on combating it.

T H Huxley[25]

With what other than condemnation is a person with any moral sense supposed to respond to a system in which the ultimate purpose in life is to be better than your neighbor at getting genes into future generations.

George C Williams[26]

The human psyche has two great sicknesses: the urge to carry vendetta across generations and the tendency to fasten group labels on people rather than to see them as individuals. Abrahamic religion mixes explosively with and gives sanction to both. Only the willfully blind could fail to implicate the divisive force of religion in most, if not all, of the violent enmities in the world today. Religion is the most inflammatory enemy-labeling device in history. Those of us who have for years concealed our contempt for the dangerous collective delusion of religion need to stand up and speak out. The historic process that caused you to exist is wasteful cruel and low. But exult in your existence, because that very process has blundered unwittingly on its own negation. Only a small local negation, to be sure: only one species and only a minority of the members of that species; but there lies hope.

Richard Dawkins[27]

Religion should never be used to justify violence.

Pope John Paul II[28]

Bringing peace back into human life has always been the ideal of religion.

Irfan Ahmad Khan[29]

Encounters between the faithful and non-believers should cease to focus on who converts whom, but on how we contribute from our own ways of faith and understanding to the universal future of the love of all things in the love of God. Our source and resource is not an energy that exploded out of nothing on the way to collapsing into nothing. The mystery is far greater than that. We are discovering all this. Hence the hope and wonder of going on.

David Jenkins[30]

It is absolutely impossible either to gloss over or ignore the very serious differences among the civilizations. However, these differences should not hinder the perception and appreciation of those ethical values and standards which are already held in common and can jointly be affirmed on religious and non-religious grounds.

Hans Kung[31]

The General Assembly [of the United Nations] proclaims:

1. All human beings are born free and equal in dignity and rights. They are endowed with reason and conscience and should act toward one another in a spirit of brotherhood.

18. Everyone has the right to freedom of thought, conscience and religion.

26. (1) Everyone has the right to education (2) Education shall be directed to the full development of the human personality and to the strengthening of respect for human rights and fundamental freedoms. It shall promote understanding, tolerance and friendship among all nations, racial or religious groups, and shall further the activities of the United Nations for the maintenance of peace.

Universal Declaration of Human Rights

The challenge we now face is for the different nations and peoples of the world to agree on a basic set of human values, which will serve as a unifying force in the development of a genuine global community.

Aung San Suu Kyi[32]

In this global age, only a true global ethic can be of real value.

Prince Hassan Bin Talal[33]

As humanity embarks on the process of globalization, it can no longer do without a common code of ethics. This does not mean a single dominant socio-economic system or culture that would impose its values and criteria on ethical reasoning. Universal human values must be brought out and emphasized as the guiding force of all development and progress [and] dialogue among religions and cultures is crucial as the basis for greater solidarity for justice and peace, human rights and dignity.

Pope John Paul II[34]

Interfaith dialogue is a precondition for human flourishing.

Andrew C Clarke, Zarrin T Caldwell[35]

Religious individuals need to look self-critically at themselves in their relationships with one another and with the wider world.

Professor Paul Weller[36]

In dialog, we cultivate self-criticism as the foundation of all criticism and the beginning of respect; we let go of outmoded prejudices; we rejoice in differences; we discover our interdependence before the sacredness that resides immanently in all things.

Alan Race, Seshagir Rao, Jim Kenney[37]

The nation-state falls short of the human and the universal and constitutes a deadly menace to the growth of the universal in man, which is postulated with increasing force by the advance of science and which the well-being of human society demands. The historical process is not a mere chain of events. It offers a succession of spiritual opportunities. Man has to attain a mastery over it to reveal the higher world operating within it.

Sarvepalli Radhakrishnan[38]

Humanity clearly needs all the inspiration and guidance it can get to move us towards sustainable ways of living together. We need God's resources to inspire and direct our faith and we need to break out beyond the smothering embrace of religion.

David Jenkins[39]

It is important to be able to make a distinction between the essence of religion – the principles of love and compassion – and the cultural aspects of a particular tradition; to examine oneself and act according to these principles. Having knowledge of religious beliefs, practitioners could use religion for purposes of exploitation and manipulation. So, as practitioners, our first responsibility is to watch ourselves. And we should also study other religious traditions through reading books, but, more importantly, meeting with people from other religious traditions to share experiences with them and learn from their traditions. Religious traditions must put forward a united front against war and conflict. But voicing opposition is not enough. We have to think seriously about the questions of disarmament, population and the world's limited resources. It is more important to create a safer kinder world than to recruit more people to the religion that happens to satisfy us. Whether or not people are religious or not does not matter much. Far more important is that they be good human beings. Those who are dedicated practitioners follow a diversity of paths. From this it becomes clear that, given our diversity, no single religion satisfies all humanity. We may also conclude that we humans can live quite well without recourse to religious faith. When I was younger and living in Tibet, I believed in my heart that Buddhism was the best way. I told myself it would be marvelous if everyone converted. Yet this was due to ignorance. Buddhism remains the most precious path for me. It corresponds best with my personality. But that does not mean I believe it to be the best religion for everyone any more than I believe it necessary for everyone to be a religious believer. Many reject religion out of convictions sincerely held, not merely because they are unconcerned with the deeper questions of human existence. It is unhelpful to try to argue on the basis of philosophy or metaphysics that one religion is better than another. The important thing is surely its effectiveness in individual cases. And there is an important distinction to be made between religion and spirituality. Religion is perhaps something we can do without. What we cannot do without are the basic spiritual qualities, whose unifying characteristic is concern for others' well-being, acknowledging human diversity and respecting the rights of all. Whether a person practices a religion or not, the spiritual qualities of love and compassion, patience, tolerance, forgiveness and humility are indispensable. Religion can play a leading role in encouraging people to develop a sense of responsibility toward others and of the need to be ethically disciplined, but until we [religious leaders] put our own spiritual teachings into practice, we will never be taken seriously. And this means, among other things, setting a good example through developing good relations with other faith traditions.

Tenzin Gyatso, 14th Dalai Lama[40]

That the colonized world, whose wealth has been plundered for 500 years, should be deemed to owe the rich world money, and that this presumed debt should be so onerous that every year $382 billion, which might have been used to feed the hungry, to house the poor, to provide healthcare, education, clean water, transport and pensions for people who have access to none of these amenities, is transferred from the poor world to the banks and financial institutions of the rich world in the form of debt repayments is an obscenity which degrades all those of us who benefit from it. Nations, like people, appear to become more selfish as they get richer. The biggest economy in the world, the United States, offers a smaller proportion of its national wealth in the form of aid than any other substantial donor – a mere 0.1% of its GDP – and this has declined as its economy has grown. In 2002, it handed $3.9 billion (three times its aid budget for all Africa) to just 25,000 US cotton farmers. This reduced world prices by about 26% destroying the livelihoods of tens of millions of farmers in the poor world. But the meanness of the dominant nations is such that they will permit no other country, if they can prevent it, from outcompeting them in any economic sector, however trivial the domestic impact may be.

George Monbiot[41]

If there is poverty in the world, it means that we still have a measure of greed in our souls. We need to transcend that within us that blinds us to our faults.

Yehuda Berg[42]

On Worship

Don't let your religion be a rut that you sink ever more deeply into.

Don Cupitt[43]

Attempts to limit truth by the formulae of any one religion are as futile as the attempt to identify a precious metal with the die which converts it into current coin. Its substance must always be distinguished from the accidents under which we perceive it, for this substance has an absolute and not a denominational importance.

Evelyn Underhill[44]

To live in the Way is but being sincere with oneself and with the universe, according to one's lights. No one can be natural and happy unless he is intellectually sincere with himself, and to be natural is to be in Heaven. The "religious" man who does good in order to get to Heaven, by implication, would not do good if he were not lured by Heaven or threatened with Hell. Doing good is its own justification. Bending to the will of Heaven is the truly religious and pious attitude.

Lin Yutang[45]

Constantly repeating the ethical teaching of Jesus is like trying to paint a wet wall with pretty colors. We first have to create a foundation for the understanding of the teaching and guide our world to a frame of mind in which the teachings of Jesus have meaning. The commandment of love means this: no one is a stranger to you; every man's welfare is your concern. Existence depends more on reverence for life than the law and the prophets. Reverence for life comprises the whole ethic of love in its deepest and highest sense. It is the source of constant renewal for the individual and mankind.

Albert Schweitzer[46]

In evolutionary terms, we are mere adolescents. Our present identity crisis prevents us from seeing the true beauty of the world. If, like the prodigal son, we return to our Father and make our peace with Him, we will see the beauty of the world, we will experience the oneness of all things, we will cease our futile search in the desert of the self, and our lives will take on meaning.

Robert Barry[47]

The man who renounces himself, comes to himself by so doing. The safety of God, the immortality of God, the majesty of God enters into that man. My country is the world and my religion is to do good.

Ralph Waldo Emerson[48]

Goodness represents the detachment of our spirit from the exclusiveness of our egoism; in goodness we identify ourselves with the universal humanity. We have to be true within, not for worldly duties, but for that spiritual fulfillment, which is in harmony with the Perfect, in union with the Eternal. Then we will act and find that service is joy.

Rabindranath Tagore[49]

Delightful as it may be for those who practice it, quiet contemplation does not rattle the cages of power.

George Monbiot [50]

Comment and Prophesy

Sectarianism, bigotry and fanaticism have long possessed this beautiful Earth, filled it with violence, drenched it with human blood, destroyed civilization and sent whole nations to despair.

Swami Vivekananda[51]

(Speech to the World Parliament of Religions, Chicago, September 11, 1893)

Religious belief is notorious for encouraging a sense of us against them and producing a narrowness of perspective. The convictions that religion fosters, and the sense of a particular community that it inculcates, can quickly become a wall of separation. Doctrine divides, but love unites. Perhaps eventually we will come to the fellowship, across historic lines of separation, of a communion of saints transcending theological divisions in the mystery of the One and the All.

Jaroslav Pelikan[52]

We have just enough religion to make us hate, but not enough to love each other.

Jonathan Swift[53]

Every one of our communities has had an enlightened one to teach us, but where is our enlightenment? Look around. It looks as if Jesus never walked among us. It looks as if Moses, Muhammad, Buddha and Confucius never walked among us. The House of Islam is broken into pieces. Where is the enlightenment? Islam is a gutter religion, as is Christianity and every community of faith that ignores its own noble teachings while people perpetuate injustice.

Louis Farrakhan[54]

The actualization of the reasoning potential of the human neocortex has been obstructed by the activities of older structures in the nervous system. Inadequate co-ordination between the old and new structures has made man's instincts and intellects fall out of step. Nature has let us down. God seems to have left the receiver off the hook and time is running out.

Arthur Koestler[55]

Our convictions are precisely that, *our* convictions, fallible intimations of a mysterious transcendent reservoir of being and value. We struggle in the making of judgments, for not everything generated by the religious imagination is conducive to human and planetary good. The failure of religious communities to cooperate has contributed to the sum total of anguish and pain in the world. Yet this history can be reversed, for the religions at their ethical best are fountains of compassion, harmony and hope.

Alan Race, Seshagir Rao, Jim Kenney[56]

Religion must become reverence for the beauty and grandeur and mystery of life, freed from the accretions which theology has accumulated and laid over its surface; freed from moral "truths" so mystified, decorated and camouflaged as to make it possible for a priesthood to make a living.

Lin Yutang[57]

The more we study natural phenomena the more we are able to know that one unifying power behind them is in control.

Nishida Kitaro[58]

The very nature of the post-modern global village affirms that the natural experience of life is to connect with its wonder and pursue our inquiry into identity and meaning. It affirms that there is an inner spirit to everything, including ourselves.

William Bloom[59]

We, who are children of the universe – animated stardust – can reflect on the nature of that same universe, even to the extent of glimpsing the rules on which it runs. The physical species, *Homo*, may count for nothing, but the existence of mind in some organism on some planet in the universe is surely a fact of fundamental significance.

Paul Davies[60]

In a society that is deprived of spiritual and moral values, those who possess material resources develop a tendency to use these resources to suck even more blood out of the poor. Likewise, those who have political or military power use it to dominate the weak and downtrodden. Even knowledge and religion can be used to exploit the illiterate masses and misguide them. A nation ought not to subordinate the principal of justice to its national interests. The root cause of most evils on the international plane lies in the fact that, as a general rule, nations do not pursue given courses of action because they are just or right, but because they are seen to serve national interests. Once a policy has been adopted, moral and legal principles are used to argue in its favor. Thus moral and legal principles do not guide our actions, they only help to rationalize actions that are actually grounded in other considerations. Such an obviously irreligious attitude presents a tremendous challenge to the world's faith communities.

Irfan Ahmad Khan[61]

The dynamic of our times is not the clash of civilizations, but the marbling of civilizations and peoples. Religious diversity will require us to create a truly pluralist society in which this diversity is not merely tolerated but becomes the very source of our strength. I might sing "Give me that old time religion, it's good enough for me!" with as much gusto as anyone, but in my heart I know that the old time religion is not good enough unless those of us who claim it are able to grapple honestly and faithfully with the new questions, challenges and knowledge posed to us by the vibrant world of many living faiths.

Diana Eck[62]

For civilization as a whole, the faith that is so essential to restore the balance now missing in our relationship to the Earth is the faith that we do have a future. We can believe in that future and work to achieve it and preserve it, or we can whirl blindly on. The choice is ours; the Earth is in the balance.

Al Gore[63]

It is impossible to establish common purpose between people whose economic lives vary as wildly as they do today. The ultra-rich will always regard the poor with terror, and the hatred that flows from terror. The extremely poor will always see the rich as a different species, placed upon the Earth to govern and oppress them. Without a great global economic leveling, we are destined always to fight each other, rather than our common problems. All those with agency are confronted by a choice. We can use that agency to secure for ourselves a safe and comfortable existence. We can use our life, that one unrepeatable product of four billion years of serendipity and evolution, to earn a little more, to save a little more, to win the approval of our bosses and the envy of our neighbors, or we can use our agency to change the world and, in changing it, to change ourselves.

George Monbiot[64]

Religion has a tendency to become obsolescent and restrictive. The pilgrimage of faith, by contrast, is maintained by a real sense of Presence and is always looking forward in hope.

David Jenkins[65]

When the light of humility dawns on the soul, the darkness of selfishness disappears and the soul no longer lives for itself, but for God, and is transformed into Him. This is the alchemy of humility. It transforms the lowest into the Highest.

Kirpal Singh[66]

A materialistic person works to overcome problems by attacking or refining the surface symptoms; a spiritually aware person sees more layers of the picture. Spirituality reveals the deeper root behind the surface problem. And the root of most problems in this world is greed.

Sharon Janis[67]

The market is functioning as a religion and needs to enter into a dialogue with other religions.

Paul F Knitter[68]

If we have no peace, it is because we have forgotten that we belong to each other.

Mother Teresa[69]

May this century be the one where the poor and marginalized come into their own and the gross social inequalities of the past are at last eradicated.

Nelson Mandela[70]

The United Nations as it is presently constituted provides a forum for governments, but individual citizens cannot be heard there. It has no mechanism whereby those wishing to speak out against their own governments can be heard. To make matters worse, the veto system currently in place opens its working to manipulation by the more powerful nations. These are profound shortcomings.

Tenzin Gyatso, 14th Dalai Lama[71]

Without world democracy, there will be no stability.

Justin de Villepin, French Foreign Minister[72]

Conclusion

We ignore the words of our nine prophets and of these modern thinkers at our peril. We raise any one above all the others at our peril. If we are to live together in a peaceful and sustainable world, we cannot cut ourselves off from either God or from humanity as a whole by arrogantly proclaiming, or acting on behalf of, just one faith or one nationality, especially as our espousal of either or both is so often determined by no more than the accident of our place of birth and/or our childhood subjection to religious or political propaganda.

Our young civilization has the potential to experience enlightenment, to build a Heaven on Earth and to connect with any Heaven beyond. We have the potential to better understand and protect our amazing planet, and to further explore the solar system, galaxy and universe(s) around us, but, if we use our free will to continue as we are doing; if, by our apathy, we allow ourselves to slide short-sightedly along the ruts we find ourselves in, or allow our leaders to do so on our behalf, then we may well be contributing to our own self-destruction – inviting God to abort this mini-experiment of humanity on Earth in favor of more deserving projects elsewhere in the vastness of the time and space that is Creation.

The signs that we are making this invitation are already rife. It is high time that we all – as individuals, as communities, and as one human family – heed the best of the visions of all nine of the prophets presented in this book, the wisdom of the thinkers quoted in this chapter, and the spirit of good purpose within ourselves (whether or not we perceive its connection to that universal spirit that some call God). It is also high time that we give more thought to establishing the global environment that will pre-empt the onset of a new dark age and allow both our human and spiritual quests to continue as one family sharing one world.

Faltering steps in this direction have been taken in the last century or more with initiatives such as the World Parliaments of Religions in Chicago (1893 & 1993), Cape Town (1999) and Barcelona (2004); the League of Nations (1920-46), its successor the United Nations, and their many subsidiary organs; and The World Social Forums in Porto Alegre, Brazil (2001, 2 & 3) and Mumbai, India (2004). But much more radical spiritual, social and political changes are needed.

Fortunately, ideas for such changes are being more and more widely discussed, if only in non-governmental organizations like the World Congress of Faiths, the World Federation of United Nations Associations, the Global Justice Movement and the World Federalist Movement. For an introduction to some of these ideas, I would refer the reader to the quarterly, *Interreligious Insight*, to George Monbiot's *The Age of Consent* (2003) and my own *The Spring of Civilization* (1973). A new dark age is not inevitable, but it will only be avoided if enough people recognize the dangers – in themselves, in their religions and in their societies – in time to deal with them before being overwhelmed by them. We need to start by accepting that many of our religious "certainties" and our evangelical or patriotic aspirations are so harmful as to be a threat to our continuing quest, rather than a part of it.

NOTES & REFERENCES

Chapter 1:
Zarathustra

1. J G Frazer, "The Worship of Nature," 1926 quoted in Geoffrey Parrinder (ed), *World Religions*, Facts on File Publications/Hamlyn, New York, 1971/1983, p32

2. This idea is developed in Leonard Shlain, *The Alphabet Versus the Goddess: The Conflict Between Word and Image*, Arkana/Penguin, New York, 1998.

3. Parrinder (op cit) p140

4. *ibid* p142

5. *ibid* p33

6. See Paul Kriwaczek, *In Search of Zarathustra*, Weidenfeld & Nicolson, London, 2002

7. See Chapters 2-9

8. Lewis M Hopfe, *Religions of the World*, Third Edition, Macmillan, New York, 1983, p296

9. Hopfe (*ibid*) p297

10. Lines from the Gathas (from Yasna 44). The Gathas are Zarathustra's original poems, hymns, psalms or prayers, preserved as part of the Zoroastrian scriptures, in the liturgy of the Yasnas. The original language of the Gathas marks them out as the oldest part of Zoroastrian scripture (the Avestan) and therefore the only part that may be directly attributed to Zarathustra, himself. As with all my quotations from the Gathas, these lines are based on Piloo Nanavutty, *The Gathas of Zarathustra*, Mappin, Ahmedabad, 1999 and *Textual Sources for the Study of Zoroastrianism* edited and translated by Mary Boyce, University of Chicago Press, 1984/1990

11. Yasna 30

12. Yasna 48

13. Yasna 30

14. Yasna 31

15. Yasna 43

16. Yasna 45

17. Yasna 43

18. Yasna 30

19. Daevas was the name given to the amoral gods of war in pre-Zoroastrian Aryan religions. The words demon and devil probably derive from this root.

20. Yasna 30

21. Yasna 30

22. Yasna 49

23. Yasna 33

24. Yasna 50

25. Yasna 51

26. Yasna 51

27. Yasna 44

28. Yasna 28

29. Yasna 30

30. Yasna 33

31. Yasna 34

32. Yasna 43

33. Yasna 46

34. Yasna 29

35. Yasna 48

36. Yasna 50

37. Yasna 48. Saoshyants, in the Gathas, probably refers to those who followed Zarathustra's teaching faithfully – perhaps equivalent to Christian saints, but in later Zoroastrian texts, which are not included here, the word is used to refer to a Savior.

38. Yasna 30

39. Yasna 51

40. Yasna 31

41. Yasna 32

42. Yasna 46. The Chinvat Bridge or Chinvat Crossing is the bridge between earth and the Kingdom of Heaven; between material and spiritual values. Crossing this bridge is described as achieving enlightenment in Buddhism and being born again in Christianity

43. Yasna 45

44. Yasna 47

45. Yasna 51

46. Yasna 53

47. Yasna 53

48. Jack Finegan, *The Archaeology of World Religions*, Princeton University Press, 1952, quoted in Hopfe (*ibid*) p310

49. See Chapter 7

50. See Chapters 2 and 5. A new religion, Manicheism, which synthesized Zoroastrianism and Christianity, arose from the teachings of the prophet Mani (AD 216-274), in Persia. The opposition of the Magi led to Mani's death in chains as a prisoner of the Persian Emperor, but his religion survived his death and spread to the Europe, Africa and the East before being destroyed by Christian and Islamic persecution

51. Jane Bradshaw, *Eight Major Religions in Britain*, Edward Arnold, London 1979

52. Queen, *One Vision*, Raincloud Productions/Queen Productions, London, 1985

Chapter 2:
Moses

1. The details of the creation, flood and ark stories have been traced back to the *Enuma Elish* (Stories from On High) and the *Epic of Gilgamesh,* and date back more than 4,000 years. They were first written down in the Sumerian cuneiform script of early Mesopotamia. The story of the Tower of Babel is probably rooted in recollections passed down about the construction of the ziggurats and temples in Babylon over 3,000 years ago. There are other examples of earlier stories from Mesopotamian writings appearing in Genesis. These include the baby-in-a-reed-basket story, transferred from Mesopotamia to Egypt to explain how the son of a slave (Moses) came to be raised in a royal court. See John Romer, *Testament – The Bible and History*, Michael O'Mara Books, London, 1988

2. Although there are no dates in Genesis, tracing back the genealogies and ages of biblical characters from the earliest dates that we can be confident about as a result of archaeological discoveries, leads to a date close to 4,000 BC for creation – many millennia after *Homo sapiens* had actually emerged in Africa. Before Abraham's journey to Canaan, Abraham is said to have lived in the city of Ur of the Chaldees; Ur became a Chaldean city during the seventh century BC, but other historical cross-references using contemporary records place the foundation of the Kingdom of Israel by his descendants over 300 years earlier. Working back through the Bible from the known dates of the history of ancient Israel to the time of the Israelites' slavery in Egypt places the plagues and the exodus toward the end of the second millennium BC, but, despite extensive records of Egyptian history throughout this period, there is no corroboration for these biblical stories – nothing to suggest any biblical scale slavery or mass migrations, either in contemporary writing or in other archaeological records. There are, however, many records of nomads coming south to the security of the settled Egyptian civilization in times of famine. Romer (*ibid*). The books of Joshua and Judges, which follow the books of Moses, are strewn with writings suggesting that God's purpose is to lead the Israelites to a

promised land at the expense of the people already living there. See the Legacy section of this chapter.

3. Deuteronomy 4.35 & 32.4

4. Genesis 1.1. The words, "The Spirit of God" also used in this passage are reminiscent of Zoroastrian writings

5. Exodus 20.2-7; Deuteronomy 5.6-11

6. Exodus 20.12-17; Deuteronomy 5.16-21

7. Exodus 20.23

8. Leviticus 18, 19 and 27; Numbers 35 and Deuteronomy

9. All the quotations from the Books of Moses and from the Proverbs and Psalms are taken from modern English translations of the Old Testament, including the New International Version, Hodder & Stoughton, 1973/1989 and the Readers Digest Condensed Version, 1990

10. The Song of Moses, Exodus 15. Tribalistic additions have been omitted

11. Exodus 34.9

12. Numbers 6.24-26

13. Deuteronomy 18.22

14. Joshua 1.4

15. Joshua 6.24

16. Romer *(op cit)* pp68-9

17. Joshua 8

18. Joshua 9.21

19. Joshua 10.11

20. Joshua 10.13

21. Joshua 11.1-20

22. Joshua 11.21

23. Judges 3

24. Judges 10.6

25. Judges 11.33

26. Judges 12

27. Judges 13.1

28. Judges 14.18

29. Judges 15.15

30. Judges 16.30

31. Samuel 15

32. 1 Kings 18.22-40

33. 2 Kings 19.35

34. Paul Johnson, *A History of the Jews*, Weidenfeld & Nicolson, London, 1987, p107. Johnson's history is a key source for much of the information presented here on pages 35-41 and covering the period from the return from Babylon until 1948

35. *ibid* p108

36. Josephus (c90AD), quoted in Johnson *(ibid)*

37. Hillel quoted in Robert Van de Weyer, *A World Religions Bible*, O Books, Alresford, Hampshire, 2003

38. Johnson *(op cit)*

39. *ibid*

40. *ibid*

41. *ibid* p163

42. *ibid* p178

43. Interview in *Radio Times* March 29-April 4, 2003

44. Bob Dylan, *Highway 61 Revisited*, Blossom Music, 1965

45. Johnson (*op cit*) p370; quoted from Encyclopedia Judaica, xiii, 570-1. This was part of the standard creed of Reform Judaism from 1895 to 1937

46. *ibid* p380; quoted from Heinrich Graetz, *History of the Jewish People* (1891), Jewish Publication Society of America, Philadelphia, 1967

47. *The Guardian*, November 14, 2003.

48. Quoted by Jacqueline Rose in "This land is your land", *The Observer*, August 18, 2002

49. Shlomi Segall, "Why I won't serve Sharon," *The Guardian*, July 18, 2002

50. *Interreligious Insight* Vol 1 #1, January 2003

Chapter 3:
Atharva

1. Mundaka Upanishad 1.1.2 in S Radhakrishnan, *The Principal Upanishads*, Indus, New Delhi, 1994

2. *ibid* 1.1

3. Key sources for this section include John Keay, *India*, Harper

Collins, 2000, and K M Sen, *Hinduism*, Pelican, 1961

4. *The Bhagavad Gita* (trans Juan Mascaro, Penguin, 1962) 2.11-2.33

5. *Interreligious Insight* Vol 1 #1, January 2003

Chapter 4:
Lao-tzu

1. Amaury de Riencourt, *The Soul of China*, Honeyglen, 1958, p11

2. Chiu Kao, *Shu Ching (Book of Documents)* quoted in Hopfe (*op cit*) p232

3. de Riencourt (*op cit*)

4. Dun J Li, *The Ageless Chinese*, Dent & Son, London, 1968, p49

5. Chiu Kao (*op cit*)

6. Hopfe (*op cit*) p234 quoting Lao-tzu's biographer, Ssu-Ma Chien (c200 BC)

7. *ibid* p234

8. I have used the English "Way" rather than "Tao" throughout my selections from the Tao Te Ching. This is to emphasize the universalism of the teaching rather than its Chinese source. From a monotheistic point of view, "Tao" implies God's Way, and I have used this expression occasionally. Generally, however, I have used the expression "The Way" so as not to lead the reader to think too much in terms of the

old Western anthropomorphic view of God. The word "Te" has been translated variously as energy, power, virtue, and "by the grace of God." "Ching" means "book." Thus the Tao Te Ching can, and has been, referred to as anything from God's Way to The Taoist Book of Virtue

9. Yen Mah, Adeline, *Watching the Tree*, Harper Collins, 2000, p23

10. Lao-tzu, *Tao Te Ching*, Dover Publications, Mineola New York, 1997; Man-Ho Kwok, Martin Palmer and Jay Ramsay, *Tao Te Ching, The New Translation*, Element Classics, Rockport MA, 1994, and Hopfe (*op cit*) are the main sources for selections from the Tao Te Ching, numbered by chapter and verse

11. Ssu-Ma Chien quoted in Dun J Li (op cit) p84

12. de Riencourt (*op cit*) p23

13. Hopfe (*op cit*) p255

14. Dun J Li (op cit)

15. C Alexander Simpkins & Annellen Simpkins, *Simple Taoism*, Newleaf, Dublin, 1999

16. de Riencourt (*op cit*) p137

17. Dun J Li (*op cit*) p269-70

18. *ibid* p383-5

19. Yen Mah (*op cit*) p7

20. *ibid* p3

21. Kang Yu Wei, Ta Tung Shu

translated by Lawrence G Thompson and quoted in Barbara Walker (ed), *Uniting the Peoples and Nations*, World Federalist Movement & World Federalist Association (USA), Washington DC, 1993, p81-4

Chapter 5:
Buddha

1. Key sources for this section include Hopfe (*op cit*); *The Story of the Buddha*, The Association of Buddhist Women in the UK, London Buddhist Vihara: G P Malalasekera, *2500 Years of Buddhism*, Buddhist Missionary Society, Kuala Lumpur; Christmas Humphries, *Buddhism*, Penguin, 1951; John Snelling, *The Buddhist Handbook*, Rider, London, 1987, and David Brazier, *The New Buddhism*, Robinson, London, 2001

2. *The Dhammapada*, trans Juan Mascaro, Penguin, 1973

3. Sangha is the name given to a community of Buddhist monks and lay people

4. Theravada means the Way or the teaching of the elders

5. Mahayana means the Great Wheel. The description is used to distinguish between the variety of religions and philosophies that developed from the original Buddhist teaching on the one hand from Hinayana (Small

Wheel) or Theravada Buddhism on the other. Theravada Buddhists prefer the term Theravada to Hinayana, for obvious reasons

6. Aung San Suu Kyi, *Heavenly Abodes and Human Development*, CAFOD, 1973

7. Sulak Sivaraksa, *Seeds of Peace*, Parallax, Berkeley, CA, 1992, pp 4, 5 and 101

8. Rick Fields, *How the Swans Came to the Lake*, Shambhala, Boston, 1992, p378

9. See Snelling & Fields (*op cit*)

10. Snelling (*op cit*) provides extensive lists

11. Buddhist Peace Fellowship, PO Box 4650, Berkeley, CA, 94707, USA

12. INEB, 127 Soi Santipap, Nares Road, Bankok 10500, Thailand; NEB (UK), Plas Plwca, Cwm Rheidol, Aberystwyth, Wales, SY23 3NB

13. Amida Trust, Sukhavati, 21 Finsbury Park, London N7 6RT

14. Sivaraksa (*op cit*) Ch4

15. *ibid*

16. Brazier (*op cit*) p25

17. *Introduction to Buddhapadipa*, Bhuddapadipa Temple, Wimbledon, London. Quoted from Douglas M Burns, *Buddhism, Science and Atheism*, 1971, Mahndarama, London.

Chapter 6:
Jesus

1. John Hunt, *Daddy, Do You Believe in God?* O-Books, 2001 contains a review of the current scholarship on New Testament writers. The book also gives an eloquent summary of the chronology of the literary transformation of Jesus from spiritual reformer to "Son of God," especially in Chapter 47

2. John 1.1. With the exception of this line all the quotations used in this section are attributed to Jesus in the gospels. The main source for the quotations is *The New Testament* in *The Bible – New International Version*, Hodder & Stoughton, London, 1973-1989. Within the New Testament, the principal source is the gospel according to Matthew, particularly the Sermon on the Mount (Matthew, Chapters 5-7). Further footnotes are used only where quotations from other parts of the New Testament have been added

3. John 3.3

4. John 3.5-7

5. Luke 17.20-21

6. Mark 10.14

7. Matthew 22.37 and Luke 10.27. When asked, "Who is my neighbor?" in response to the injunction, "Love your neighbor," Jesus uses the parable

of the good Samaritan (Luke 10.29-37) to show that this love should extend beyond other Jews

8. Mark 9.50 and Luke 17.3

9. Matthew 22.21. This injunction is repeated in the other gospels; a clear statement that religious activity should be kept separate from political power

10. Luke 12.15 and 21.34

11. Mark 13.38-40

12. Luke 12.11

13. Mark 4.9

14. Matthew 4.17. See also the parables in Matthew 20 and 21, which make the point that it is never too late to repent

15. Luke 12.35

16. Luke 14.33

17. Luke 22.46

18. Luke 18. The parable of the persistent widow

19. Matthew 18.7 and Luke 17.1

20. Luke 11.28. See also Note 2

21. Luke 14.15. See also Note 2

22. Luke 18.15. See also Note 2

23. Luke 18.17. See also Note 2

24. Matthew 13.11. See the whole of Matthew 13 for the parables that show that this Prophecy, often quoted out of context, refers only to the Kingdom of Heaven, and does not have a more general application

25. Luke 12.48

26. John 3.20-21

27. John 8.31

28. Luke 15.7

29 Luke 21.10-11. The gospels contain many more prophecies that deal with the end of Jesus' life and the imminent end of the world. Neither set of prophecies has been included in this section. The former, which refer to Jesus' crucifixion and resurrection, have been excluded as the events prophesied are also described in the same narratives, which were written at least 20 years after Jesus' crucifixion, and could easily, therefore, have been added retrospectively. The latter, being written during a time of the final conflict between the Jews in Judea and Rome (see Chapter 2), could be seen as prophesizing the end of Judea, which did soon happen – without the prophesied divine intervention; or they could be seen as prophesies about a literally imminent end of the world – a view still held by some Christians – but, 2,000 years on, such an end can no longer be considered as imminent with respect to Jesus' time, and these prophesies have not, therefore, been included in the Vision section. Some of them are, however, discussed in the Legacy section

30. Paul Johnson, *A History of*

Christianity, Weidenfeld & Nicolson, London, 1976, p55

31. Luke 1.3

32. Matthew 21.12

33. Mark 11.15

34. Isaiah 56.7

35. John 2.16

36. Romans 3.21-25

37. Luke 3.38

38. Matthew 27.52-3

39. Luke 23.46

40. John 20.19

41. John 21.16

42. 1 Corinthians 15.22

43. Acts 9

44. Ephesians 2.8-9

45. 1 Corinthians 11.15

46. 1 Timothy 2.13-15

47. 1 Timothy 5.9

48. Titus 2.10

49. Galatians 9

50. James 2.17

51. James 3.17-18

52. 1 John 3.3

53. Romans 13.1-2

54. Mithraism: worship of one of the old Persian gods, Mithra, a god of light and power (like the Roman god, Sol Invictus) whose stories had also been mixed with those of Jesus (virgin birth, teaching, miracles, resurrection). Gnosticism: from the Greek, knowledge, the name was given to a range of spiritual movements aimed at release from the bondage of the material world. Stoicism: a philosophy holding that virtue depends on living in harmony with nature, founded by Zeno of Citium (c300 BC) and developed by Seneca, Epictetus and the Roman Emperor Marcus Aurelius. Manicheism: a fusion of Zoroastrianism and Christianity developed by a Persian priest, Mani (c AD216-276). It explained the problem of good and evil by an absolute dualism – it saw God as light and goodness, evil as matter and darkness. Platonism: a religion of idealism developed from the works of the Greek philosopher, Plato (427-347 BC)

55. The imperial position on monotheism was reversed in 681

56. The Church prohibited image worship again in 815 then reinstated it again in 843

57. See Jonathan Barker, *No-Nonsense Guide to Terrorism*, New Internationalist, Oxford, 2003, and Ronald Wright, *Stolen Continents*, Pimlico, London, 1992. In the United States the slavery would go on until the civil war of 1861-5 and the genocide would continue until 1890, when the Wounded Knee massacre would bring the last stand of the decimated plains

Indians to a bloody end

58. Harvey Gillman, *A Light That is Shining*, Quaker Home Service, London, 1988

59. Walter Martin, *The Kingdom of the Cults*, Bethany House, Minneapolis, 1985

60. BBC *Horizon* April 19, 2003

61. Mary Pat Fisher, *Religion in the 21st Century*, Routledge, London,1999, p62

62. Pentecost: Jewish feast day remembering the revelation of the Law to Moses; also celebrated as Whitsuntide by Christians in memory of the day on which Jesus' disciples received the holy spirit and spoke in tongues (Acts 2)

63. Fisher (*op cit*) p63

64. *ibid* p97

65. Stewart Lamont, *Church and State*, Bodley Head, London, 1989

66. David Jenkins, *The Calling of a Cuckoo*, Continuum, London, 2002

67. US figures from U of Pennsylvania & Gallup polls quoted in *Research News and Opportunities in Science & Religion*, Vol 3 #9, May 2003

68. Greg Palast, *The Best Democracy Money Can Buy*, Robinson, London, 2003

69. Richard Dawkins, *A Devil's Chaplain*, Weidenfeld &

Nicolson, London, 2003

70. Michael Moore, *Stupid White Men*, Penguin, London, 2002

71. Katherine Gun, former UK Intelligence employee

72. As 68 and 69

73. The attacks on Libya and Sudan and the 1998 attack on Afghanistan were all responses to terrorist attacks on US targets overseas. The Libya attacks followed the bombing of an airliner over Lockerbie, Scotland. The 1998 Afghanistan and Sudan attacks were directed at Al-Qaida targets

74. The inclusion of Iraq is not a reference to the 1991 Gulf War, which did have UN sanction, but to some of the subsequent air attacks over the "no-fly zones" in north and south Iraq. The inclusion of Yugoslavia is not a reference to the NATO peacekeeping action in Kosovo, but to the bombing of Belgrade

75. John Pilger, *Breaking the Silence*, ITV, September 22, 2003

76. Nuremberg Tribunal Report quoted by John Pilger in *New Statesman* April 14, 2003

77. Quoted in *New Statesman* April 14, 2003

78. *ibid*

79. Jackson Browne, *The Rebel Jesus*, Elektra Entertainment, 1997

80. Jackson Browne, *Lives in the Balance*, Elektra Entertainment, 1997

81. *Interreligious Insight* Vol 1 #2, April 2003

82. *ibid*

Chapter 7:
Muhammad

1. The Koran, translated by N J Dawood, Penguin Classics, London, 1956

2. *Hanif* (deviant) referred to a person whose behavior and beliefs differed from the traditional norms of the society

3 Dawood, op.cit.

4. The Koran goes on to elaborate the good tidings: "They shall dwell in gardens watered by running streams. Whenever they are given fruit to eat, they will say, "This is what we used to eat before," for they shall be given the like. Wedded to chaste virgins, they shall abide there forever." The Koran is littered with promises like this for believers. Such promises, some of which are referred to in the Legacy section of this chapter and in Notes 11-14 below, can clearly form no part of any eternal and universal truth and also conflict with appeals to seek spiritual enlightenment in the Selected Highlights from the Koran used in the Vision section of this chapter. They were probably added to the original recitations by political leaders of early Islam (perhaps even Muhammad himself) as a false means of increasing the popularity of the new religion, particularly among the desert nomads, and hence manipulating them in order to increase Islam's political influence. Sadly, these promises continue to be used to manipulate the gullible. They remain very much a part of Islam today, and are surely a factor in allowing the ongoing recruitment of suicide bombers from among young Islamic fundamentalists

5. Words added here include: "you may marry other women who seem good to you – two, three or four of them, but if you fear that you cannot maintain equality among them, marry one only, or any slave girls you may own."

6. Words added here include: "If a man is slain unjustly, his heir is entitled to satisfaction, but let him not carry his vengeance too far, for his victim will in turn be assisted and avenged." This is clearly not an expression of eternal and universal truth, but simply advice for a society not yet under the rule of law

7. Although this injunction gives credibility to the idea of

swearing oaths, it is action rather than words that count. This is stated directly later in the recital (24.53)

8. Words added here include: "to draw their veils over their bosoms and not to reveal their finery except to their husbands, fathers, husbands' fathers, sons, step-sons, brothers' sons, sisters' sons, slave-girls, household eunuchs and children who have no carnal knowledge of women, and let them not stamp their feet in walking so as to reveal their hidden trinkets." Such details are clearly intended for the ambient culture. The universal and eternal in this verse should be taken as an injunction against any behavior that may encourage male irresponsibility and promiscuity, or constitute "walking proudly" (17.37)

9. This verse has been abstracted from the Koran's longest chapter, "The Cow." While it may be read as divinely inspired and universally acceptable advice, albeit addressed to a society with a liberal but misogynist attitude to divorce, much of the more specific advice on women in the rest of the chapter is clearly compromised by the mores of the society. For example: "Women are your fields. Go then into your fields as you please."(2.223), "Women shall with justice have rights similar to those exercised against them, although *men have a status above women.*"(2.228), "Divorce may be pronounced twice, then the woman must be retained in honor, or allowed to go with kindness."(2.229), "Mothers shall suckle their children for two whole years, *if the father wishes the suckling to be completed.*"(2.233), "Widows shall wait, keeping themselves apart from men for four months and ten days after their husbands' death."(2.234)

10. This verse has been abstracted from the chapter entitled, "Women." Less holy verses from this chapter include the following: "Men have authority over women because God has made one superior over the other, and because they spend their wealth to maintain them. Good women are obedient. They guard their unseen parts because God has guarded them. As for those from whom you fear disobedience, *admonish them and send them to beds apart and beat them.*"(4.34), and "if you have relieved yourselves or had intercourse with women while traveling and can find no water, take some clean sand and rub your faces and hands with it."(4.43)

11. Additional promises included

here, and still taken literally by some Muslims, include: "the righteous shall dwell amongst gardens and fountains. They shall recline on couches face to face, a band of brothers. Toil shall not weary them, nor shall they ever leave their Paradise."(15.47 & 48)

12. This Koranic advice was, at some point, tempered as follows: "Blessed are the believers who restrain their carnal desires, except with their wives *and slave girls, for these are lawful to them.*"

13. The Koran goes on: "God will reward the believers with robes of silk and the delights of Paradise. Reclining there upon soft couches, they shall feel neither the scorching heat nor the biting cold. Trees will spread their shade around them and fruits will hang in clusters over them. They shall be served with silver dishes and beakers as large as goblets – silver goblets, which they themselves shall measure, and cups brim-full with ginger-flavored water from the Fount of Selsabil. They shall be attended by boys graced with eternal youth who to the beholder's eyes will seem like sprinkled pearls. They shall be arrayed in garments of fine green silk and rich brocade, and adorned with bracelets of silver. Their Lord will give them pure beverage to drink."(76.10-20)

14. The Koran adds the following description of the reward: "with gardens watered by running streams."(85.11)

15. Here, the Koran again adds details of the reward: "God will reward them with the gardens of Eden; gardens watered by running streams, where they shall dwell forever."(98.8)

16. The word, Islam, derives from the word, salam, meaning peace. It could, therefore, be translated as meaning "being at peace with God", but a more usual Muslim interpretation is "submission to the Will of God," and, to a traditional or fundamentalist Muslim, this also means submitting to the Koran in its entirety, as canonized some 30 years after Muhammad's death, accepting it as the literal Word of God, and even seeking to destroy those who cannot accept that the entire Koran is the literal Word of God

17. See, for example, the Koran, Chapters 2, 3, 6, 14, 21, 38 and 51

18. *ibid* Chapters 2, 5 and 19

19. *ibid* Chapter 5

20. *ibid* Chapters 14, 21 and 71

21. *ibid* Chapters 21 and 27

22. *ibid* Chapter 19

23. *ibid* Chapters 12 and 38

24. *ibid* Chapters 2, 14, 21, 27, 28, 51, 73, 79, 87 and 89

25. *ibid* Chapter 2

26. *ibid* Chapters 2, 21 and 27

27. *ibid* Chapter 2

28. *ibid* Chapters 2, 21, 27 and 34

29. *ibid* Chapter 34

30. *ibid* Chapter 38

31. *ibid* Chapters 48 and 68

32. *ibid* Chapter 6

33. *ibid* Chapters 6 and 19

34. *ibid* Chapters 4, 19, 33 and 66

35. *ibid* Chapters 4, 6, 19 and 33

36. *ibid* Chapters 18, 27, 38, 41 and 58

37. *ibid* Chapters 18, 27

38. *ibid* verse 4.164

39. Karen Armstrong, *Muhammad*, Gollancz, London, 1991, p90

40. Ahmed (= the promised one) is generally accepted as a reference to Muhammad

41. The Koran 2.143

42. Armstrong (*ibid*) p143

43. Al Gore, *Earth in the Balance*, Earthscan, London, 1992, 2000, p261

44. Farhad Daftary, *A Short History of the Ismailis*, Edinburgh University Press, 1998, gives a detailed history of the Nizaris in particular. Another extant group with Ismaili roots is the Druze community. Followers of Al Darazi, an 11ᵗʰ-century Ismaili opponent of the Fatimid Caliph, Al-Hakim in Egypt, they emphasized direct communication with God as a living presence and fled persecution in Egypt to settle in Lebanon, Palestine and Syria. Now around a million worldwide, about half in Lebanon, many are active in business and education: the International School of London, for example, is Druze-owned

45. Martin, Woodward and Atmaja, *Defenders of Reason in Islam*, One World, Oxford, 1997

46. Karen Armstrong, *Islam*, Weidenfeld & Nicolson, London, 2000

47. Ali Issa Othman, *Islam and the Future of Mankind*, Alhani, London, 1993

48. The Guardian, July 23, 2002, p11

49. Other Muslim-majority areas still fighting for separation from larger Muslim countries include Aceh in Sumatra (under Indonesian control) and Kurdistan, currently divided between Turkey, Syria, Iraq and Iran

50. Lebanon has had the particular misfortunes of inheriting a constitution that deliberately divided the community on religious lines (Maronite

Christians, Sunni Muslims and Shia Muslims) and of being Israel's northern neighbor – thus having to host tens of thousands of Palestinian refugees on its already crowded land

51. UNESCO figures quoted in *Asad Abu Khalil, Bin Laden, Islam and America's new "War on Terrorism,"* Seven Stories, New York, 2002, p48

52. Samuel P Huntington, *The Clash of Civilizations and the Remaking of World Order*, Simon & Schuster, London, 1997

53. Hassan Hathout quoted in Diana L Eck, A New Religious America, Harper, San Francisco, 2001, p268

54. Shabbir Mansuri quoted in Eck (*op cit*) p267

55. Eck (*op cit*) p265

56. *ibid* p252

57. Othman (*op cit*) p29

58. *ibid* p30

59. Ziauddin Sardar, *The Future of Muslim Civilisation*, Croom Helm, London, 1979

60. Ziauddin Sardar, *The Observer*, 21 October, 2001, p25

61. Abdul Rashied Omar, *Interreligious Insight*, Vol 1 #4, October 2003

Chapter 8:
Nanak Dev

1. Guru Granth Sahib, *Japji* p1 English translation as quoted in Patwant Singh, *The Sikhs*, John Murray, London, 1999, p23

2. *ibid* p21, *Japji* p5

3. *ibid* p30, *Var sarang* p1237

4. *Japji* p2. English translation as quoted in Hopfe (*op cit*) p219 from S E Frost (ed), *Sacred Writings of the World's Great Religions*, McGraw-Hill, New York, 1943

5. *Japji* p4. Hopfe (*op cit*) p221

6. Quoted in Al Gore, *Earth in the Balance*, Earthscan, London, 1992, 2000, p261

7. *Rehras* p9 quoted in Singh (*op cit*) p22

8. *ibid* p31, *Rag Bhairon* p1128

9. *ibid* p19, *Asa* p471

10. *ibid* p20, *Asa* p141

11. *ibid* p20, *Japji* p4

12. *ibid* p27, *Asa* p473

13. *ibid* p26-7, *Var Mag* p141

14. *ibid* p22, *Asa* p467

15. *Japji* p1 Hopfe (*op cit*) p218

16. *Japji* p3 Hopfe (*op cit*) p220

17. *Asa* p141 quoted in Singh (*op cit*) p20

18. *Japji* p2 quoted in Hopfe (*op cit*) p219

19. *Japji* p1 quoted in Hopfe (*op cit*) p218

20. *apji* p3 quoted in Hopfe (*op cit*) p220

21. *Japji* p5 quoted in Hopfe (*op cit*) p222

22. *Rag Bhairon* p1136 quoted in Singh (*op cit*) p18

23. *Japji* p3 quoted in Hopfe (*op cit*) p220

24. Singh (*op cit*) p24

25. The Mogul Empire survived in name until 1857, but fell into disarray after 1707, only to be revived as a nominal entity within British India. The pretence of Mogul rule was finally abandoned by the British in 1857 in the aftermath of the Indian Mutiny

26. Singh (*op cit*) p39

27. *ibid* p40

28. *ibid* p47-48

29. *ibid* p 48 (Guru Granth Sahib, *Slok 16* p1427)

30. *ibid* p51

31. *Interreligious Insight*, Vol 1 #1, January 2003

Chapter 9:
Mirza Husain Ali Nuri

1. The first name, Sayyid, represents a family claim to direct descent from the prophet, Muhammad

2. Peter Smith, *A Short History of the Bahai Faith*, One World, Oxford, 1996, p37

3. *Baha'ullah, The Hidden Words*, translated by Shoghi Effendi and friends, Bahai Publishing Trust, London, 1932; *Gleanings from the Writings of Baha'ullah* translated by Shoghi Effendi, Bahai Publishing Trust, London, 1949. Excerpts used are identified with the letters H (Hidden Words) or G (Gleanings) followed by the verse numbers

4. Quoted in Smith, op cit

5. Baha'ullah, Gleanings 165, op cit

6. *ibid* Gleanings 19

7. *ibid* Gleanings 54

Chapter 10:
Collected Visions

The collected visions are drawn from the same sources as the Vision – Selected Highlights incorporated in Chapters 1-9. Superscripts refer to the notes on Chapters 1-9 as appropriate.

Chapter 11:
The Quest Continues

1. Leonard E Barrett, *The Rastafarians*, Beacon, Boston, 1997

2. L Ron Hubbard, *Certainty Magazine*, Vol 5, #10, Los Angeles

3. L Ron Hubbard, *Professional Auditor's Bulletin #31* quoted in Walter Martin: *The Kingdom of*

the Cults, Bethany House, Minneapolis, 1985

4. *ibid*

5. L Ron Hubbard, *Scientology 8-8008* quoted in Martin (*op cit*)

6. Owen Flanagan, *New Scientist* May 24, 2003

7. BBC *Horizon*, April 19, 2003

8. *ibid*

9. Richard Dawkins, *A Devil's Chaplain*, Weidenfeld-Nicolson, London, 2003

10. See, for example, *Research News & Opportunities in Science & Religion*, Vol 3 #9, May 2003.

11. Jaroslav Pelikan (ed), *The World Treasury of Modern Religious Thought*, Little Brown & Co, Boston, 1990

12. *ibid*

13. *ibid*

14. Quoted by Dorothy L Sayers in Pelikan (*op cit*)

15. in Pelikan (*op cit*)

16. in Dawkins (*op cit*)

17. *ibid*

18. David Jenkins, *The Calling of a Cuckoo*, Continuum, London, 2002

19. in Pelikan (*op cit*)

20. *Radio Times* interview May 2003

21. in Pelikan (*op cit*)

22. Quoted in Julia Cameron, *The Artist's Way*, Pan, London, 1995

23. *ibid*

24. in Pelikan (*op cit*)

25. Quoted in Dawkins (*op cit*)

26. *ibid*

27. *ibid*

28. Speech in Assisi, January 24, 2002

29. *Interreligious Insight*, Vol 1 #1, January 2003.

30. Jenkins (*op cit*)

31. *Interreligious Insight*, Vol1 #1, January 2003

32. *ibid*

33. *ibid*

34. *ibid*

35. *Interreligious Insight*, Vol 1 #2, April 2003

36. *ibid*

37. *Interreligious Insight*, Vol 1 #1, January 2003

38. in Pelikan (*op cit*)

39. Jenkins (*op cit*)

40. H H Dalai Lama, *The Heart of the Buddha's Path*, Thorsons, London, 1995 and *Ethics for the New Millennium*, Riverhead, New York, 1999

41. George Monbiot, *The Age of Consent*, Flamingo, London, 2003

42. Yehuda Berg, the Power of the Kabbalah, Hodder Headline, London, 2003. (Berg was born into a Kabbalist family in Israel, emigrated to the USA and settled in LA)

43. From the introduction to David A Hart, *One Faith?*, Mowbray, London, 1995

44. in Pelikan (*op cit*)

45. *ibid*

46. *ibid*

47. Robert Barry, *A Theory of Almost Everything*, One World, Oxford, 1996

48. in Pelikan (*op cit*)

49. *ibid* plus Sharon Janis, *Spirituality for Dummies*, Hungry Minds, New York, 2000

50. Monbiot (*op cit*)

51. Quoted in *Interreligious Insight* Vol 1 #2, April 2003

52. Pelikan (*op cit*)

53. Quoted in Koestler, *The Ghost in the Machine*, Hutchinson, London, 1976

54. Quoted in Eck (*op cit*)

55. *ibid*

56. *Interreligious Insight*, Vol 1 #1, January 2003

57. in Pelikan (*op cit*)

58. *ibid*

59. From the introduction to William Bloom (ed), *Holistic Revolution – The Essential New Age Reader*, Penguin, London, 2000

60. Paul Davies, *The Mind of God*, Penguin, London, 1992

61. *Interreligious Insight*, Vol 1 #1, January 2003

62. Eck (*op cit*). Eck was referring specifically to American society here; the word "American" was deleted from the original quotation to give her words global applicability

63. Al Gore, *Earth in the Balance*, Earthscan, London, 1992 and 2000

64. Monbiot (*op cit*)

65. Jenkins (*op cit*)

66. Quoted in Janis (*op cit*) p193

67. *ibid* p222

68. Paul F Knitter and Chandra Musaffar, *Subverting Greed*, Orbis, New York, 2002

69. Quoted in Janis (*op cit*) p183

70. Speech to British Labour Party Conference, October 2000

71. H H Dalai Lama (*op cit*)

72. BBC Dimbleby Lecture, October 2003

INDEX